Phrase Structure

Generative Syntax

General Editor: David Lightfoot

Recent work in generative syntax has viewed the language faculty as a system of principles and parameters, which permit children to acquire productive grammars triggered by normal childhood experiences. The books in this series serve as an introduction to particular aspects or modules of this theory. They presuppose some minimal background in generative syntax, but meet the tutorial needs of intermediate and advanced students. Written by leading figures in the field, the books also contain sufficient fresh material to appeal to the highest level.

1 *Government and Binding Theory and the Minimalist Program*
  Edited by Gert Webelhuth

2 *Logical Form*
  Norbert Hornstein

3 *Minimalist Analysis*
  Howard Lasnik

4 *Phrase Structure: From GB to Minimalism*
  Robert A. Chametzky

Forthcoming

5 *More! A Minimalist Theory of Construal*
  Robert Hornstein

Phrase Structure
From GB to Minimalism

Robert A. Chametzky

Copyright © Robert A. Chametzky 2000

The right of Robert A. Chametzky to be identified as the author of this work has been asserted in accordance with the Copyright, Designs and Patents Act 1988.

First published 2000

2 4 6 8 10 9 7 5 3 1

Blackwell Publishers Inc.
350 Main Street
Malden, Massachusetts 02148
USA

Blackwell Publishers Ltd
108 Cowley Road
Oxford OX4 1JF
UK

Library of Congress Cataloging-in-Publication Data
Chametzky, Robert.
    Phrase structure : from GB to minimalism / Robert A. Chametzky.
        p.   cm. — (Generative syntax ; 4)
    Includes bibliographical references and index.
        ISBN 0–631–20158–0 (alk. paper) — ISBN 0–631–20159–9 (pbk. : alk. paper)
            1. Phrase structure grammar.   2. Generative grammar.   3. Grammar,
    Comparative and general—Syntax.   I. Title.   II. Series.
    P158.3.C478   2000
    415—dc21   00–023100

British Library Cataloguing in Publication Data
A CIP catalogue record for this book is available from the British Library.

Typeset in 10 on 13pt Palatino
by Graphicraft Limited, Hong Kong
Printed in Great Britain by M.P.G. Books, Bodmin, Cornwall

This book is printed on acid-free paper.

Contents

For

Max Nicholas Fennell-Chametzky
Jules & Anne Halley Chametzky

with love,
from the guy in the middle.

The truth is rarely pure, and never simple.
Oscar Wilde, *The Importance of Being Earnest*

Preface

Form follows fashion. Also convention, and, so I have heard, occasionally a rational plan. This is a book in which "form" in various of its senses is deeply implicated. The presumption is that the work falls more on the side of planned rationality than fashionable conventionality.

"Syntax" *is* form, in the sense that things behave syntactically, have a syntax, insofar as they behave due to their *shapes*. So, any book in or about syntax is a book in or about form, whether it says so or not. "Phrase structure" is one hypothesis about the form of natural language syntax, about the nature of the shapes that characterize the grammar(s) of natural languages. So, a book about phrase structure is a book about the form of form. Any book about anything itself has a shape (we hope), some form or other. The form of this book about the form of form is, in fact, unconventional.

Much of this book takes the form of close reading of and argument with three existing books: Chametzky (1996), Kayne (1994), and Chomsky (1995). This is not the way of most linguistics (text)books. I do it this way because I think that these specific books contain complex and subtle ideas about phrase structure that repay engaged scrutiny, because I think that doing things this way creates precisely the path that our subtitle (*from GB to Minimalism*) promises, and because I very much think that this is how we actually think when we think well. That is, I think that we think well when we enter deeply into a dialectic with the articulated products of a(nother) mind. Consequently, I think that a proper introduction to something is some kind of immersion in some of the actual thinking it takes to do whatever is being introduced. I suppose this means I also think that sometimes form follows function.

Acknowledgments

It was Norbert Hornstein's idea that I write a book on phrase structure for this series. David Lightfoot, the series editor, has read and commented extensively on my manuscript, as has Teresa Satterfield. Only they can judge just how much better the book could still have been had I followed yet more of their respective suggestions than I ultimately did. Peggy Speas and Dave Lebeaux each gave much appreciated encouragement to some early portions of the manuscript.

Without the support of my wife, Ann Fennell, whose "firmnes drawes my circle just, And makes me end, where I begunne", there would have been no light visible through my tunnel vision.

Introduction

Our topic

A book about "phrase structure" – as opposed to, say, the ECP, the Projection Principle, or the PRO Theorem – subtitled *from GB to Minimalism* might be accused of looking "neither out far nor in deep" (Frost 1934). Not *in deep* because "phrase structure" does not begin with Government & Binding (GB) theory and not *out far* because other approaches not in the GB-to-Minimalism line also make use of it. This Introduction both previews what is in the book and explains some things the book is not about and why it has the particular blinders it does.

The book is about the current state of Phrase Structure (PS) theory in Principles and Parameters (P & P) approaches to syntax.[1] The goal is both to explicate and clarify the theoretical issues and the positions that are in play as of the time of writing, and to develop tools and concepts for the evaluation and comparison of the positions. Theoretical issues – e.g., primitive and derived concepts, theoretical architecture, simplicity and naturalness of extensions of basic ideas, internal coherence and consistency, explanatory adequacy – are stressed throughout, which means that relatively little space is devoted to the analysis of natural language phenomena. Though the presentation of all views attempts to be fair, I should say at the outset that I am not merely a disinterested commentator on these matters.

The book first explicates and analyzes the crucial concepts in current PS, then examines how these are treated within three alternatives within the P & P approach.

Plan of the Book

This Introduction deals with "phrase structure" – the very idea. There is very briefly some pointing at the history of the concept and at formal language theory, in section 1; section 2 asks the question "phrase structure instead of what?"; and section 3 says something about X-Bar Theory. Finally, I explain why none of these interesting subjects is exactly our subject here. The work begins in earnest in Chapter One, which takes up concepts/themes which are central to PS in P & P. Among them are: headedness and endocentricity, the relation of argument structure to syntactic structure, Functional vs. Lexical Categories, X-Bar Theory and its status, and the respective statuses of precedence and dominance. Their treatment within the three alternative approaches is the organizing principle of the book. I explicate and analyze the concepts in this chapter, thus preparing the reader for the particular discussions to come. Among the specific issues that come up are the following: are all constructions endocentric; is there a unique Head; position of Subjects in PS; status of Adjuncts (that is, non-argument modifiers of a head) and adjunctions (that is, the results of non-substitution movement); what is the theoretical justification for the "generalization of X-Bar" to Functional Categories; if X-Bar rules should not be explicitly stated, how are their effects to be derived; are there two formal primitives for PS, or just one?

The alternatives: there are three chapters here. Chapter Two deals with a *Late Classical GB* approach to PS, Chametzky (1996), building on Speas (1990). Chapter Three discusses the *Mannerist P & P* of Kayne (1994). Chapter Four takes up the *Minimalism* of Chomsky (1995). I discuss each briefly in turn.

(1) *Late Classical GB* approach. This marks the culmination of a line of inquiry begun especially in Stowell (1981) and for which Speas (1990) remains perhaps the fullest statement. The central idea here is that D-structure is both a pure representation of theta-grids (Speas) or the argument-of relation (Lebeaux 1988), and also the locus of X-Bar restrictions, though explicit X-Bar rules are analyzed away. The focus is on the theoretical refinements and elaborations in Chametzky (1996).

(2) *Mannerist P & P*. Kayne (1994) develops a theory based on the idea that if x precedes y in the linguistic string, then XP must asymmetrically C-command YP in the syntactic phrase marker. He both argues for the theoretical plausibility of this restriction and traces out various of its consequences. Issues discussed of relevance to our concerns include: the question of the status of precedence in PS; the issue of Adjuncts; and the derivability of X-Bar conditions.

(3) *Minimalism*. Chomsky (1995) brings together Chomsky's papers developing the minimalist program (MP).[2] A central point in MP is the giving up of all distinguished syntactic strata other than one that corresponds, more or less, to what has been called LF in earlier P & P work – there is neither D-structure nor S-structure. Another desideratum is to keep syntactic operations to as close to "virtual conceptual necessity" as possible. The theory is strongly derivational: the single phrase marker is constructed from items drawn from the lexicon, with partial structures being licit insofar as they are the result of the "minimal" operations. In line with the general thrust of MP, much of the PS theory that preceded it is apparently analyzed away as unnecessary.

Conclusion: in this chapter, I briefly consider two points. One is the status of "derivational" versus "representational" theories, an issue that arises in the discussion of MP in Chapter Three. The second is the status of phrase structure itself.

Having seen where we are heading, I shall get us back on route.

1.0   Phrase structure, the past

The term *phrase structure* (PS) enters linguistics as part of an argument. The argument is that made by Noam Chomsky against structural linguistics, primarily in its American Descriptivist version, beginning in the late 1950s. *Phrase Structure Grammar* (PSG) is the name Chomsky gave to a (family of) formal system(s) which, he claimed, reconstructed the unformalized descriptive syntactic practice found, for example, in Bloomfield (1933), Bloch (1946), or Harris (1946, 1951). This practice was called *immediate constituent* (IC) analysis (see particularly Wells 1947). The conclusion of Chomsky's argument is that PSG systems are inadequate for the description of natural language syntax and so, *a fortiori*, IC analysis and structural linguistics are also inadequate.[3] Thus, the need for *transformational* grammar.

What are WE to make of this? The following: PS, as we shall use the term – and this is in accord with how it is used within the P & P writings that we scrutinize herein – indicates something very much like the intuitive idea behind IC analysis. That is, it refers to an iterative part/whole analysis of a linguistic string (NB, though sentences are not the only units with a PS analysis, we will not be concerned with morphological "PS" analysis) which analysis results in a hierarchical branching structure. It does not include reference to rules of a particular form, nor, indeed, to rules at all. Nonetheless, *phrase structure* begins its life in linguistics as part of the name for a certain kind of rule, and it continues to function in such a capacity, so now we turn to a very brief look at this tradition.

1.1 PS rules and grammars

Chomsky's work which introduced *phrase structure* begins what is known as formal language theory. This (mathematical) inquiry examines rule systems of various sorts (that is, with different restrictions on the form of rule allowed), the languages which these systems generate/accept/enumerate, and relations between these rule systems and other formal devices (e.g., automata). This ongoing inquiry is now, I think it is safe to say, pursued largely by computer scientists and computational linguists. It moves sporadically in and out of the field of vision of most linguists, intruding or surfacing (as they might characterize it) at unpredictable moments with odd sounding results that apparently carry great import for linguistics. The issue of concern to linguists has been the (formal) (in)adequacy of phrase structure grammars for the description of natural language.

Again, none of this has anything much to do with our project here. There are different senses of "phrase structure grammar", and once we are clear on this, and on what they are, we can proceed to investigate our favored sense of "phrase structure" without becoming embroiled in disputes and controversies that are simply beside the point. Our decks, however, are not yet entirely clear.

2.0 If not phrase structure, what?

Everyone agrees that sentences are organized. PS, as we understand it, organizes sentence structure in terms of constituent hierarchies. We shall look very briefly at two other approaches to the organization of sentence structure in this section. The first is "dependency theory" (DT) and the second is "categorial grammar" (CG).

2.1   Dependency theory

DT has been called by one of its proponents "the 'indigenous' syntactic theory of Europe" (Hudson 1990: 107). It is, arguably, a more traditional approach to sentence structure than is phrase structure theory (Matthews 1993: 111–12, 146–51).[4] The basic difference between DT and phrase structure is the (nearly) total absence of larger phrasal units in the former approach. The syntactic structure of a sentence in DT is given by a set of (pairwise) relations between words, where the essential relations are those of Head and Dependent. DT is thus essentially relational, and the derived concepts are also relational; for example: subject (of), object (of), complement (of), adjunct (of), governor (of). We might note that these relation types are commonly used in current phrase structure based approaches, and we might ask questions about this fact (see Hudson 1990: 103–13 and Brody 1994 for some discussion).

There are broadly two possible positions with respect to the use of dependency relations in phrase structural approaches. One is that this shows that the bases of phrase structure are ill-conceived; when it comes to actual analyses of linguistic phenomena, it is necessary to import concepts that have no natural place in such a theory. The other is that the ability of phrase structural approaches to define relations and identify relata solely in terms of a structural vocabulary shows the nonbasic nature of such information; even if such relations are essential for adequate analysis, this does not entail that they are building blocks for theory. I shall not attempt to adjudicate this dispute. Evidently, it is only on the basis of well worked out analyses couched within the alternative approaches that such an adjudication might be attempted. At that point, the adequacy of the analyses, and the coherence of the theories in which they are worked out, could be evaluated. Note that the more adequate analysis of a given phenomenon might not appear as such, as it might be given within a theoretical approach that is inhospitable to that analysis. So, for example, if certain dependency relations required relatively baroque (or even rococo) definitions and stipulations within a structural theory, an analysis dependent on these might well seem ill-conceived or wrong. Translation into (some version of) DT might, however, make the analysis relatively straightforward and perspicuous, and thus insightful and plausibly correct, as well. The point here is merely to briefly take note of DT approaches and both how they differ from phrase structural approaches and how there is nonetheless convergence, at least at the level of analysis, between them.

2.2   Categorial Grammar

The approach to syntax found in Categorial Grammar (CG) "is akin to that of dependency grammars" (Wood 1993: 1).[5] This similarity is remarked on also by Hudson (1990: 109–10). Wood (1993: 3) even goes so far as to characterize CG as "a valency or dependency grammar rather than a phrase-structure grammar" (see also Wood 1993: 30). The crucial idea in CG for our purposes is that "language is seen in terms of functions and arguments rather than constituent structure" (Wood 1993: 3). Function and argument status are directly encoded in terms of syntactic category. CG work begins with a (small) set of "primitive" (Pollard 1988: 393; Bach 1988: 20), or "atomic" (Wood 1993: 7–8) categories and on the basis of these recursively defines a(n) (infinite) set of categories containing both these and "complex" categories (Oehrle et al. 1988: 1; Bach 1988: 23–5). The complex categories are "functor categories" which are "incomplete– 'unsaturated', in the terms of a valency grammar – and need some other expression(s) to occur with them to complete them" (Wood 1993: 8). Note that the primitive or atomic categories are not "incomplete" in this sense.

So, for example, what we pre-theoretically call a "transitive verb" might be categorized as follows. It is a function which combines with (takes as its argument) a noun (phrase) to form a new function which itself combines with a noun (phrase) to form a sentence, where the categories of noun (phrase) and sentence might well be atomic. Similarly, an "intransitive verb" could be categorized as a function which combines with a noun (phrase) to form a sentence. The work that would have been done in PSGs by phrase structure rules is here done by "fine-grained" complex categories (Bach 1988: 25; Wood 1993: 4). This difference grounds a "distinction between the tree-theoretic basis of phrase-structure description and the functional basis of categorial description . . ." (Wood 1993: 6) in virtue of which "all of the configurational notions, such as c-command and the like . . . are up for grabs" in CG (Bach 1988: 31). This is true despite the long- and well-known *weak* generative capacity equivalence between CGs and context-free PSGs (Bar-Hillel et al. 1960; see Wood 1993: 24; Pollard 1988: 392–5 for brief and helpful discussion).

The basic difference between both DT and CG, on the one hand, and phrase structural approaches, on the other, was already characterized by Chomsky (1963: 414) over 35 years ago.

> There is, in fact, a traditional view that identifies grammar with the set of grammatical properties of words or morphemes (cf. de Saussure, 1916, p. 149), and it might reasonably be maintained that the approach just outlined [CG–RC] gives one precise expression to this notion.

3.0 X-Bar Theory

X-Bar Theory is a theory of the what and why of the labelling of nodes in a phrase marker.[6] It derives its name from a notation in which different subtypes of a single syntactic category type (viz., nominals or verbals) are indicated with some number of "bars" above (or, often, "primes" next to) the symbol for the category. So we might have, in the "prime notation" : N, N', N", N''', N''''. The central issue is whether the labels on a mother and its daughter(s) are nonarbitrarily related. As observed already by Lyons (1968: 235), in a PSG of the sort discussed in section 2 above, there need be no nonarbitrary relation. So, for example, a rule with "NP" on its left need not have any sort of nominal category symbol on its right: the format and restrictions on the rules do not require that "Noun phrases" be in any way related to other nominals. Among other things, X-Bar Theory attempts to end this state of affairs. It does so by importing into phrase structure based syntax a notion of "Head", which, as we have seen, is the core notion of DT.[7]

Having accepted a notion of Head as syntactically necessary, it is a basic tenet of (most versions of) X-Bar Theory that all constructions are endocentric (see Richardson 1984). Once this idea is introduced, mother-daughter labels immediately cease to be arbitrarily related, at least for the case of the Head daughter. It also becomes possible to introduce into the phrase structure based theory such further DT concepts as Complement and Adjunct. As discussed above, in keeping with the nature of the approach, however, these concepts are given a structurally mediated conception. So, for example, a Complement might be a sister to the Head.

We can see, then, that a central tendency of X-Bar Theory is to bring PS-based approaches to syntax closer to DT.[8]

There are other aspects of X-Bar Theory. One concern has been called "cross-categorial harmony" (see e.g., Hawkins 1982). Here the issue is to what degree the various categories (viz., NP, VP, AP etc.) have the same internal syntax with respect to such questions as position of Head or number and position of Complements. A related issue is sometimes called "uniform projection" – the question here is whether the number of "bar-levels" (how many subcategory types indicated by number of bars or primes) is the same across all categories. Along with this comes a question about Maximal Projections: is there a number of bars beyond which grammar does not go, and, if so, is it uniform across categories (e.g., Jackendoff (1977: 36) posits a "uniform three level hypothesis")? A basic thread running through all such work is an attempt to develop a theory of phrase structure with more linguistic content, which can thus bear more of the burden of syntactic description and explanation, than in early PSG literature. This is often cast in terms of "the base component" versus "the transformational component" but this is overly narrow, as approaches which eschew transformational analysis entirely (hence have no "base component") nonetheless can and do embrace or elaborate versions of X-Bar Theory (see, e.g., Bresnan 1982; Gazdar, Klein, Pullum, and Sag 1985; Pollard and Sag 1987; Sadock 1991).

4.0   And so what?

Most of what we've run through (or over) in the preceding few pages we will now simply leave behind. This is for several reasons. One is that there are already works which discuss various of the individual topics, as I have tried to indicate, and there seems no great need for yet one more. Another is that a single work by a single author that tried to do justice both to the separate topics gestured at or lightly touched on above and to their various connections is quite hard to imagine, let alone write: it verges on being an encyclopedia of syntax. Finally, with respect to our rather restricted topic – the current state of

PS play within P & P syntax – the concepts most useful for explication and understanding are for the most part simply different ones. We therefore now turn our attention to developing those concepts.

Notes

1   I take P & P as a cover term for the GB-to-Minimalism lineage.
2   In his chapter 4 he directly takes up PS issues. He explicitly discusses Kayne (1994). I have discussed Chomsky's chapter 3, published in 1993, in Chametzky (1996).
3   Whether or not Chomsky's argument is a good one is not our concern here. Manaster-Ramer and Kac (1990) and Matthews (1993) are indispensable on this and more generally on the history of IC/PS grammar, and its treatment within generative grammar.
4   Tesniere (1959) is the *locus classicus* for DT; Mel'cuk (1988) is a more recent proponent; Hays (1964), Robinson (1970) and Venneman (1977) all have interesting things to say about DT and PS-based syntax.
5   Wood (1993) is an especially accessible source for linguists interested in CG. I have relied on it and, to a lesser extent, the Introduction and papers by Bach (1988) and Pollard (1988) in Oehrle et al. (1988). Some of the most compelling CG work from the point of view of theoretical linguistics is in a remarkable series of papers by Steedman; see his (1985, 1987, 1988, 1990).
6   The X-Bar literature is enormous. The most useful (conceptual) history of X-Bar Theory is Stuurman (1985: chs. 1 and 2). Crucial works include Chomsky (1970), Jackendoff (1977), and Speas (1990); Kornai and Pullum (1990) study X-Bar Theory formally.
7   There is good discussion of some of the background and general issues here in the Introduction to Corbett, Fraser, and McGlashan (1993); Zwicky (1985) and Hudson (1987) provided some direct impetus for this volume.
8   See Chapter Four, note 29.

Chapter one

Phrase Structure in Principles and Parameters Syntax

The issues

This chapter explains and analyzes the concepts which we examine in the three alternative P & P approaches to PS. As these concepts are to orient and guide us through the subsequent chapters, it is crucial that we have a tolerably clear under-standing of them at the outset. However, it is not necessary to try for absolute clarity (whatever that might be) – largely because it is not possible. It is not possible, of course, because ultimately theoretical concepts such as the ones we explore in this chapter can only be truly well understood within a particular theoretical setting. One of the signal benefits of working at the end of the 20th century is that we no longer labor under the delusion that in empirical inquiry we must "define our terms", preferably at the outset. We *discover* what our terms mean in a constant, reciprocal process of refining and bootstrapping as we engage in both theoretical and analytic work.[1] So, we shall rough out the contours of our investigations here, and in the later chapters we will see just how they are sharpened and articulated in different settings.

We have already listed some concepts and questions explored in this chapter.[2] I repeat that listing now.

1 The relation of argument structure to syntactic structure:
>   What is the position of Subjects in PS?
>   What are the statuses of Adjuncts (that is, non-argument modifiers of a Head) and adjunctions (that is, the results of non-substitution movement)?
2 Headedness & endocentricity:
>   Are all constructions endocentric?
>   Is there a unique Head?
3 Functional vs. Lexical Categories:
>   What is the theoretical justification for the "generalization of X-Bar" to Functional Categories?
4 X-Bar Theory and its status:
>   If X-Bar rules should not be explicitly stated, how are their effects to be derived?
>   Is all branching binary?

5 The respective statuses of precedence and dominance:
    Are there two formal primitives for PS or just one?

Though there is inevitably a large degree of interconnectedness among them, hence some degree of arbitrariness in doing so, I shall nonetheless now take them up in the order just presented.

1.0 Structuralization and argument alignment

The basic issue here is: how does lexical information get "structuralized"?[3] The guiding idea here is that there must be some systematic relation between individual lexical requirements (i.e., argument structure) and syntactic structure – lexical items cannot appear in arbitrary places in a well-formed sentence – and that characterizing this relation is to some large degree what the theory of PS is about and for. In particular, then, there must be (a set of) "canonical structuralizations" which are the systematically encoded/decodable syntactic representations of lexical information. The reasoning behind this view is pretty familiar and clear. We are interested in what one knows when one knows a language. Part of that knowledge is knowledge of lexical items. Part of what it means to know a lexical item is to know the particular restrictions that item carries with it in terms of what it can or must cooccur with. This sort of lexical knowledge is not, strictly, grammatical knowledge, and has to be rendered in a format appropriate to (knowledge of) the grammar, given that grammar is the means by which lexical information is made recoverable for wider cognition (i.e., thought). In the P & P tradition, this systematic grammatical format is PS. The issue then is sharpened: what are the forms of information in the lexical entry, how much of this information is structuralized, and according to what principle(s)? Borer (1994) calls this "the lexical-entry-driven-approach" and credits Ann Farmer's 1980 MIT dissertation (cf. Farmer 1984) with its first explicit statement.[4] Stowell (1992: 11–13) refers to this central issue as "argument alignment"; Speas (1990) provides discussion within "standard" P & P; Pesetsky (1995) offers a detailed nonstandard approach.[5] We shall only indicate briefly some main lines of inquiry and dispute.

Chomsky (1981) suggested that syntactic subcategorization information is structuralized as D-structure using defined predicates such as "government" to regulate the mapping. Grimshaw (1979, 1981) argued that as well some sort of semantic selection was required in the lexicon and in structuralization. Chomsky (1986b), drawing on David Pesetsky's unpublished 1982 MIT dissertation, argued that only the semantic selection (s-selection) was needed, and that syntactic selection (c-selection) was redundant. Rothstein (1991a, 1991b) countered that not all c-selection is in fact eliminable.

Chomsky (1981, 1986b) also suggests that D-structure is "a pure representation of theta structure" (1986b: 100). This idea is taken up and its implications extensively traced out by Speas (1990), Lebeaux (1988, 1990), and Chametzky (1996).[6] An influential proposal concerning argument alignment was put forward by Baker (1988) in his Uniformity of Thematic Assignment Hypothesis (UTAH), given in (1); Bouchard (1991) proposed a Relative Theta Assignment Hypothesis (RTAH), given in (2).[7]

(1)   UTAH: Identical thematic relationships between items are represented by identical structural relationship between those items at the level of D-structure. (Baker 1988: 46)

(2)   RTAH: The argument which is relatively highest in LCS [Lexical Conceptual Structure – RC] is linked to the position which is relatively highest in syntactic structure, and so forth, for the second highest, etc. (Bouchard 1991: 28–9)

We may note that RTAH differs from UTAH in that the former, but not the latter, seems to presuppose some sort of hierarchy of semantic/thematic arguments and that this hierarchy mediates structuralization. However, this is a misleading way to characterize Bouchard's proposal. In fact, Bouchard is revising Jackendoff's (1983) Conceptual Structure (CS), and the notion of "higher" in (2) is basically one of constituency both in LCS and syntax. Structuralization on this view means that "... all syntactic nodes correspond to CS constituents ..." and "two nodes A and B in SS [syntactic structure – RC] ... correspond to two nodes A' and B' in CS ..." (Bouchard 1991: 24, 25). This is in contrast to "true" hierarchy positions with respect to argument alignment, which date back to Fillmore (1968) (see also Jackendoff (1972)), in which there is an ordered set of thematic/semantic roles, and these are structuralized in accordance with their positions in this order.

Stowell (1992: 12–13) points out that this approach is not usually one found in P & P work, as it is possible to map more directly from such a hierarchy to a "surface" string, without mediation by means of phrase structure. Thus, as he notes, such hierarchies are generally found in work that is not exclusively or at all PS-based, and this forms one area for disagreement among approaches to syntax. However, Speas (1990: 14–16) does adopt a version of the hierarchy approach, with the proviso that she is not committed to "... claiming that some primitive device like [the hierarchy she gives] exists as a part of the grammar. The thematic hierarchy *describes* the order of the arguments in the theta grid" (emphasis in original).[8]

More commonly accepted within P & P work is an asymmetry between an *external* and all *internal* arguments (Williams 1981).[9] The external argument is the "most prominent" argument of a lexical item, and is structuralized in a position outside a Maximal Projection headed by that item and containing any internal arguments. Which argument is the external argument is typically taken to be part of the lexical information specified in a lexical entry.[10] This distinction also leads us directly to the next subtopic, the position of Subjects in PS.

1.1   Subjects in PS

The intuition that Subjects are somehow different from any other arguments is an old one. The notion of "external argument" provides one way to begin to theoretically reconstruct this intuition. It does not by itself, however, have necessary implications for a PS mediated interpretation of the intuition.[11] There are several issues in play with respect to Subjects and PS. Does the Subject appear within a Maximal Projection of the item of which it is an argument? Does it appear outside such a Maximal Projection? Are these mutually exclusive options? What principle(s) determine the answers to these questions? Are there principles which refer to Subjects as such?

Much, perhaps most, P & P work seems to accept the following idea: ". . . all of the arguments of [a] predicate are in some sense internal to a projection of the predicate."[12] Speas calls this idea the Lexical Clause Hypothesis (LCH), and it is one of the main (though not the only) justifications for the currently widespread view that Subjects originate structurally within VP (or, more generally, any maximal category headed by a predicate).[13] The basic idea here is theoretical parsimony: if structure is a representation of lexical information, and if an argument-taker licenses structure within which its arguments are to be found, then the simplest proposal is that all of its arguments are to be so found. Accepting the LCH still leaves open the question of what category a Subject is sister to, however.

It might seem that this is not so. If Subjects are within maximal projections, then, presumably, they are not also sisters to them. This is the position of Speas (1990). Yet many proponents of versions of the LCH in fact have Subjects as both daughters and sisters to maximal projections.[14] There are both empirical and theoretical reasons for so doing. Speas herself (1990: 128–38) provides a range of empirical evidence that strongly suggests "that the underlying structure of English is hierarchically organized in such a way that the subject is structurally superior to the objects and is outside of a maximal constituent of VP" (Speas 1990: 138). Theoretical grounding is provided by the theory of Predication (Williams 1980; Rothstein 1985).

Predication Theory is a syntactic theory, and one that explicitly refers to Subjects. As developed by Rothstein (1985: 7) there are three central claims:

(3) a. A predicate is an open one-place syntactic function requiring SATURATION.
     b. The syntactic unit which may be a predicate is a maximal projection.
     c. APs, VPs, and PPs must always be predicates; NP and S' may be predicates.

A Subject, on this view, just is that argument which saturates a Predicate. As Predicates must be maximal projections, it follows then that a Subject is outside of the maximal projection of which it is the Subject.[15] If you want both Predication Theory and the LCH, then Subjects are going to be both within and outside of the maximal projection of the verb.[16] But, as Speas (1990: 102) points out, such a proposal places the Subject ". . . in an underlying adjunction configuration [actually, an *adjunct* configuration–RC], which violates the strictest forms of X-bar theory. . . ." This means that in order to combine Predication Theory and the LCH, one needs an account of Adjunct structure. But one needs that anyway, and it is our next subtopic.[17]

1.2   Adjunct(ion)s

Here we double back to the notion of "canonical structuralization" in that these are exactly cases of **non**canonical structures, as explained below. There are two distinct topics here which are often run together.[18] One is *adjunction*, a syntactic movement operation, one often taken to mediate, for example, the S-Structure-to-LF relationship. The other is *Adjuncts*, nonargument modifiers of a Head.[19]

It is not really so surprising that these two have been treated together. They share, so it seems, a structural configuration unique to them, exemplified in (4). As noted, this is a noncanonical structure. The crucial fact is that the mother and one of the daughters have the same label.[20]

(4)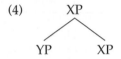

I begin with adjunctions, then move on to Adjuncts.

Adjunctions actually relate the structure in (5a) to that in (5b), not that in (4).

(5)   a.   b.

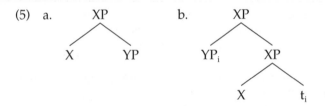

The crucial properties of the adjunction rule are (1) it is a movement rule, (2) it creates a new node, (3) the new node is the after movement mother of the moved element and a second node, and (4) the new mother node bears the label of its nonmoved daughter (the host). Adjunction is taken to mediate both the S-Structure-LF mapping, as noted previously, and the D-Structure-S-Structure relationship. The issue for PS theory is how, if at all, the theory helps explain the existence of a rule with the four properties just listed. PS theory is only indirectly relevant to property (1). It is this property which marks adjunctions as noncanonical structures; that is, the attempt to develop an account of the nature of noncanonical structures within a PS-based approach to syntax is the essence of "movement". So, PS theory may not shed any direct light on the movement, but the fact that the overall approach is strictly phrase structural throughout effectively requires movement if noncanonical structures are to be incorporated and, it is hoped, explicated. However, PS theory could or should shed light on each of the other three, as these involve elements (nodes) or relations (mother, labelling) ostensibly from PS theory.

For property (2), the issue is the status and licensing of nodes. Most P & P theorists take nodes as a basic building block of PS.[21] A theory that did not presumably could not have a rule with the second property; either there is no adjunction rule in such a theory, or there is some variation on (2) that does not invoke "nodes". Regardless of how this issue is resolved,[22] there is a deeper one: should a **rule** be such as to license additional structure? This engages two more fundamental issues. First, how is structure generally licensed – are rules involved or not? Second, what is the status of **additional** structure: is it necessary? if it is not necessary, how is it possible? why and how is it allowed? We should like our theory of structure to give us insight into the creation and licensing of all structure, canonical and noncanonical.

A relatively popular approach to adjunctions stems from work by May (1985, 1989; see also Chomsky 1986a).[23] May stipulates a rule with the four properties above and offers redefinitions of the basic PS predicates *dominates* and *category* to accommodate structures as in (5) above.[24]

In addition to issues about nodes (structure), there are issues about labels (categories).[25] What mechanisms and principles are involved? Given that there are both canonical and noncanonical structures, we need to consider how and why each are labelled as they are. Are the mechanisms and principles the same for both canonical and noncanonical structures? If not, how do they differ and how are they related? May, for example, assumes the same restrictions apply,[26] and that this apparently requires distinct mechanisms.[27] Speas (1990: 42–6) adumbrates an approach to labelling which "collapses the labeling function of X-bar theory with the implicit free generation of hierarchical structures" (Speas 1990: 43). Chametzky (1996: 17–19, 91–5) revises this position, uncollapsing labels and structures.[28] Chomsky (1995) takes a quite different approach to labels and labelling.[29]

Chomsky (1986a: 6) put forward a proposal for adjunctions, though at best for empirical reasons, it seems. His proposal is a two-part stipulation: (1) that adjunction to an argument is prohibited and (2) that only maximal projections may be hosts. This latter has been dropped in much subsequent work, including that by Chomsky, as Heads have been widely used as hosts. A number of theoretical issues are raised here. If the stipulations are useful, we should, of course, prefer to derive rather than demand their effects. And if they are not useful – as, for example, many find the restriction on hosts – then the theoretical investigation into the nature of possible adjunctions is entirely wide-open.[30]

We see with respect to adjunctions, then, that there has been widespread agreement – though little real theoretical work – both on the existence and nature of such a rule,[31] with the dissent of Chametzky (1994, 1996), and on the basic nature of nodes and labels, with the dissent of Chomsky (1995). Moreover, even putting aside the dissents, there are questions and issues that come up about adjunctions which PS theory could and should answer and address. We turn now to Adjuncts.

Adjuncts, recall, are nonargument modifiers of a Head. There are several diagnostics (NB, *diagnostics* are not a *definition*): (1) they are not mandatory[32] (2) they appear farther from the Head than do arguments (3) they iterate and (4) they do not appear in a specific order with respect to one another. Typical Adjuncts are, for example, locative and temporal PPs for V(P)s and relative clauses for N(P)s. Some examples illustrating the diagnostics are provided in (6).

(6) a. Kim announced the winners.
     b. *Kim announced in the auditorium.
     c. *Kim announced at three o'clock.
     d. Kim announced the winners in the auditorium.
     e. Kim announced the winners at three o'clock.
     f. *Kim announced in the auditorium the winners.
     g. *Kim announced at three o'clock the winners.
     h. Kim announced the winners in the auditorium at three o'clock.
     i. Kim announced the winners at three o'clock in the auditorium.

Though the phenomena are distinct, similar questions and issues arise here as arose with adjunctions: why do we see the structure we do (that in (4))? How is this structure licensed: by rule? by general principle(s)? Why? Is there node creation? How is the labelling licensed? Is there any restriction on the label which a host may bear? Notice that if we can answer these questions satisfactorily with respect to Adjuncts, then we might actually have reason to doubt the existence of an adjunction rule with all the properties listed in the discussion above. In particular, as no one analyzes Adjuncts by means of a movement rule that creates and labels a new node, if we find we are able to license and label a new node without such a rule in this case, we would want to know why whatever was involved did not carry over to the situation of the new node and label in adjunctions. It could be, of course, that there would be good theoretical reasons ruling out such carry over; but then we would be faced with a situation in which these two phenomena would have entirely distinct routes to their convergence on a common structure found only in these cases. Not impossible, by any means, and reminiscent of the distinction in evolutionary biology between homologous and analogous traits; but still, in generative grammar at least, a highly disfavored theoretical state of affairs.

Within the approach to structuralization explored by Lebeaux (1988, 1990) and Speas (1990), which, as noted above, takes D-structures to be "pure representations of theta grid requirements" there is no obvious way to include Adjuncts – definitionally not required by theta considerations – at D-structure.[33] The approach thus offers a relatively transparent explication of the noncanonical status of Adjuncts, though no straightforward clue as to how to integrate them into structure.[34]

For adjunct(ion)s as in (4) (repeated here), then, the crucial point, to reiterate, is that the mother and one daughter bear the same label. We have the following issues and questions. Is (4) correct in that the host is always a maximal projection; why should this be either true or false? Why, in the case of adjunction, do we not see some other adjunction – daughter-adjunction, for example?[35] Why not a label distinct from either that of the host or that of the adjoiner? How are nodes licensed: is this separate from labels; is it done by rule or by principle? Given the noncanonical nature of such structures, might it be appropriate to invoke revisions of basic predicates and relations to license them? Why should there be noncanonical structures anyway? Should we expect the same licensing principles to apply to Adjuncts and to adjunctions?

(4)   XP

    YP   XP

In discussing Adjuncts, crucial mention (and use) has been made of the notion "Head". We now turn to directly examining this concept.

2.0   Heads in PS

"Head" is the basic notion of DT; central to X-Bar theory has been the importation of this concept into PS-based syntax.[36] A Head is generally taken to be the lexical item which determines the syntactic nature of a larger unit (a phrase) of which the Head is a part. Typically, a Head is taken to determine the syntactic category of the larger unit, to be a mandatory constituent of that phrase, and to determine to some degree what else, if anything, may or must also occur in the phrase. Though there are questions and problems concerning the notion "Head" itself, we shall not address them.[37] Instead, we shall simply accept that "Head" is a real syntactic notion, with a role to play, as is now customary in PS-based P & P work. Our questions come down to the two already raised on p. 8. (1) are all constructions endocentric? and (2) is there a unique Head? These questions are related, since, if (1) is false, then (2) must be also, and if (2) is false, we might wonder about whether (1) is true. They are also related to the topic of the next section, Functional Categories, as these often are taken to expand the set of phrases to which (1) and (2) might or must pertain. "Head" is also crucial to the nature of X-Bar Theory.[38]

Endocentricity is largely assumed to hold for all phrases in current P & P work. Sometimes it is simply written into a set of rule schema (e.g., Chomsky 1986a); others, such as Speas (1990), Chomsky (1995), and Bouchard (1995) attempt an explication and analysis. PS-based work antecedent to or outside of P & P (e.g., Jackendoff 1977; Pullum 1991) does not always accept this view, and instead allows for exocentric analyses. The P & P analyst typically uses new categories (viz., Functional Categories) to cover those phenomena analyzed as exocentric by others. We shall presently have occasion to inquire into this move; for now, we simply note it.

Head uniqueness is also generally assumed in P & P work. Indeed, it seems to be taken as hardly worth discussion, more or less an inevitable result of other aspects of the theory (viz., endocentricity, the nature of "projection"). However, Bouchard (1995) and Williams (1994) disagree. Bouchard (1995: 75; 457, fn. 5) proposes a parameter of "endocentricity value" by which specific languages allow only one or more than one Head. Williams (1994: 11f.) argues specifically that coordinate structures and clauses are doubly headed. More generally, Williams (1994: 45–51) develops a notion of "relativized head" that goes along with, and is dependent on, the more usual notion, which he calls the "absolute head". This notion allows a non (absolute) Head to have some Head-like properties (e.g., feature projection) in a given configuration.

We should also take note of the question of "empty Heads". The issue here concerns when or if there is projection from a Head. Given the "lexical-entry-driven" approach, this comes down to what must there be in a lexical entry for a Head to project? This can have some important implications, particularly for the theory of movement.[39] We shall briefly mention two proposals.[40]

Speas (1994: 186, her (11)) proposes "a principle of Economy" on representations (7). As she notes, this can only do any work if its notion *content* is itself given content. She therefore suggests (8) (Speas 1994: 187, her (13)):

(7)   Project XP only if XP has content.

(8)   A node X has content if and only if X dominates a distinct phonological matrix or a distinct semantic matrix.

Speas includes both phonological and semantic matrices because "all structures must be interpreted at both of the interface levels, PF and LF . . ." (1994: 187). She applies (8) to a structure as in (9) (1994: 187, her (12)) in the following way (emphasis in original):

> If XP in [(9)] dominates no phonological material except that which is in the complement YP, then XP dominates no <u>distinct</u> phonological matrix. Similarly, if XP dominates no semantic material except that which is in the complement YP, then XP dominates no <u>distinct</u> semantic matrix. (1994: 187)

The implications for movement are explicitly drawn by Speas (1994: 187): "Thus, radically empty projections with the sole purpose of serving as landing sites for movement are disallowed."

(9)

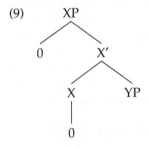

Bouchard (1995: 25) develops an approach to syntax which arrives at basically the same conclusion that "there cannot be semantically unlicensed 'open' positions, which only appear as landing sites for syntactic operations." He argues (1995: 93) for a particularly strong version of the "lexical-entry-driven" approach: "[t]he null assumption . . . is that the semantic formatives in the lexical representation of an item are all identified in some way in the sentence where the item occurs." He enforces this assumption, which drives his entire theoretical undertaking, with (10), his Principle of Full Identification (1995: 93–4, his (31)).

(10) *Principle of Full Identification*: Every syntactic formative of a sentence must have a corresponding element in the semantic representation. Every formative of a semantic representation must be identified by a morphosyntactic element in the sentence with which that representation is associated.

The point in bringing up this issue is the following. If one adopts both some version of the "lexical-entry-driven" view of PS and some kind of "account-ability" requirement (Bouchard 1995: 95)[41] on what can and must appear in a syntactic structure, then the justification of "empty Heads" can become a problem. It may be possible to dissolve the problem (Chomsky 1995), but it should not be assumed that analyses developed within other assumptions can be simply carried over without problem. Very often, I think, analytic work proceeds without this sort of theoretical reconnoitering, sometimes, at least, to bad effect.

Even this brief roughing out of the Head territory has proven impossible to do without reference to the topic of the next section, Functional Categories. So we move directly to that discussion.

3.0   Functional vs. Lexical Categories

The founding notion of the P & P approach to PS is that structure is not arbitrary, but is rather a means of representing information carried by lexical items in their lexical entries, where this information is both the category of the lexical item itself and restrictions on its cooccurrence with other items or phrases.[42] Understandably enough, this project began with those items which tradition-ally were thought to carry such lexical information: Nouns, Verbs, Adjectives, some Prepositions – the categories traditionally dubbed "content words" or, more theoretically, "Open Class items" or "Lexical Categories". Opposed to these are the "function words", or "Closed Class items" or "Functional Categories": Determiner, Complementizer, INFL, perhaps Conjunction.[43] A striking feature of much P & P work of the last decade has been the extension of the struc-turalization relation from Lexical Categories to Functional Categories, along with a concomitant proliferation (or, perhaps, discovery) of further Functional Categories.[44]

For the PS theorist, the basic question is what theoretical justification is there for this development. There may be a temptation to point to various analytic successes that this development has afforded, but, while analytic success is, of course, the ultimate arena of evaluation, it is not the only such arena. And, from a theoretical point of view, we need not be overly impressed, perhaps, by the analytic successes, as it should be expected that expansion of the theoretical apparatus leads to increased analytic coverage. More interesting is to achieve greater analytic coverage without expanding the theoretical apparatus. None-theless, there is no inherent virtue in waiting for theoretical or conceptual clearance for expansion before proceeding with analytic work, and, indeed, such pusillanimity may create a pointless obstacle to inquiry.[45] But as we are here engaged in theoretical analysis and inquiry, we do ask for something other than analytic justification. And, indeed, the discussion in this subsection will ultimately be more evaluative than has so far been the case, as we shall see.

3.1   Chomsky (1986a) and the "generalization" hypothesis

Though early in P & P work (e.g., Chomsky (1981), Stowell (1981)) it is suggested that the syntactic constituents then labelled S and S', and which were only problematically analyzed endocentrically,[46] might better be seen as headed by INFL or COMP, these constituents were nonetheless not afforded "full projection" status until Chomsky (1986a). Chomsky there asks whether the system regulating Lexical Categories "extend[s] to the nonlexical categories as well." He immediately answers, "[e]vidently, the optimal hypothesis is that it does" (1986a: 3). This is the extent of the theoretical argument and justification. The argument is familiar and not uncompelling: if there is a set of clear cases (in this instance, the Lexical Categories) for which we have a theoretical proposal, then the null hypothesis is that this carries over to less clear or central cases (Functional Categories) until and unless there develops strong evidence to the contrary.[47]

So, starting with Chomsky (1986a), we get IP and I (= INFL), CP and C (= complementizer), and then the further "generalization" to DP and D (= determiner) (this is developed especially in Steven Abney's unpublished 1987 MIT dissertation), the "splitting" of IP into AGRP and AGR (= agreement) and TP and T (= tense) (beginning with Pollock (1989)), along with subsequent or contemporaneous suggestions for various other Functional Heads and Categories (e.g., NEGP and NEG for negation, ASPP and ASP for aspect). Spencer (1992: 313) calls the general idea the Full Functional Projection Hypothesis (FFPH).[48]

(6)   Full Functional Projection Hypothesis
       Any morphosyntactic formative which corresponds to a Functional Category in a given language is syntactically the head of maximal projection.

Despite its apparent status as a null hypothesis, there is nonetheless a basic theoretical question we might ask of the FFPH. If the guiding idea in P & P approaches is that PS is indeed "lexical-entry-driven", why should Functional Categories be involved? Really, this is just questioning that FFPH is the null hypothesis. Sharpening the question a bit: given that *everyone* seems to agree that there is some real difference between the two sorts of categories, is it truly so obvious and straightforward to "generalize" as Chomsky (1986a) suggests?

There are a number of possible positions that some sort of negative answer to this question allows. Most radical is simple denial of the generalization, limiting projection to Lexical Categories. No one in P & P seems to take this position explicitly, so we leave it (for now).[49] Instead, analysts suggest ways of maintaining both the distinction and the generalization. We shall look at Fukui and Speas (1986) (FS, hereafter) and Fukui (1995), Speas (1990) and unpublished works by Abney (1987), Grimshaw (1991), and Lebeaux (1988). We should bear in mind, however, that there is a tension between the "distinction" and the "generalization": the greater the one is, the less motivation there is for the other, and any particular attempted reconciliation may strike us as unstable.

3.2   Fukui and Speas (1986), Fukui (1995), and Speas (1990): Functional Heads

FS (1986: 5–6) and Fukui (1995: 14) list the following four properties as ways in which Functional Categories contrast with Lexical Categories.

(11)   (i)   Functional Heads have one and only one (i.e., non-iterable) Specifier, while the Specifiers of Lexical Heads may be iterable ones.

(ii)   The Specifiers of Functional Heads are often (in our model, always) moved from within their complement.

(iii)   All Functional Heads can have Specifier positions; it is not at all clear that all Lexical Heads have Specifier positions.

(iv)   Languages which lack Functional Heads also lack Specifier positions.

Fukui (1995: 12, 13) also incorporates the observations that Functional Categories, unlike Lexical Categories, do not "have theta-grids or 'Lexical Conceptual Structures'" and, citing Abney (see below), that Functional Categories "are closed-class items, that they lack the sort of semantic value associated with Lexical categories, and that they always select a unique complement."

Having characterized a distinction between Functional and Lexical Categories, FS (1986: 13–16) and Fukui (1995: 27–30) distinguish between two kinds of Functional Categories. They do this on the basis of *Functional Features* (*F-Features*). The idea here is to generalize the commonly accepted difference between tensed versus infinitival AGR/INFL (or whatever) in that the former, but not the latter, assigns nominative Case. The generalization is the suggestion that every Functional Category includes some such distinction, with F-Features being the cover term for the class of assigned properties. Besides nominative Case, genitive Case, assigned by *'s* and +WH, assigned by a WH-COMP are given as F-Features. A further new term Kase is also introduced, where this is defined as in (12) (Fukui 1995: 27, his (29)). Functional Categories have a specifier position only when Kase is assigned to that position.

(12)   Kase = Case U F-Features

The paradigm in (13) is derived on these assumptions (FS 1986: 14; Fukui 1995: 28, his (30)).

(13)

	C	I	DET
Kase assigner	+WH	Tense/AGR	's
non-Kase assigner	that	to	the

These authors go on to work out various consequences and extensions of these ideas, but these do not directly concern us. The point, rather, is to get a sense of how they flesh out the bare suggestion of generalizing "projection from the lexicon" from Lexical Categories to Functional Categories.

Speas (1990: 110–16) revises somewhat the proposals made in FS. Speas (1990: 112) points out that FS made "an implicit assumption that the theory of phrase structure is relevant in restricting the occupants of the specifier position for functional categories, and that bar level is a primitive which may vary both cross-linguistically and from category to category." Both of these ideas are rejected in Speas (1990), though the elaboration of Kase Features is retained and is used to account for the facts which the rejected assumptions accounted for in FS.

Speas also adumbrates an account of grids and Lexical Conceptual Structures (LCS) for Functional Heads, "grids which specify what sort of complement they take, and specify the Kase features that they have" (Speas 1990: 114). The examples of functional LCS are those for DET and INFL, which are analyzed as "theta binders" rather than "theta assigners", with concomitant differences in LCS form:

> The difference between lexical and functional heads is that the position in the Kase grid of a functional head is never linked to a variable in LCS. The reason is that there are no referential variables in the LCS of a functional head. A functional head is in an informal sense semantically parasitic on a predication, and so although it has Kase features to assign, it has no relevant variable in its LCS to which these might be linked. (Speas 1990: 116)

We see, then, that Speas (1990) disagrees with Fukui (1995) with respect to whether Functional Heads have LCSs, but agrees with the notion, which Fukui gets from Abney, "that they lack the sort of semantic value associated with Lexical categories". Speas also carries over the restriction on number of specifiers of a Functional Head (see (11i) above), though now rejecting the PS account given by FS. Again, our point is not what can be done with the generalization once it is effected, but rather how and to what extent, if at all, the distinction between Lexical and Functional Categories is maintained given this generalization. We turn now to the work of Abney (1987), already alluded to by Fukui (1995).

3.3   *Abney (1987): Functional Elements*

Fukui (1995) takes over some ideas from Abney for characterizing Functional Categories.[50] Abney (1987: 64) also notes that the Functional versus Lexical distinction seems to play a role outside of grammar proper, in that children acquire the former later than the latter, and that in some aphasias there can be loss of ability to process Functional, but not Lexical, Categories. Abney (1987: 64–5) lists the following five properties, stressing that "none of the following properties are <u>criterial</u> for classification as a functional element. . . ." (emphasis in original)

(14)   (i)   Functional Elements constitute closed lexical classes.
       (ii) Functional Elements are generally phonologically and morphologic-
             ally dependent. They are generally stressless, often clitics or affixes,
             and sometimes even phonologically null.
       (iii) Functional Elements permit only one complement, which is in
             general not an argument. The arguments are CP, PP, and . . . DP.
             Functional Elements select IP, VP, NP.
       (iv) Functional Elements are usually inseparable from their complement.
       (v)   Functional Elements lack . . . "descriptive content". Their semantic
             contribution is second-order, regulating or contributing to the
             interpretation of their complement. They mark grammatical or
             relational features, rather than picking out a class of objects.

Though they differ in their respective statuses (e.g., (iii) is evidently theory internal in a way that (i) and (ii) are not), none of these by now seem especially surprising or novel. Abney takes (v) to be the central characteristic, and it is crucial for motivating his distinction between *c-projection* and *s-projection* (Abney 1987: 57–8). C-projection (= "category projection") is just the usual notion of syntactic projection (viz., V to VP, I to IP, etc.). S-projection (= "semantic projection") "is the path of nodes along which its descriptive content is 'passed along'." Thus, Functional Categories are part of the s-projections of Lexical Heads, as Functional Elements have no "descriptive content" of their own, and serve to "pass along" the content of the Lexical Heads. Abney gives the following definition (1987: 57, his (47)):

(15)   b is an s-projection of a iff
       a.   b = a, or
       b.   b is a c-projection of an s-projection of a, or
       c.   b f-selects an s-projection of a

"F-selection" is the name Abney (1987: 56) gives to "the syntactic relation between a functional element and its complement." He gives the example in (16) (1987: 58, his (48)), where the circled nodes are, respectively, the c-projection and s-projection sets of the lower V. We note that CP is the maximal s-projection of V, I, and C.

(16)   a.   b.

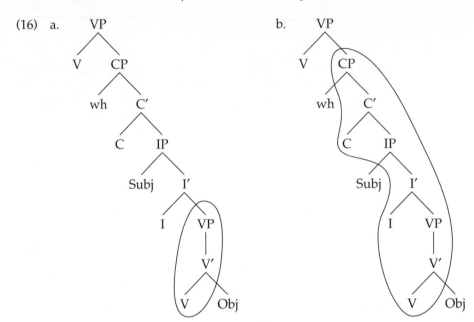

As always, we shall not pursue the various analytic consequences of these observations and definitions. And, indeed, Abney's notions of c-projection and s-projection lead rather nicely to the discussion of Grimshaw (1991).

3.4   *Grimshaw (1991): from Extended Projection to a theoretical impasse*

Grimshaw (1991: 1) explicitly refers to and draws on Fukui, FS, and Abney. She calls this tradition "functional head theory" and introduces the terms *F-head* (functional head) and *L-head* (lexical head). Grimshaw's basic idea is the following. Each F-head is categorially non-distinct from some L-head, and this affords insight into the combinatoric (im)possibilities of Heads and their complements. We now provide the mechanics.

Grimshaw (1991: 3) analyzes syntactic categories as triples, where one member of the triple is the categorial specification (done in terms of the features [+/−N] and [+/−V]), one is the bar-level specification, and the third, novel, member is the specification for a non-categorial feature F (= functional). Crucial are two points: (1) F is not part of the category specification, so items differing in F value but identical in N/V values are of the same category and (2) F is not binary valued. As to this second, F takes one of three values: 0, 1, or 2. The first value means that the item is an L-head, not an F-head; the second two values distinguish among F-heads, as shown directly. Grimshaw (1991: 3, 6 her (2) and (8)) provides the following analyses for some Heads; under this analysis, V, I, and C are of one syntactic category, while N, D, and P are of another, and the relations within each category are the same as those in the other (viz., higher F values take lower F values as complements – see (19d) below).[51]

(17) V   [+V,–N]   {F0}   (L0)
      I   [+V,–N]   {F1}   (L0)
      C   [+V,–N]   {F2}   (L0)
      N   [–V,+N]   {F0}   (L0)
      D   [–V,+N]   {F1}   (L0)
      P   [–V,+N]   {F2}   (L0)

Grimshaw (1991: 3, 4, 9, her (3), (4), and (12)) also provides the following definitions for *perfect Head/projection, extended Head/projection,* and the *Generalized Theta Criterion* (GTC). Perfect projection is just ordinary projection, as the F-feature is effectively irrelevant. Extended projection allows and constrains projection in terms of the F-feature value.

(18) x is the *perfect head* of y, and y is a *perfect projection* of x iff
      (a) y dominates x
      (b) y and x share all categorial features
      (c) all nodes intervening between x and y share all categorial features
      (d) the F value of y is the same as the F value of x

(19) x is the *extended head* of y, and y is an *extended projection* of x iff
      (a) y dominates x
      (b) y and x share all categorial features
      (c) all nodes intervening between x and y share all categorial features
      (d) If x and y are not in the same perfect projection, the F value of y is higher than the F value of x

(20) *Generalized Theta Criterion*
      Every maximal projection must either
      a.   receive a role or
      b.   be part of an extended projection that receives a role.

As noted above, the goal of the analysis is to explain (im)possibilities in the combinatorics of Heads and their complements. Grimshaw (1991: 8 her (9)–(11)) provides the following three classes of cases. In (21) we find combinations which form extended projections as defined in (19) – an F-head with a complement that it is both categorially identical to and higher valued on the F-feature value than. In (22) we have combinations of an L-head with a complement. In (23) are combinations of an F-head with a complement with which it cannot form an extended projection. The combinations in (21) and (22) are common ones which must be licensed, while those in (23) do not occur, and thus must not be licensed.[52]

(21) C-IP, P-DP
      I-VP, D-NP
      C-VP, P-NP

(22) V-PP, V-DP, V-NP, C-CP, V-IP, C-VP
      N-PP, N-DP, N-NP, N-CP, N-IP, N-VP

(23)   I-NP, I-DP, I-PP, I-CP
       D-VP, D-IP, D-CP, D-PP
       C-NP, C-DP, C-NP, C-VP
       P-VP, P-IP, P-CP, P-NP
       C-CP, P-PP, I-IP,   D-DP

The two clauses of the GTC (20), along with the assumption that only the complements and specifiers of L-heads can be theta-marked, will distinguish the cases. The maximal projection complements in (22) fall under (20a), theta-marked complements of L-heads, while those in (21) fall (potentially) under (20b), as they form extended projections with F-heads which may be theta-marked. But those in (23) fall under neither, as they are complements of F-heads, but not ones with which they form extended projections. The combinations in (23) are impossible in principle: the complement can neither be theta-marked by the F-head nor form an extended projection with the F-head, and so cannot be assigned a role, as the GTC requires. As Grimshaw observes (1991: 9) this provides an account of a property we have seen already (emphasis in the original): "each f-head ... occurs only with a very limited set of complements, quite typically only with one. This will follow if *f-heads take only complements that they form extended projections with.* ..." Given the definitions and category analysis, L-heads cannot form extended projections with their complements: L-heads and their projections are {F0}, and so the projection cannot have a <u>higher</u> F-feature value than a complement, as required by (19d) for an extended projection.

The *perfect projection* versus *extended projection* distinction is clearly very similar to Abney's *c-projection* versus *s-projection* distinction.[53] Indeed, it is not unreasonable, I think, to see Grimshaw's work as something of a culmination of the entire line of Functional-Head Theory inquiry. So, before moving on to Lebeaux (1988), which, as we shall see, is importantly different from these other works, it is appropriate to look somewhat more closely at this line, and its zenith in Grimshaw (1991).

As we have noted at the outset of this section, everyone agrees that Functional and Lexical Categories are different. And, again as pointed out earlier, the issue in Functional-Head Theory is to investigate these differences within a framework that generalizes PS theory from Lexical to Functional Heads. Grimshaw develops Functional-Head Theory most directly and explicitly, and reaches the statement in (24) (1991: 41 her Principle 1.)

(24)   Only Lexical Heads Select, Syntactically and Semantically.

As a corollary of this, Grimshaw states that "[f]unctional heads have no selectional powers at all." She argues for this view as follows (1991: 39–40). The usual view in Functional-Head Theory is to suppose that the generalization to Functional Categories is essentially a generalization of the *selection* relation from Lexical Heads to Functional Heads. But this position then takes the combinatoric (im)possibility facts illustrated in (21)–(23) above as arbitrary facts. And it ignores the salient dissimilarities between the two cases; Grimshaw (1991: 40) cites the familiar facts that Functional Heads take only one category as a complement and that, as a result, there is little or no lexical variation within Functional Categories with respect to complement categories. Further, it ignores what Grimshaw (1991: 40) calls the "stability" of the relations between Functional Heads and their complements "both within a language and cross-linguistically." Grimshaw cites as an example the fact that "C is always on top of I rather than vice versa. . . ." Again, this is unexpected if the mechanisms in play are "isolated stipulations about what goes with what." She concludes (1991: 40) "that there is nothing substantive to the claim that the relationship between an F-head and its complement is one of selection." Making the claim "does not bring to bear a set of principled restrictions; it merely allows the description of any observed combination."

Grimshaw's alternative is that not selection, but rather projection, determines the nature of complements to Functional Heads. Her notion of extended projection (along with the GTC and her analysis of categories) completely determines the range of (im)possible complements to Functional Heads. And, correspondingly, because Lexical Heads do not form (extended) projections with their complements, projection, whether extended or perfect, plays no role in determining the complements of Lexical Heads (1991: 41). "The character of the relationship between a functional head and its complement," Grimshaw writes (1991: 40), "is quite dissimilar from that between a lexical head and its complement."

I think there can be no denying but that Grimshaw is correct in her theoretical arguments and conclusions. Using *selection* as the mechanism to account for the relation between Functional Heads and their complements is unprincipled, uninsightful, and, ultimately, no more than word play. In this, she, and now we, disagree with the Functional-Head Theory tradition; so much the worse for the tradition. However, we might now want to inquire a bit more closely into Grimshaw's own approach. For if the tradition's view of things is theoretically hopeless, it would be nice to know that the alternative bears up under some scrutiny, as otherwise a considerable problem arises. I happen to think Grimshaw's approach does not bear up very well at all, and that there is, indeed, a considerable problem. I move first to Grimshaw, then the problem, and finally to Lebeaux (1988), who suggests a way out, I believe.

The {F} feature is crucial to Grimshaw's project.[54] There are two crucial aspects of the {F} feature. First, it is not categorial. Second, it is not binary. We take up each in turn. Because it is not categorial, specification for {F} does not distinguish e.g., DP from NP. In order to help understand what {F} is, Grimshaw invokes "Bar-level specification", represented as the feature (L), as also neither categorial nor binary. But it is an interesting fact about the most careful contemporary analyses of X-Bar theory – viz., Speas (1990) and Kornai and Pullum (1990) – that they do away with "Bar-level" as a primitive of the theory.[55] While this is not itself sufficient to give up on {F}, it is not particularly encouraging, either. We need to look a bit more deeply. We need to ask what it can mean, syntactically, to say, as Grimshaw (1991: 3) does, that "a category label . . . is analyzed as a triple" only one part of which is categorial. We need to ask how it is that information in a category label that is not categorial is available in and for syntax. Notice that if we did still believe in the need for "bar-levels", there would be a disanalogy here between (L) and {F}. It is certain that no one would want to maintain the position that, say, N, N′ and NP are all *identical* in category. It was precisely the point of X-Bar projection that these are both not identical syntactic categories and also closely related syntactic categories.[56] This is of no small importance, as to claim that syntactic entities are of identical syntactic category is to be committed to their having identical syntactic behavior. At least, it is to be so committed within a PS-based approach to syntax. There just is no other sort of information in such an approach other than the syntactic category labels, based in word classes, and the constituent structure positions of such category labels. Grimshaw (1991: 2) says, "[t]he {F} value of a node is, in this theory, not part of its categorial analysis." But this is to say that it is not part of syntax "in this theory"; either the feature makes a categorial contribution, distinguishing subcategories, or it is syntactically invisible and inert. Grimshaw herself makes the salient point, though she does not draw our conclusion:

> The categorial theory which is the basis for extended projection makes explicit the hypothesis that a functional category is a relational entity. It is a functional category by virtue of its relationship to a lexical category. Thus DP is not just a functional category it is the functional category <u>for N</u>, as IP is <u>for V</u>. (Grimshaw 1991: 3, underlining in original)

The point to stress is that PS-based syntax can refer to a "relational entity" only if it is definable in PS terms. This is why, for example, we have the famous structural/categorial definitions of Subject and Direct Object as, respectively, NP immediately dominated by S and NP immediately dominated by VP.[57] This is not to say that Grimshaw's observation might not be correct. It is to say, rather, that how to encode this observation in the vocabulary of PS-based syntax is none too obvious.[58] One may attempt to do as Grimshaw has done, but this changes the theory in obscure ways, allowing noncategorial information to play a categorial role.

It might be objected that I have placed undue weight on a name. That is, I have read too much into Grimshaw's use of "categorial" for the [+/−N +/−V] features. If some other term had been used – say, "lexical" – no one would be so tempted to make the argument I have. What we have is not, on this view, some kind of major theoretical incoherence, but rather, at worst, a relatively minor terminological equivocation. This response is serious, and requires an answer. My answer depends on examining Grimshaw's practice in two areas. One is what she says about the category status of Functional versus Lexical Categories. The other is how the {F} feature is actually put to use – which leads us back to our second aspect of the {F} feature, its nonbinarity. I note that this answer may not totally convince a hard-liner in that Grimshaw could be wrong or confused in her practice and this would not necessarily undermine the theoretical concepts: *abusus non tollit usum*. However, there would be considerable prima facie evidence in favor of my position, and a substantial burden of argument would be placed on my hypothetical interlocutor.

Grimshaw says explicitly (1991: 2) "D and N are of the same syntactic category, once we have abstracted away from the lexical/functional distinction." This may still seem equivocal. Again perhaps equivocally, she writes (1991: 24) "the neutralizabliity of N and V holds equally for D and I, P and C, since these are categorially the same as N and V." However, Grimshaw also says (1991: 2), "[s]ince I and D are of the same category as their lexical counterparts, V and N, they must be distinguished by another property. . . ." And, later, she writes of C, I and V (1991: 39) that "[t]hese three are of the same syntactic category, and have F values which permit them to form an extended projection." These seem to me about as unequivocal as could be hoped for. I think it is fair to say that for Grimshaw, at least, the terminological choice is a motivated, not an arbitrary, one: the "categorial" features alone really do determine an item's syntactic category.

Let us now consider the use of {F}. How does Grimshaw account for the differences in distribution between, e.g., NP and DP? It is here that we confront the second crucial aspect of {F}, its nonbinary nature. For, of course, Grimshaw must use {F} to distinguish DP and NP, as they are categorially identical. It is in conditions (18d) and (19d) of her definitions for perfect and extended projections, repeated here, that the crucial distinctions are made. Given these, the analyses of DP as {F1} and NP as {F0}, and the GTC, also repeated here, DP and NP will not be licensed in the same environments. Thus, as argued above, noncategorial information not reducible to some combination of the PS conceptions of category and structure is used to account for syntactic distribution, a theoretical development entirely new in – because it goes against the basic theoretical commitments of – PS-based theory. Notice, too, how much depends on a notational convention, viz., that {F} should have values for which "higher than" can be defined. This is not a necessary consequence of a nonbinarity; imagine that the three values in question were notated by #, @, and $, to pick three symbols pretty much at random from the keyboard in front of me. We could then stipulate an ordering among them, of course, but we would do so only in order to be able to state the definitions as in (18) and (19). I think we are entitled to serious suspicion when apparently deep linguistic properties hinge on the vagaries of notation. As Gauss said, "*non notationes, sed notiones.*"

(18)   x is the *perfect head* of y, and y is a *perfect projection* of x iff
    (a)   y dominates x
    (b)   y and x share all categorial features
    (c)   all nodes intervening between x and y share all categorial features
    (d)   the F value of y is the same as the F value of x

(19)   x is the *extended head* of y, and y is an *extended projection* of x iff
    (a)   y dominates x
    (b)   y and x share all categorial features
    (c)   all nodes intervening between x and y share all categorial features
    (d)   If x and y are not in the same perfect projection, the F value of y is higher than the F value of x

(20)   *Generalized Theta Criterion*
    Every maximal projection must either
    a.   receive a role or
    b.   be part of an extended projection that receives a role.

And, in fact, it is not even clear that the apparatus Grimshaw sets up does the work she claims it does – or, at least, not in the way she claims. Consider again the set of "impossible combinations" (23), repeated here. In particular, consider the last row: C-CP, P-PP, I-IP, D-DP.

(23)   I-NP, I-DP, I-PP, I-CP
        D-VP, D-IP, D-CP, D-PP
        C-NP, C-DP, C-NP, C-VP
        P-VP, P-IP, P-CP, P-NP
        C-CP, P-PP, I-IP,   D-DP

Grimshaw's claim and point, recall, is that "[i]t is only combinations of L-heads and complements that are not governed by projection" (1991: 40). Or, put the other way round, the combinatoric (im)possibilities of F-heads are governed by projection. Grimshaw points out (1991: 6) that such con-figurations as in the last line of (23) are ruled out by (19d). True, but they are all allowed in by (18d). While they cannot form extended projections, they are (perfectly) in accord with the conditions on perfect projections. Notice, further, that what would rule out such combinations in traditional Functional-Head Theory, viz., a stipulation on the "selectional" properties of the Functional Head in question – is not possible for Grimshaw, given that she has shown that selection plays no role with respect to Functional Heads and their complements.

Now, as it happens, these perfect projections do run afoul of (20), the GTC. They do so because in a structure such as (25), in which all the DPs form a perfect projection, none of the lower ones are in accord with either clause of the GTC. They are not assigned a role *simpliciter*, clause (20a), because, unlike the topmost DP, they are not complements of a Lexical Head. And because they form a perfect projection, not an extended projection, they cannot fall under clause (20b). But now, contrary to Grimshaw's stated claim, it is not just the theory of projection which accounts for the combinatoric (im)possibilities of Functional Heads and their complements. While evidently not in itself any sort of theoretical catastrophe, it does indicate a theoretical weakness in exactly the place where the claim is for most theoretical strength.

(25)

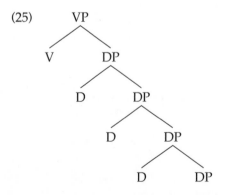

To sum up: I have pointed to two sorts of problems with the {F} feature. One is that it seems to advance a merely notational approach to a presumably deep linguistic issue. Second, the major theoretical advantage it claims to afford, viz., directly and entirely accounting for the combinatorics of Functional Heads and their complements, is not exactly true (though, perhaps, not exactly false, either). I now claim that such technical problems are exactly what we should expect to find in an approach that is in fact conceptually unsound, as I have already argued Grimshaw's is. Foundational problems ought to – presumably must – give rise to technical problems at some point. If there were not the sort of unsoundness I have demonstrated, then we could count the technical problems merely as defects in the particular analysis or analyst. Now, however, there would be a terribly heavy burden of argument on one who would take such a position.

But now where are *we*? Grimshaw has shown us that the usual Functional-Head Theory is unsatisfactory, even empty, in crucial areas. Her own alternative is unsound conceptually and technically flawed. As these approaches – one based in selection, the other in projection – would seem to partition the ways in which to carry out the generalization of structuralization from Lexical to Functional Categories, the prospects for a theoretically contentful "generalization" do not look promising. This should not really be so surprising, given Grimshaw's argument that selection has essentially nothing to say about the role of Functional Heads in syntax and her observations concerning the "stability" of the relations Functional Heads do have in syntax. The central issue with respect to structuralization and PS, recall, is precisely to tame the (selectional) idiosyncrasies of individual lexical items. But if Functional Heads have no such idiosyncrasies, then there just is nothing for the generalization to do. Hence the theoretical emptiness of the traditional selectional approach and the conceptual unsoundness of Grimshaw's projectionist alternative. I think the work of Lebeaux (1988), to which we now turn, can offer us a way out of this impasse, though the way out does, in fact, require giving up rather a lot of what is generally taken as established by the "generalization" within P & P approaches to PS. What we will not have to give up, however, is *some* way of integrating Functional Categories into a PS-based approach to syntax. Instead of a spurious "generalization", Lebeaux's work offers us an alternative that respects, indeed takes as fundamental, the distinction between Lexical and Functional Categories, and constructs a theoretical architecture for structuralization that is explicitly based in and builds on this distinction.

3.5 *Lebeaux (1988): Closed Class items and a theoretical opening*

Lebeaux asks us to take language acquisition facts into serious account when hypothesizing a syntactic architecture. In particular, Lebeaux (1988: 65, his (37)) suggests that syntactic theorizing be constrained by what he calls the *General Congruence Principle* (GCP), given in (26). Crucial from our perspective is the well-known acquisitional stage of "telegraphic speech" (see Lebeaux 1988: chapter 1 and 225f.) in which Closed Class items are absent.[59]

(26)   General Congruence Principle:
       Levels of grammatical representation correspond to (the output of) acquisitional stages.

Lebeaux argues for a radical reorganization of the syntax.[60] He suggests separate representations for Theta and Case relations, where these comprise, respectively, Open Class elements and Closed Class elements. These two representations undergo an operation called Merge, as in (27) (Lebeaux 1988: 243, his (43)). Each representation is "a pure representation of the particular vocabulary it invokes (Case theory vs. theta theory), and indeed, the crucial categories that are mentioned in each theory (determiner vs. nominal head) are distinct as well" (Lebeaux 1988: 242).

(27)

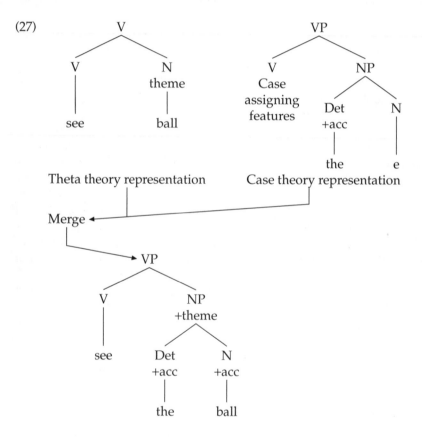

Lebeaux characterizes the two representations as follows. The Theta representation has as its vocabulary "theta roles . . . and category labels of the 0 bar level." And it includes Open Class items instantiating the terminal nodes (Lebeaux 1988: 243), as these are the relata in Theta relations. The Case representation "factors out the closed class aspect of the V-NP representation in a principled way. What it contains is the following: (1) a subtree in the phrasal syntax (it projects up to at least V'), (2) where the case assigning features of the verb are present, but not the verb, and (3) in which Case has been assigned to the determiner" (Lebeaux 1988: 244).[61]

The Merge operation is also characterized by Lebeaux (1988: 244):

> First, it inserts two lexical items into the slots provided by the case frame: the head verb and the theta governed noun. Second, it percolates the theta relation already assigned to the noun to the NP node (theme, in this case). Third, it copies the Case that was originally associated with the determiner position onto the head noun. This means that *ball*, as well as *the*, is marked for (abstract) accusative case.

Finally, he notes that "the fixed character of the closed class elements is modelled by having such elements be the frame into which the theta representation is projected" (Lebeaux 1988: 245).[62] As he puts it at the start (1988: 1) "it is the need for CC [closed class–RC] elements to be satisfied which gives rise to phrase marker composition from more primitive units." This is a crucial observation from our perspective. We need to know what this "satisfaction" for Closed Class items is supposed to come down to.

In fact, Lebeaux has put things somewhat badly here. It is not, in fact, that Closed Class items must be satisfied; it is, rather, that Open Class items must be syntactically licensed. We require some further analysis of the general situation. Any item that receives a semantic interpretation must, presumably, be both semantically and syntactically licensed. Those are the respective functions of the theories of Theta and Case; the former is semantic licensing, the latter is syntactic. Roles and Cases must be assigned and borne, or else some element will be unlicensed. Now, Lebeaux's insight is to see that the theories of Case and Theta are rather more separate than has usually been supposed; and this is to say that syntactic and semantic licensing are more separate than generally supposed. The two kinds of licensing correspond to the two kinds of elements, Closed and Open Class. Open Class elements license semantically, Closed Class elements license syntactically, giving rise to two distinct representations. In order for all meaningful elements to be both syntactically and semantically licensed, the two representations must merge and the distinct licensings must "spread" within the newly composed structure, as Lebeaux (1988: 240f.) proposes. So, it is not quite right to say, as I did above, that what is required is for Open Class elements to be syntactically licensed. While true, this misses the point, which may have been what Lebeaux was getting at, that Closed Class elements are also in need of further licensing. If NPs require Case, and Case is assigned to D Heads, and Ns bear Theta roles, and Ds are Theta binders (as Speas 1990 suggests), then in order for both the Open and the Closed Class item to be both syntactically and semantically licensed, the merger must bring them together.

But there remains a difference between the two sorts of elements and their representations. Closed Class items, to repeat, create the "frame into which the theta representation is projected" (Lebeaux 1988: 245). Theta structures have just enough of the vocabulary of syntax to undergo merger. And theta structures are themselves usable, and used – by adults as well as children – without merger; that, after all, is what telegraphic speech is.

We can now see just what is wrong with the Functional-Head Theory/ "generalization" tradition. It takes Functional Elements to be part of the problem, when in fact they are a part of the solution. The problem, recall, is the systematic structuralization of the idiosyncratic (selectional) properties of Lexical (Open Class) elements. Having made headway on this issue, the tradition extends – generalizes – its findings to Functional elements, despite the fact that there is no corresponding problem. This has allowed for an ever increasing inventory of Functional Heads and their projections, with apparently no theory guiding or constraining these "discoveries".

Lebeaux, on the other hand, argues that the Functional versus Lexical elements distinction is a fundamental one, not just in the lexicon, but in the architecture of the syntax as well. Functional elements and Lexical elements give rise to distinct representations incarnating distinct licensing conditions, which representations ultimately are merged into a single object. Notice that, in a sense, this simply extends the common "lexical-entry driven" approach to structuralization while respecting the different kinds of elements in the lexicon. Moreover, and this is crucial, Lebeaux's approach suggests that there are principles and constraints on the inventory of Closed Class elements and their structuralizations. The idea here – not one that Lebeaux himself advances – is the following. Functional elements and their structuralizations provide the syntactic licensing which Lexical elements require – recall the example of the Case marking on D spreading to the N(P) which requires Case for syntactic licensing. This means that analysts should posit Functional elements and their structuralizations only if it can be plausibly argued that there is an independent syntactic licensing relation which can both legitimate that Functional element and spread to a Lexical element that requires such licensing.[63]

We find ourselves, then, not with a new set of answers and analyses, but rather with a new way of looking for answers and analyses. There remain obscurities of both conception and detail in Lebeaux's work. It is not at all clear which findings and analyses from the tradition would carry over, nor in what form. But the advantages are real enough, I think. First, different theoretical kinds (in the lexicon) are kept distinct, instead of being simply and unthinkingly assimilated. Second, this distinction forms the basis for a network of distinctions that are otherwise thought unrelated (e.g., Case vs. Theta representations in syntax, stages in acquisition), creating a theoretical architecture that is much more integrated and deductively complex than previously. Finally, the beginnings of a contentful theory of Functional Heads and their structuralizations is adumbrated, so that Chomsky's (1986a: 3) original question of whether the system for structuralizing lexical categories "extend[s] to the nonlexical categories as well. . . ." no longer takes the null hypothesis "yes" as its answer.

I have taken rather more space, and been rather more argumentative, in this subsection than in previous ones. I think it has been warranted, in that the issue is an important one, and the discussion would not find a natural home in the later chapters. The positions I have argued for might be controversial; in any event, they are certainly minority views. In the next subsection, I return to the less tendentious mode.

4.0 X-Bar Theory

We consider two issues here. The first is the status of rules (or rule schema) in the grammar. The second is branching: is it always and only binary?

4.1 *Rules*

Stowell (1981) initiated the program of "X-Bar reduction" that reached its zenith in Speas (1990). A crucial enabling observation for the program is the following. Once an independent lexicon was introduced by Chomsky (1965), the grammar contained a massive redundancy, in that essentially the same information was specified in both the phrase structure rules and subcategorization frames. Eliminating the redundancy could evidently proceed in one of two ways: get rid of the phrase structure rules, or get rid of the sub-categorization frames. The Stowellian project pursues the former line.[64] Despite some criticism, notably by Pullum (1985) and Kornai and Pullum (1990), this is the standard view in P & P work.[65] Speas (1990) is the fullest working out of this line of inquiry, and contains much valuable review and criticism of other work. Despite this widespread agreement, there is still occasional equivoca-tion about the status of rule schema, if not rules themselves. It is sometimes the case that rule schema such as those in (28) are given and it is claimed that "categories are projections . . . in terms of . . ." these schema (Chomsky 1986a: 2–3). However, the status of these schema is generally not explicitly discussed, and concomitantly it is left obscure just how and why structuralization is "in terms of" them.[66] If there is a commitment to elimination of phrase structure rules, we should be told explicitly what other commitments afford this elimina-tion; a desire for reduction in redundancy does not, by itself, count.

(28) a. $X' = X \ X''^*$
      b. $X'' = X''^* \ X'$

4.2 *Binary branching*

There are two issues here, though typically only one gets discussed. One, the usual topic, is whether there is more than binary branching in a phrase marker (i.e., can any mother have more than two daughters?). The other is whether there is less than binary branching (i.e., can any mother have fewer than two daughters?). Most discussion of the first question traces itself back to Kayne (1981). Kayne there proposed an "unambiguous path" condition on various syntactic relations, and for this condition to hold, branching would have to be, by and large, at most binary.[67] Unlike many who purport to follow him in this line, Kayne does not stipulate that branching is at most binary. Instead, binary branching is required if there is to be an unambiguous path mediating some other syntactic relation, so it is an effect, rather than a cause.

There is relatively little actual attempt to motivate at most binary branching in the literature. Such argument as there is generally amounts to observing that such a restriction would restrict options analytically (or acquisitionally), hence is desirable, and therefore it will be assumed. Often virtually no consideration is given to the fact that there are empirical reasons to suppose branching may be more than binary,[68] though Williams (1994: 30–1) notices that such facts result in no more than binary branching having effects on the "locality" requirement on the "argument-of" relation, viz., that if a predicate has more than one argument, then not all the arguments can be sisters of that predicate. Williams seems to prefer giving up no more than binary branching to weakening the locality condition, as he finds the latter independently justified.

Kayne (1994) advocates no more than binary branching, once again, it seems, requiring this for satisfaction of some other syntactic relation (here his central Linear Correspondence Axiom rather than his earlier unambiguous path concept) rather than stipulating it outright for its own sake. Chomsky (1995: chapter 4) appears to take the position that no more than binary branching is required by "virtual conceptual necessity" (1995: 249). Chametzky (1996: 35–6, 112) allows that no more than binary branching might be justified as an empirical generalization and that it provides help in the analysis of Adjuncts. This issue will loom large in our Conclusion.

We turn now to the other issue, whether branching must be at least binary; that is, is there nonbranching domination? Often those who proscribe more than binary branching seem to allow for less than binary branching. The matter itself is examined in detail in Richardson and Chametzky (1985: 337–40) and resumed in Chametzky (1996: 27–8). They argue that no well-behaved PS theory ought to have such a relation.[69] There are two parts to their argument, a conceptual and an analytic. The conceptual portion is simply to observe that constituency is a part-whole relation, and to claim that a whole with one part is in the same relation to that part as a whole with two (or more) parts is to its parts is to make a nonobvious, quite plausibly spurious, claim. That the whole in the latter case is distinct from the parts seems clear, perhaps necessary; that this is so in the former case is not at all clear, though possible. The analytic portion is an examination of the actual range of cases of nonbranching domination in the literature. There are some four types examined; two have some antecedent plausibility.[70] One is the relation between lexical items and the "zero level" categories in a phrase marker. This, however, is not the part-whole relation of constituency, so the use of dominance is inappropriate.[71] The final case is that as in (29), nonbranching within a single Head's projection. The alternative suggested is multiple labelling of a single node; both formal and substantive reasons are advanced for supposing this is possible, even desirable.[72] The general conclusion is the following. If nonbranching domination is conceptually unsound, then there ought to be no clear and compelling instances of it – and there are not.

(29)   X″

X′

X

We move now to our final question, the statuses of precedence and dominance.

5.0   How to order a phrase marker

The issue here is whether phrase markers are specified as formal objects with two ordering relations or only one. No one suggests that the *dominance* ordering relation does not formally specify a phrase marker (though there is some disagreement with respect to whether this relation is reflexive or not[73]), so the question comes down to whether a *precedence* ordering relation also does. The issue really only arises once PSRs are given up; PSRs specify both immediate dominance relations among mother and daughters and linear precedence relations among daughters.[74] Within the P & P tradition, it is typically assumed that these two dimensions are separable and separate.[75] Following the lead of Stowell (1981), it is also typically assumed that precedence relations are the result of the interactions of various substantive subparts of the theory (see Speas 1990: 19–24 for discussion); this provides one type of "precedence rejection". A different type is argued for by Chametzky (1995, 1996: 6–14) where a novel argument against precedence as a basic ordering relation specifying phrase markers as formal objects is given.[76] Notice that the first, more common, type of "rejection of precedence" does not require this second type, while this second type still allows for the first. Under the first type, precedence relations are derived in substantive syntax, rather then specified in some sort of rule. But this is nonetheless consistent with a formal requirement that a precedence ordering relation be part of the specification of phrase markers. Under the second sort, there can be no such formal requirement, but it can still be the case that substantive syntactic considerations result in a precedence ordering.

Williams (1994: 178–98) provides a spirited, and unusual, defense of precedence as "a fundamental syntactic notion" (178). Most of the argument is with Larson's (1988) development of "shells" and use of verb movement to solve problems in binding theory, given the assumption that binding relations are mediated entirely by hierarchical (command) relations, and not at all by precedence. Williams's brief is that over a range of data types and analyses, Larson's approach is empirically worse than alternatives that do use precedence. Williams also examines two other areas, the Nested Dependency Condition and Weak Crossover, with similar results. However, it is not actually clear even if Williams is correct that therefore either of the "rejectionist" stances outlined above need be given up. If independent substantive syntactic considerations result in a precedence ordering, then it may well be open to the "rejectionist" to refer to this ordering in accounting for the empirical phenomena Williams discusses. What such a "rejection of precedence" would actually then amount to might be less than entirely clear; indeed, it might be empty or pointless.

Kayne (1994) makes much of precedence facts. Indeed, that entire book is an attempt to make something theoretically deep and revealing out of precedence facts. Interestingly, however, I do not think that Kayne's theory requires taking precedence to be a formal ordering relation that is part of the specification of phrase markers. Chomsky (1995: 335–40) discusses Kayne (1994) and explicitly relegates precedence relations to the nonsyntactic portion of the grammar (viz., the "phonological component").

This concludes our preliminary investigations. We turn now to the particular cases, the works through which we inquire into the fate of our concepts and questions, and of phrase structure more generally. Examination of the PS concepts and questions with which we are now familiar will structure much of our inquiry.

Notes

1   See Chametzky (1996: xvii–xviii) on *theoretical* versus *analytic* work.

2   See p. 2.

3   This is often called "projection" in the literature. I use the less elegant, but more transparent, "structuralization" in Chametzky (1996).

4   Borer rejects the lexical-entry-driven-approach and adumbrates an alternative driven by "the part of the subpredicate dealing with the verb in combination with aspectual projections" (1994: 45).

5   There is an extensive literature on the form and content of lexical information and its relation to syntactic structure. Besides Speas and Pesetsky, within P & P beginnings can be made with: Grimshaw (1990) and Levin and Hovav (1995).

6   We shall examine details in Chapter Two.

7   Compare these with Perlmutter and Postal's (1984) Universal Alignment Hypothesis (UAH) in Relational Grammar (RG). Rosen (1984) is an important discussion of argument alignment couched within RG assumptions. Chapters 1 and 2 of Pesetsky (1995) extensively review problems and prospects for what he calls U(T)AH, combining both UAH and UTAH. It should be noted that Bouchard (1995) elaborates an alternative general approach to these issues (and to syntax, semantics, and their relation) that he argues makes such statements as U(T)AH and RTAH – and explicit statements concerning PS – unnecessary.

8   Williams (1994: 159–61) has insightful remarks on argument ordering, including what he calls *t-normal order*: "ordering of elements according to theta roles . . . simply one of the factors that determines order, and a weak factor at that" (1994: 160).

9   This distinction remains absolutely central to the rather different theory developed in Williams (1994).

10   Speas (1990) accepts that there may be a "most prominent" argument lexically, but does not accept that it is structuralized outside a Maximal Projection of the lexical item of which it is an argument.

11   See note 15 below.

12   See, e.g., Speas (1990: 17–18, 102, and the works cited in her footnote 12, p. 25).

13   Whether Subjects which so originate also move to another position is a separate question, one that will not much concern us.

14   Chametzky (1996) is one example.

15   Well, almost. You also need a structural relation to mediate the Subject–Predicate relation; typically, some command relation (Barker and Pullum 1990; Chametzky 1996: ch. 2) is invoked, where the Subject must X-command the Predicate. See Chametzky (1987: 58–65) for some discussion of alternatives suggested by different versions of Predication Theory.

16 Chametzky (1996: 130–4) makes exactly this proposal.

17 Williams (1994: 141–51) develops an approach based in Predication Theory that neither obviously accepts nor denies the LCH.

18 Here and below I follow the discussion in Chametzky (1996: ch. 4).

19 Recall that "Adjunct" names a dependency relationship. It is not an essentially PS relationship.

20 A terminological note: I call the XP-daughter – the adjoined-to element – the "host". I here ignore nonmaximal hosts, viz., "adjunction to a Head". See below, however.

21 As we shall see in Chapter Four, however, Chomsky (1995: 244–5) does not.

22 We return to this issue in Chapters Four and Five.

23 It should be noted that May never discusses Adjuncts, hence never distinguishes them from adjunctions.

24 I have gone over this ground before, in Chametzky (1994, 1996: 89–106), and do so again in Chapter Two, section 2.3, so I will refrain from further comment here.

25 As pointed out in Chametzky (1996: 1) *structure* and *category* are the two basic **concepts** of the theory of syntax. *Immediate constituent node* and *word class label* are the **conceptions** given these concepts in virtually all P & P work. See, e.g., Rawls (1971: 5–6) or Dworkin (1977: 134–6) on the *concept* versus *conception* distinction.

26 Whether these are the result of similar, or any, principles, is not discussed, however.

27 Though this is somewhat unclear, as May does not explicitly discuss labelling and he may be assuming already labelled nodes as his primitives.

28 See Chapter Two.

29 See Chapter Four. Bouchard (1995: 85–6) adopts what was to become the position found in Chomsky (1995).

30 We note that Kayne (1994) relies on adjunctions to a very great degree; this is discussed in Chapter Three.

31 Bouchard (1995: 109–13) rejects all movement transformations, including adjunctions.

32 A more syntactic way to approach the same fact is to say Adjuncts do not subcategorize a Head.

33 Kornai and Pullum (1990: 44) in their formal (and somewhat hostile) analysis of "X-Bar grammars" notice this property as well.

34 We might also suggest that the approach appears to make the very existence of Adjuncts something of a surprise. That the existence of Adjuncts might pose a theoretical issue in need of explanation has not been explicitly raised before, to my knowledge. I think the theory in Chametzky (1996) can shed some light on this, as discussed in Chapter Two. We shall explore these problems and seeming conundra in some depth, particularly in section 2.3 of Chapter Two and section 3.3 of Chapter Four.

35 Or sister-adjunction – these are from the Standard Theory (see, for example, Bach 1974: 86–7).

36 See sections 2.1 and 3.0 of the Introduction.

37 See the references in note 7 of the Introduction. Croft (1996) argues for a "semantic definition of headhood" (1996: 69). I am not exactly sure what Croft takes the significance of his argument to be; we can note, however, that inability to *define* "Head" syntactically might be what one would expect were it a syntactic **primitive**. This is hardly a novel idea; it is basically the conclusion reached by Johnson (1977: 690) with respect to the failed attempt by Edward Keenan to define "Subject" in syntax, for example:

the best interpretation of K[Keenan]'s results is that they provide a reductio ad absurdum argument in favor of the RG view that grammatical relations such as SUBJ be taken as primitive, theoretical terms. As such, they are neither defined in terms of, nor directly connected to, observables or antecedently understood concepts. As uninterpreted, theoretical terms, however, they are indirectly connected to observables and/or antecedently understood concepts via the empirically testable predictions resulting from the statements in which they occur.

38   See section 4 below.

39   This is alluded to in Chametzky (1996: 182, fn. 16).

40   See also Emonds (1987) on his Empty Head Constraint.

41   As, for example, Bouchard's Principle of Full Interpretation (10), or Speas's statement, quoted above, concerning interpretation "at both interface levels."

42   In the terminology of the structuralist tradition, these might be seen as information concerning the "paradigmatic" and the "syntagmatic" dimensions.

43   Prepositions, famously, seem to cross-cut the classifications, being both "ClosedClass" and "Lexical". See, for example, the discussion in Emonds (1985: chs. 4, 6, 7) and Grimshaw (1991).

44   It should be noted that Jackendoff's (1977) "Uniform Three Levels Hypothesis" was not limited to Lexical Categories, but also included Article, Degree, and Quantifier Phrases.

45   See Kitcher (1983: 213–17, 229–41, 268–70) for insightful discussion of these issues in the context of "rigorization" in mathematics, with special reference to the difference in the development of calculus in Britain and on the European continent after its discovery by Newton and by Leibniz. A belief in the need to get a "legitimate inquiry license" may go along with the belief in the need to antecedently "define your terms" alluded to on p. 8.

46   See Chametzky (1987a) for discussion.

47   As Fukui and Speas (1986: 4) remark, *functional categories* is a much better term than *nonlexical categories* because on this view these categories "are projected from the lexicon and have independent lexical entries." Abney (1987: 54) makes a similar observation, using the term *functional element*.

48   Spencer, it should be noted, is critical of this position. Other critical discussion of "generalization" work can be found in Iatridou (1990), Ernst (1992), Janda and Kathman (1992), Joseph and Smirniotopoulos (1992), and Janda (1993).

49   Bouchard (1995: 255; 457, fn. 5; 479, fn.1) almost does, but in fact disallows only "contentless functional categories".

50   Abney uses the terms *Functional Element* and *Thematic Element* in his discussion.

51   Grimshaw (1991: 6) justifies the {F2} analysis of P and C as follows. "They do not act like the lexical categories, because they do not occur as complements of functional categories. They do not act like the functional categories because they do not take lexical complements. . . . P stands in the same relationship to DP and NP as C does to IP and VP."

52   There are some analytic details to consider here, as the generalization just stated is recognized by Grimshaw to be not obviously true. We shall not pursue the apparent counter examples or Grimshaw's attempts to explain or deny them.

53   Grimshaw (1991: 14) notes the similarity, and points out that the problems that require these moves are "more general – involving not just semantic relations but syntactic ones. . . . Hence, the solution must also be more general."

54 Though Grimshaw (1991: 8) writes, ". . . the theory of extended projection in no way rests on reference to the {F} feature; the same results will always be obtained even if the work of {F} is taken over by other parts of the theory." This is true enough, but, in the absence of anything remotely like a suggestion as to what such "other parts of the theory " might be, only abstractly and uninterestingly so.

55 As noted in Chametzky (1996: 20–1), these authors converge in some striking ways in their analyses of what is baby and what is bath water with respect to X-Bar theory, despite their rather different starting points and rather different goals.

56 One can understand the differences in bar-levels as differences in subcategories of the categories determined by the "categorial" features, as subcategory distinctions are needed anyway.

57 Obviously, whether or not these definitions are current or correct is not the point or issue. It is the necessity of some such definition that is crucial.

58 Recall here the discussion in section 2.1 of the Introduction with respect to the general issue of encoding dependency relations in PS syntax, of which this is evidently another example.

59 Lebeaux uses the terms *Open Class* and *Closed Class items* for what we have hitherto been referring to as Lexical and Functional elements. I shall follow his terminology in discussing his work.

60 Lebeaux argues not just from acquisitional facts and assumptions, but also from "pure" syntactic ones, which he does "not really differentiate between" (Lebeaux 1988: 6).

61 Lebeaux (1988: 16f) argues that the set of Case features on verbs is Closed Class, while the set of verbs is Open Class.

62 Lebeaux uses *Project-a* as another name for his Merge operation.

63 There must also be semantic licensing of the Functional element if it is to receive a semantic interpretation, of course.

64 Gazdar and Pullum (1981), within Generalized Phrase Structure Grammar, observe the same redundancy and pursue the alternative course, eliminating the subcategorization frames.

65 Speas (1990: 35–8, 56–60) discusses Pullum (1985); Chametzky (1996: 20–2) comments on this discussion and on Kornai and Pullum (1990).

66 See Chametzky (1996: 153–6) for discussion of this problem with respect to Chomsky (1993).

67 Chametzky (1996: 32–6) criticizes the "unambiguous path" concept.

68 See, e.g., Carrier and Randall (1992); Pesetsky (1995: chapter 7).

69 The theory of Lasnik and Kupin (1977), in fact, does not. Or, rather, in this framework nonbranching domination is a symmetric relation, so it effectively disappears.

70 The other two cases are exocentric labelling and using "functional" labels such as "subject" or "topic".

71 See Chametzky (1996: 5, and references cited there).

72 See Richardson and Chametzky (1985: 339–40); Chametzky (1996: 14–15, 27–8); Chapter Two in this volume, section 5.2.

73 Chomsky (1995: 338) takes dominance to be irreflexive. Chametzky (1996), following the normal practice in formal grammar theory, takes it to be reflexive. See Chapter Four and Chapter Two, respectively.

74 More accurately, PSRs are generally interpreted as specifying such relations among mothers and daughters; the rules can also be interpreted simply as string-to-string rewrite instructions, which can be further related to mother and daughter

relations. These matters, while of intrinsic interest, are orthogonal to our concerns (see McCawley 1968; Partee, ter Meulen, and Wall 1990).

75   See Gazdar and Pullum (1981) for elaboration of a rule formalism that separates these two within Generalized Phrase Structure Grammar: what they call ID/LP (immediate dominance/linear precedence) format.

76   We return to this in Chapter Two.

Chapter two

The School of Athens

The work

The book we examine in this chapter, *A theory of phrase markers and the extended base* (Chametzky 1996; TPM hereafter), is a piece of what we can call *Late Classical GB*.[1] TPM is a *theoretical* work of a relatively stringent and disputatious sort; it is, in particular, a work largely concerned with refining an existing theoretical approach to PS, that developed most notably in Speas (1990). Considerations of theoretical simplicity, coherence, and elegance have pride of place, while empirical argument of the type familiar in most syntactic work is at most only rarely in evidence. The overall goal of the work is to trace out theoretical implications of a relatively impoverished set of initial assumptions, enlarging the set only insofar as theoretical justification can be adduced. A recurrent mode of argument relies on finding either the presence or absence of (theoretical/natural) *kinds* as justification for pursuing or abandoning a particular path of inquiry, either one in TPM itself or one in other works.

In the rest of this section, I give more detailed exposition of TPM's general project. We then turn to the fates of the specific PS concepts and issues of Chapter One.

1.0   A theory of phrase markers

1.1   *TPM's two part harmony*

There are, as the subsection title indicates, two major concerns in TPM. One is the theory of phrase markers (PMs). The issues here are how PMs are formally specified and why, and what implications, if any, resolving these issues might have for more substantive syntactic concerns. The second concern is with theoretical architecture. Slightly more concretely, the concern is with specifying a plausible "base component" given some relatively common assumptions about D-structure. TPM develops distinct forms for these two lines of investigation. In the first, TPM takes an essentially formal line, while for the second, pushing forward implications of the "D-structure as argument-of structure" assumption of Speas and Lebeaux, TPM engages in substantive syntactic theory construction. We discuss each in turn.

1.2   PM theory

TPM develops a position called there *Minimal Phrase Structure Theory* (MPST), in which a reduced substantive conception of X-Bar theory (basically, though not exactly, that in Speas 1990) dovetails with a reduced formal conception of PMs. Rather than pursuing the substantive reduction of X-Bar theory to other principles of GB syntax, TPM argues for reducing the set of ordering relations in the formal theory specifying PMs to just *dominance* (ultimately, *immediate* or *direct* dominance), rather than both dominance and *precedence*.[2] An ultimately crucial aspect of the overall position (though this is not strictly a part of the argument presented against precedence) is that the substantive program of reduction as realized by Speas (1990) dovetails with this independent formal inquiry. Speas (1990: 43ff) proposes "one rule of the base", viz., **Project Alpha** (her (41)), which presupposes the dominance relation.[3] Thus, the single formal assumption of the single principle of the substantive theory is also the single ordering relation of the formal theory. This is the convergence of the formal and substantive inquiries.

(1)   Project Alpha: a word of syntactic category X is dominated by an uninterrupted sequence of X nodes.

There are two theoretical points here worth discussing a bit more. One is the importance of the convergence. If we did not have the two (formal and substantive) independent routes to the elimination of precedence, but rather just either one and not the other, then we would be faced in either case with a theoretical conundrum. Why, in the one instance, if the two relations were on a par as formal ordering relations for PM specification, should substantive syntactic investigation find an asymmetry? And, conversely, if there were only one such ordering relation, why would substantive investigation treat the two relations as on a par with one another? Indeed, the formal argument against precedence offers an explanation for the substantive findings: the ability to reduce precedence relations to effects of other syntactic relations is grounded in the lack of a basic precedence ordering relation for PMs. And, correspondingly, the formal argument is strengthened by the substantive reductions, which are just what one would expect with no basic precedence relation formally specifying PMs.

The second point is that the formal argument does not deny that there are or can be significant precedence relations in syntax. Rather, the point is that there is no precedence based *kind* in syntax, while there is a dominance based kind. The dominance based kind is (what is left of) X-Bar Theory. There is, and will be, no analogous such kind – or module – based in precedence (*pace* Gazdar and Pullum 1981). Precedence relations are ultimately based in and on the existence of *formatives*, and this lends such relations a parochial character quite unlike the general nature of dominance relations. This is the reason that precedence mediated relations and predicates are often parameterized, unlike dominance mediated relations and predicates, which are universal.[4]

Once again, the formal argument offers an explanation for substantively discovered patterns in syntax.

TPM follows standard formalizations (e.g., Partee, ter Meulen, and Wall 1990 443–4) in understanding PMs to be collocations of nodes and labels. The theory of such collocations is the theory of well formed PMs, viz., the theory of the base. As belabored above, TPM departs from standard formalizations in arguing against there being two basic ordering relations in the specification of PMs. From this it follows that TPM also differs from standard views in rejecting Exclusivity and Nontangling as conditions specifying PM well-formedness.[5] TPM also rejects the condition that requires the relation between nodes and labels to be a *function* from nodes to labels, as this arbitrarily limits nodes to bearing a single label; TPM allows for the possibility of multiple labelling of nodes. Formally, then, PMs in the MPST are collocations of nodes and labels, where there is a (many-to-many) relation between these two sets, and one relation: a binary relation D (immediate/direct dominance) on the set of nodes; we then define D*, the reflexive, transitive closure of D as well. MPST PMs are rooted and connected, and have no loops (TPM: 14–16; 173, fn. 12; 175, fn. 5). The MPST also rejects the widespread but erroneous view that the relation between lexical items and leaves ("zero-level categories") in a PM is the dominance relation. This is not the part/whole relation of constituency at all, but is an exemplification relation we can call *instantiation* (Richardson 1982). Lexical items do not constitute syntactic nodes distinct from those they instantiate.[6]

Turning now to the substantive portion of the MPST, Speas (1990: 43ff) proposes, in addition to (1), repeated here, definitions for Projection Chain, Maximal Projection, and Minimal Projection (her (42) and (43)).

(1)   Project Alpha: a word of syntactic category X is dominated by an uninterrupted sequence of X nodes.

(2)   Projection Chain of X $=_{def}$ An uninterrupted sequence of projections of X.

(3)   Maximal Projection: $X = X^{max}$ iff $\forall G$ which dominate X, $G \neq X$.

(4)   Minimal Projection: $X = X^0$ iff X immediately dominates a word.

Given that instantiation, rather than dominance, is the actual relation between lexical items and Minimal Projection nodes, we revise (1) and (4) (TPM: 18).

(1')   Project Alpha: an instantiated node labelled X is dominated by an uninterupted sequence of X labelled nodes.

(4')   Minimal Projection: $X = X^0$ iff X immediately dominates nothing.

For Speas, Maximal and Minimal Projections are relativized to a given projection and are given a general structural definition; officially, all labels in a Projection Chain are the same. And, indeed, intermediate levels, while they exist, have no theoretical status, and cannot be referred to by grammatical rules or principles. TPM revises these positions somewhat: Maximal and Minimal Projections have labels of their own (with (3) and (4′) now functioning as well-formedness conditions) and the suggestion is made for a distinguished, theoretically potent intermediate level and label (TPM: 134–9).[7] Note that (1) "collapses the labelling function of X-bar theory with the implicit free generation of hierarchical structures. . . ." (Speas 1990: 43), while (1′) uncollapses labelling and generation of structure.[8] To collapse the two is to lose the possibility of having independent theories converge, which we have argued is one of the strongest points in favor of the MPST (TPM: 18–19). We also see that Speas (1990: 102) assumes that ". . . all of the arguments of [a] predicate are in some sense internal to a projection of the predicate . . ." and (1990: 1–2) "that D-structure is a pure representation of the theta grid of a lexical item." The MPST accepts these assumptions; it follows that Adjuncts are not licensed by the MPST. Also following Speas, the MPST does not impose any restrictions on number or position of non-heads. Other principles, lexical or structural, determine these. We turn now from what the MPST is to what it can do.

1.3　*C-command*[9]

The MPST provides a theoretical matrix in which we can, for the first time, understand in a deep way both what C-command is and why it has the syntactic role(s) that it does. Two points are crucial. First, from Richardson and Chametzky (1985, R/C hereafter), we reorient our understanding of C-command, taking "the point of view of the commandee"; that is, we no longer ask "Does Node A C-command Node B?"; instead, we ask "What is the set of all and only the nodes which C-command Node B?". Second, we recognize that in an approach to PMs with only the ordering relation of dominance, there will be many nodes which do not stand in this relation to one another. Given this, if any such nodes are to be related to one another in some substantive syntactic way, some other formal relation, complementary to yet parasitic on dominance, is required to relate these nodes. C-command is that relation. Thus, while the R/C conception of C-command is available to any approach, the precedence-free MPST motivates it.

The R/C shift means we can understand C-command as in (5). C-command is a generalization of the sister relation.[10] As noted above, dominance is reflexive.

(5)　For any node A, the C-commanders of A are all the sisters of every node which dominates A.

If we consider the tree diagram in (6) and a "target" node – that labelled G, say – (5) returns the set {F,E,B}. This is the correct set, and notice, there is nothing linguistic about it, in the sense that no specifically linguistic predicates or relations are needed to derive it. The labels are nonlinguistic, and the relations required are merely dominance and sister, both definable in terms of immediate/direct dominance, itself a nonlinguistic predicate.

(6)

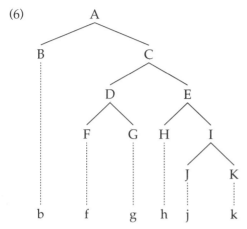

Moreover, and most significantly, the set {F,E,B} provides the *minimal factorization* of the PM with respect to G.[11] That is, there is no other set of nodes which is smaller than (has fewer members, a lesser cardinality) than {F,E,B} and also, when unioned with {G}, provides a complete, nonredundant constituent analysis of the PM. This is true for the set of C-commanders with respect to any target node. Put more perspicuously: C-command *is* the minimal factorization of a PM with respect to a target node. It is a natural, almost expectable, relation, given the MPST, as we now clarify.

MPST PMs are ordered only by dominance. Suppose we want to find candidate nodes for further substantive syntactic relations with a target node in a PM, nodes with which the target node does not stand in a dominance relation. We might simply take all those nodes not related to the target by dominance. But notice that such a set – for G, in (6), for example, it is {B,F,E,H,I,J,K} – would typically ignore the fact that a PM is hierarchically structured, in that it contains nodes which are constituents of other member nodes. If we are correct in assuming that dominance is the single basic ordering relation for PMs, we should be surprised to find it utterly ignored in this way, and the usefulness of a relation which is both nonbasic and totally indifferent to the basic relation should make us question our initial commitment to dominance as that basic relation. Alternatively, we might take the smallest set relatable by dominance to, but not in a dominance relation with, the target: the set of sisters of the target. But this set, while plausibly useful, seems too constrained for our initial goal: finding a set of candidate nodes in the PM for further substantive syntactic relations with a given node. What we want is a set that both is relatable to our target by means of dominance, though there is no dominance relation between the target and any set member, and which utilizes the full PM while respecting the hierarchical structure which the dominance relation imposes.

Returning to (6), repeated here, there would be three candidates with respect to G: {B,F,E}, {B,F,H,I}, and {B,F,H,J,K}. Only these sets provide complete, nonredundant analyses of the PM with respect to G.[12] {B,F,H,I} is simply an arbitrary factorization, but the other two are distinguished: {B,F,E}, as we have noted, is the minimal factorization; {B,F,H,J,K} is the *maximal* factorization. But the maximal factorization suffers from a

(6)

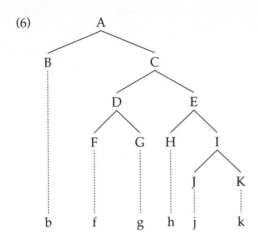

familiar problem: it denies the relevance of the full hierarchical structure imposed by the dominance relation in that it is just the set of (pre)terminals not in a dominance relation with the target node G. Indeed, it arguably does worse on this score than even the set of all nodes not in a dominance relation with the target, considered and rejected above. That set *ignores* the structure dominance imposes, but at least redundantly contains all the nodes; this set *denies* the structure, entirely leaving out the nodes indicating hierarchical organization. Thus, the minimal factorization is the only nonarbitrary set which requires and respects the full branching hierarchical structure dominance imposes on a PM.

We note, as well, that C-command is the basic command relation (Barker and Pullum 1990). All other command relations are supersets of C-command. It is a formal, graph-theoretic relation, a generalization of the sister relation, which founds a family of further command relations, themselves typically involving substantive syntactic predicates.[13]

We have seen, then, that the MPST virtually requires some further formal relation other than dominance for relating nodes not related by dominance. If it is correct that dominance is the sole basic ordering relation for PMs, then this further relation should be complementary to but parasitic on – constructible from and respectful of – dominance. The R/C conception of C-command, we have argued, is unique in that it is a nonarbitrary such relation. The R/C conception is independent of – indeed, antedates – the MPST, but the MPST provides motivation for it that no other framework does.[14] The discussion so far has been largely about PMs. We turn now to the Extended Base.

1.4   Extending the base

The theory of well-formed PMs is the theory of the base. According to the MPST, well-formed PMs are pure structuralizations of "argument-of" relations specified in the lexicon. The evident appeal of this view should not blind us to the fact that not all sentences are entirely pure structuralizations of "argument-of" relations specified in the lexicon. What then of such sentences? In particular, how is the theory to accommodate Adjuncts, which are nonargument modifiers of the Head of a Projection Chain, and coordinate structures, which can, for example, "overload" a predicate with more arguments than it has places for? There are basically two options, if the theory is correct: (1) such sentences do not have well-formed base PMs or (2) the set of well-formed base PMs contains members which are not straightforward structuralizations of the "argument-of" relation.

It might seem that neither option is consistent with the theory being correct. If these are the options, then the theory is refuted. It cannot be the case that such thoroughly unexceptional sentences as those in (7) have no well-formed base PM.

(7) a. Kim ate lunch in the kitchen.
     b. Pat ate some oysters and some clams.

This leaves only the second option. But that seems to be simply a bald contradiction of the basic assumption of the MPST. So, neither option is possible, given the theory.

Nonetheless, the notion of the "Extended Base" is exactly the second option. The contradiction is sidestepped by combining well-formed PMs that are pure structuralizations of Theta-grid requirements, such combinations themselves being subject to the requirements of the MPST (viz., Project Alpha, the definitions for Maximal and Minimal Projections). The idea here is basically an algebraic one: we have a set of PMs and some combining operations defined on that set, the operations enlarging the set of PMs.

The contradiction is sidestepped in the following way. The "unextended" base is both a syntactic representation and an interface with the nonsyntactic lexicon. There are two sorts of conditions which regulate it. One sort regulate it as syntax, e.g., Project Alpha, Minimal & Maximal Projection definitions. Another sort regulate it as interface, e.g., the requirement that structures represent Theta-grid requirements, the requirement that all arguments of a predicate be realized within the projection of the predicate. The Extended Base, however, is not regulated by the interface requirements – it is formed *from* the structuralizations, not formed *as* (or *by*) structuralization; it is constituted purely as syntax, so it is regulated only by the syntactic requirements.

The operations which extend the base combine well-formed PMs. They are, then, "generalized transformations", in the sense of Chomsky (1957).[15] There need to be two such operations, one for coordinate structures, and one for Adjuncts (NB, *Adjuncts*, not *adjunctions*). We can approach this issue from another point of view. We can ask a more formal question. Supposing that we want to expand the set of well-formed PMs, what resources does the MPST give us for so doing? Recall that formally PMs are collocations of nodes and labels, ordered by a single relation, dominance. We discover, then, that the MPST allows us two dimensions for PM combining, or "joining":[16] (1) join at a node or (2) join at a label.

Quite remarkably, these analyze adjuncts and coordinate structures, respectively.[17] As with C-command, here again the formal bases of TPM afford deep theoretical insight into domains hitherto given at best only analytical investigation.

The theory of coordinate structures is a version of the "union-of-phrase markers" approach adumbrated in Goodall (1987) and more fully investigated and formalized in Chametzky (1987). In this approach, coordinated constituents are "parallel structures" in the sense that they are not syntactically related to one another, though they have the same syntactic relations to other elements in the sentence. The analysis is placed here within a more general theoretical context, one that does not always share specific assumptions of earlier work. One such change is that given the argument against precedence in TPM, there is no longer any need to alter the definition of PM to allow for nodes which stand in neither a dominance nor a precedence relation to one another, as there was previously. The primary empirical desideratum is to derive the central (though not entirely unproblematic) fact about coordinate structures: that only like syntactic categories conjoin. This follows on the TPM account because sharing a node will generally entail sharing a label, which will require (type) category identity.[18] The crucial point is that the single shared node is part of more than one Projection Chain, one for each conjunct, and Projection Chains are subject to the conditions of the MPST.

The formal nature of the joining relies on the fact that PMs, which are 4-tuples,[19] correspond to sets of pairs of labelled nodes, called D*–sets, where the first member of each pair dominates the second member.[20] Coordination comes down to union of two such D*–sets: union is just the combining of sets, and so on this view then, coordination is just the combining of PMs. More importantly, it turns out that the formally most general partitioning of the union of two sets – into the intersection of and the symmetric difference between the sets – is virtually all that is needed to derive the central empirical fact of like category coordination.[21] Recall that our formal question was how to combine PMs to extend the base. We saw that the MPST allowed for two joining possibilities: join at a node, or join at a label. We now reconstrue PMs as sets of pairs of (labelled) nodes, and do the obvious combining operation available on pairs of sets: set union. This analyzes coordination.

A crucial fact about set union is that it adds nothing new. This has a striking implication for the conjunction words (*and, or, but*): either they are present in the input(s) to the union, or they are not present at all in the syntax. The TPM position is that they are not present at all in the syntax.[22]

This finishes the discussion of coordination in TPM. The theory of Adjuncts is discussed below in section 2. It is worth stressing again that the theoretical vocabulary and architecture of TPM unite these two, and explain why they constitute a syntactic kind. This theoretical finding serves as one of the bases for TPM's inquiry into Islands, to which we now turn. The discussion of Islands concludes our general description of TPM.

1.5   Islands: PS of no return

The goal of the TPM inquiry into Islands is explanatory on two fronts. First, it asks why these particular structures are *Islands*. Second, it asks why these *particular* structures are Islands. Unlike the second question, which seems to motivate virtually all other approaches to Islands, this first question seems to be rarely, if ever, asked. TPM's answers are, it develops, closely intercon-nected – which is as we should hope, once both questions have been raised. Naturally enough, the approach to Islands in TPM is phrase structural. In particular, TPM finds a syntactic kind in Complex NPs (both relative clauses and noun complements) (CNPs), Coordinate structures, Subjects, and Adjuncts in that all of these structures are *rule-licensed phrase structure.*[23] Such structure is called *non-canonical phrase structure* (NCPS) in TPM. Coordinate structures, Subjects, and Adjuncts are all licensed by generalized transformation;[24] CNPs are licensed by explicit PS rules. Subjects and Adjuncts are discussed in sec-tion 2 and PS rules are discussed in section 5 below. NCPS is further shown to be Periphery, rather than Core grammar, because it is rule-licensed.[25] It is Island structure because it explicates the concept *characteristic structure* from the Learnability Theory of Wexler and Culicover (1980). I now elaborate on these evidently somewhat cryptic statements.

In proving that an *Aspects*-style grammar is learnable from input of "Degree 2" (having only structures with no more than two embedded clauses), Wexler and Culicover (1980: 119–20) require what they call the **Freezing Principle** (FP, hereafter), given here with their explication.

(8) **Definition**: If the immediate structure of a node in a phrase marker is nonbase, that node is **frozen**.

(9) **Freezing Principle** (FP): If a node *A* of a phrase marker is frozen, no node dominated by *A* may be analyzed by a transformation.

They explain the significance of the FP (Wexler and Culicover 1980: 120) as follows:

> We may think of the base grammar as providing *characteristic structures* of the language. Transformations sometimes distort these structures, but only these characteristic structures may be affected by transformations. . . . The freezing prin-ciple leads to a very important property of the learning system, namely the ability to learn grammar from the exposure to relatively simple sentences. The crucial property of FP is that **only base structures may be used to fit transforma-tions**. (bold added – RC)

The TPM claim, then, is that NCPS – the extended base – is **non**characteristic structure in the sense relevant to (something like) the FP.[26] The **un**extended base is the set of characteristic structures. Given (some version of) the FP, the structures it picks out are going to form a set of Islands. What we need now is a way to pick out this set of structures that is independent of the analysis of Islands – without this, the claim is not much more than a stipulation. We need an independent analysis of "noncanonical phrase structure".

This is what the analysis of Core versus Periphery of Fodor (1989) pro-vides.[27] The central point TPM takes up is that the Periphery may contain rules, while the Core is not a rule system. This distinction dovetails with the architecture of TPM in that the Extended Base is rule licensed (by generalized transformations), while the unextended base is not (the MPST has no rules). This does not yet give us a way to license CNPs, however. For these, as noted above, PS rules are suggested (TPM 134–8).[28]

The PS rules proposed license a theoretically potent "intermediate label". This introduction of PS rules and an intermediate label do not, however, constitute the reintroduction of full-blown X-Bar Theory. If there are to be PS rules, there is nothing for them to do but license an "intermediate label": recall that Maximal and Minimal Projection labels are licensed by their position in a specific Projection Chain, so that anything new licensed by PS rules could be nothing else except intermediate. On account of its familiarity, the "bar notation" is used for this label in TPM, but it has no content other than "neither Maximal nor Minimal (and theoretically potent)". Further, given the Core versus Periphery distinction, the existence of PS rules is almost a corollary of the claim that the former does not contain rules, while the latter does (or may). The Core with respect to phrase structure licensing in the base is the MPST, hence its rulelessness. The Periphery, if it is also to license phrase structure in the base, virtually by definition then will contain some sort of "phrase structure rule". So, there is basically nothing new to the proposal. It comes down to accepting and fleshing out the following: (1) the MPST positions on how unextended base structures are licensed and what those structures consist of; and (2) the Core versus Periphery distinction in terms of no rules versus rules. In the context of (1), an instance of (2) pretty much has to have the form and content suggested.

There are two significant theoretical points to make here. First, we are able to give specific content to the Core versus Periphery distinction, clarifying the relation between the two systems in an unprecedented way. The rules which can extend the base – Periphery – though **not required** by the MPST, are nonetheless **consistent with** and **constrained by** the MPST – the Core. This is because they serve exactly to extend the base, of which the MPST is the theory. So, properties of Core grammar are directly relevant to the nature of the Periphery. Further, it is the structures which are **required by** the MPST – the unextended base, the Core – which are the "base structures" of the FP.

Second, we see that formally dissimilar types of rules – generalized transformations, PS rules – come together as a theoretical kind in the analysis. Outside of the current context of the MPST architecture, finding in these distinct rule types a theoretically significant kind seems unlikely. Yet within the MPST they share the crucial property of licensing structure not otherwise available (in the Core). This property is crucial because it aligns the Core versus Periphery distinction in terms of rulelessness versus rules with the unextended versus Extended Base distinction. In this way, our MPST-internal categorization based on a property (licensing Extended Base structures) that cuts across formal rule type (generalized transformations, PS rules) converges with an independently arrived at analysis (rulelessness versus rules) of a taxonomy of the syntactic component (Core versus Periphery).

We see, too, that both points serve to give, perhaps for the first time, principled content to the Core versus Periphery distinction. Further, and at least as significantly, we see that within the MPST the Core versus Periphery distinction does serious linguistic work – again, perhaps for the first time.

I now sum up the proposal. Wexler and Culicover (1980)'s Learnability proof requires identifying a set of *characteristic structures* licensed by a grammar. Only these structures may be inputs to/deformed by transformations. Other structures fall under their FP and would be, *a fortiori*, Islands. For Wexler and Culicover, it is base structures that are characteristic structures. Within the MPST, however, base structures are themselves differentiated as between unextended and Extended Base structures. Only unextended base structures are characteristic structures. Extended Base structures, then, would fall under (some version of) the FP, and so be Islands. But why – other than the fact that this would afford an account of Islands (no small thing, but arguably question-begging) – should only unextended base structures be characteristic structures? Because Extended Base structures are all of them rule-licensed phrase structure, whereas unextended base structures are not rule-licensed, and the rule versus rulelessness distinction is itself already available as the Core versus Periphery distinction. Core grammar gives us characteristic (base) structures; the Periphery gives us Islands through the FP. The proposal thus links together concepts from apparently disparate areas of syntactic research for the first time, doing so naturally within the vocabulary and architecture of the MPST, and in the process affording new insights into all the concepts involved. Note, too, that by deriving Islands (in part) from considerations in Learnability Theory, we approach explanatory adequacy (Chomsky 1965) by linking grammatical facts to the solution to the acquisition problem.[29]

This concludes the discussion of Islands and of the general review of TPM. We turn now to how the concepts and questions of Chapter One are dealt with in TPM.

2.0   Syntactic structure and argument structure

We discuss three subtopics in this section. The first is structuralization and argument alignment. The second is the position of Subjects. The third is Adjuncts and adjunctions.

2.1   *Structuralization and argument alignment*

TPM adopts the "D-structure as 'argument-of' structure" position of Speas (1990) and Lebeaux (1988; 1990).[30] Lebeaux's work offers the most explicit defense and explication of why the "D-structure as 'argument-of' structure" might be plausible to begin with. The basic idea is that different modes of licensing correspond to different syntactic structures, which structures are ultimately composed into a single PM. As Lebeaux (1988: 141, his (32)) puts it:

(10)   (Every) D-structure is a pure representation of a single licensing condition.

Notice that this says both more and less than "D-structure is 'argument-of' structure". It says more in that it is about particular "little" D-structures, which are (or can be) composed into a "full" D-structure, and less because it does not say that the single condition is always "argument-of". Lebeaux (1988: 139–44) argues that this condition is the "argument-of" relation by invoking the Projection Principle. He suggests that D-structure is simply where the Projection Principle, and nothing but the Projection Principle, holds. Lebeaux's position can be reconstructed as follows.

(1) Different licensing conditions give rise to different syntactic structures; call this "Lebeaux's Conjecture". (2) The Projection Principle points out that lexical argument requirements must be represented in structural syntax. (3) Lexical argument requirements are one sort of licensing condition; call this condition "argument-of". (3) Given Lebeaux's Conjecture, there is, therefore, a syntactic structure that represents only the licensing condition "argument-of". (4) Call this "D-structure" as it represents the absolute minimum that must be represented syntactically given lexical requirements.[31]

In sum: TPM has nothing of any originality or novelty to say in these areas.[32] This might be a strength of TPM, as it apparently leaves TPM open for integration with the best account of argument alignment. On the other hand, argument alignment may be viewed as no mere trivial detail of PS theory, and it could reasonably be asked of a PS theory that it support some sort of counterfactual statement in this area. To be either entirely underdeveloped or completely vague in this area is not obviously a desirable theoretical property. If Lebeaux's Conjecture is on the right track, TPM at least explicitly subscribes to one of its main entailments, if not to the Conjecture itself.[33] We move now to Subjects.

2.2   Subjects

TPM both follows and disagrees with Speas (1990) on this issue.[34] Speas is followed in that her Lexical Clause Hypothesis (LCH) – the view that Subjects are within a projection of the verb at D-structure and that this is so for reasons essentially of theoretical parsimony (all arguments are thereby structuralized within the projection headed by the item of which they are arguments) – is adopted. However, TPM (129–33) disagrees with Speas with regard to what the sister of the Subject is: Speas (17–18, 106–9) holds that the sister is a nonmaximal projection, while TPM opts for a Maximal Projection sister. Both take the mother of the Subject to be a Maximal Projection.

This is a disagreement of consequence and with consequences. In the TPM theory, Subjects have Adjunct structure, and this is crucial to the account of Islands previously canvassed.[35] If Subjects do not have Adjunct structure, then it is hard to see how or why they would be an instance of NCPS. Still, while this is a nice result, nice results typically are not thought to be sufficient grounds for adopting proposals that immediately lead to them, if no other grounds are also offered.[36] So, we shall examine this dispute.

Speas adopts the nonadjunct structures for principled reasons, the principle one being that there are no Adjunct structures in D-structure (48–53), given the definitions of Maximal and Minimal Projections.[37] Speas follows Lebeaux (1988) in having Adjuncts added by generalized transformation, post D-structure.[38] There is a bit of a glitch, however. Speas "discovers" a class of Adjuncts which she feels compelled to argue *are* present in D-structure, which she calls "thematic Adjuncts" (56).[39] A crucial contrast, for her, is that in (11) (52, her (61)), where the Adjuncts are the fronted PPs.

(11) Temporal vs. locative:
   a.   On Rosa$_i$'s birthday, she$_i$ took it easy.
   b.   *On Rosa$_i$'s lawn, she$_i$ took it easy.

Now, Speas gives no arguments for her assertion that locative PPs are some-how thematically related to their verbs in ways that temporal PPs are not. Further, neither the formalism she adopts and adapts from Higginbotham (1985; 1989) (60–72) nor the proposal she makes with respect to which phrases are present at D-structure and which may be added by generalized trans-formation (72) serve to distinguish these two sorts of PP.[40] The TPM position on this is that calling a recalcitrant phenomenon names and hoping it goes away is an inadequate response. TPM asserts that there simply is no coherent way to have these two sorts of Adjuncts in either the theory of Speas (1990) or TPM. TPM argues that the sorts of data seen in (11) refute the claim that all (or, indeed, any) Adjuncts are added post D-structure. Luckily, the TPM notion of the Extended Base allows us to develop a coherent theoretical position. We turn to the TPM account.

The TPM account of Subjects combines the LCH, the theory of Adjuncts, and Predication Theory (Rothstein 1985).[41] We recall the basics, then elaborate. According to the LCH, (thematic) Subjects are found within the projection of the verb of which they are arguments. According to TPM's theory of Adjuncts, Adjuncts are placed by generalized transformation as part of the creation of the Extended Base. The outputs of this joining operation are themselves still D-structures, subject to the (syntactic portions) of the theory of the base, the MPST. Finally, Predication Theory (Rothstein 1985: 7) makes the three follow-ing claims:

(12) a.   A predicate is an open one-place syntactic function requiring SATURATION.
   b.   The syntactic unit which may be a predicate is a maximal projection.
   c.   APs, VPs, and PPs must always be predicates; NP and S' may be predicates.

Putting these together, we get the following picture. Subjects are required due to the Saturation requirement (12a) (the syntactic unit which saturates a Predicate is definitionally that Predicate's Subject). If the Subject is thematic, the LCH insists it must be internal to the verb's projection at D-structure. However, the Maximal Projection requirement (12b) insists that a Predicate must be maximal. There thus is a clear clash between the requirements of the LCH and those of Predication Theory.[42] However, TPM's theory of Adjuncts allows us to resolve the conflict. (Thematic) Subject placement is part of the formation of the Extended Base, done by the generalized transformation that creates Adjunct structure.[43]

There is still an issue to be resolved, it would seem. Namely: why and how are both the mother and the sister of the Subject labelled with a Maximal Projection label? The idea is straightforward enough. The Projection Chain of the verb in the unextended base has a topmost node, which thereby meets the definition for Maximal Projection. Hence only that label can be licensed at that position. But after the Subject is added and we have an Extended Base structure, we now have a new node that needs a label. If it is to be a member of the verb's Projection Chain, then it is now the topmost such element, and so must bear the Maximal Projection label. What then of the unextended Maximal Projection label? It remains what it was, given the null (and usual) assumption that labels do not change in the course of derivation.[44]

But so far all we have done is argue that TPM can have the Adjunct structure which the approach of Speas (1990) would not allow. The only reason proffered has been TPM's account of Islands – no small thing, but, as observed, perhaps not enough. Another theoretical support is that we can adopt Predication Theory, an independent and general theory of the Subjects and Predicates, and integrate it rather elegantly into our architecture. Speas (109), by contrast, must use a suggestion from Borer (1986) involving agreement indexing in English in order to cover the "Extended" part of the Extended Projection Principle (viz., the obligatory nature of Subjects), and concludes that "[t]here is no requirement that all verbs have a subject in underlying structure." The interaction of general, independent subtheories characteristic of the TPM account should appeal to current tastes.

There are also some empirical issues. Speas (1990: 106–8) argues that traditional movement and deletion constituency tests show only that under the LCH the mother of the Subject position must be maximal, not that the Subject's sister must be as well. We can grant this, as the facts seem entirely neutral. But Speas (128–38) also reviews a fairly wide array of data types which converge to suggest "that the underlying structure of English is hierarchically organized in such a way that the subject is structurally superior to the objects and is outside of a maximal constituent of VP" (138). This is an interesting, even powerful, conclusion, but not one we should have expected her to reach. It is quite impossible to see how she could reconcile this with her explicit positions on the LCH and the nonmaximal status of the sister of the Subject in D-structure. And, indeed, there is no attempt to do so. Happily, TPM has no such problem, and all the facts and principles push and pull in the same direction.[45] Subjects (when thematic) are indeed arguments, but as the evidence Speas reviews indicates, they are not just like other arguments. TPM nicely explicates this status.

We have already had several occasions to refer to the treatment of Adjuncts in TPM. We move now to that topic, and the related, though distinct, topic of adjunctions.

2.3   Adjunct(ion)s

We begin with Adjuncts – nonargument modifiers of a Head. TPM follows the logic of the theory in Speas (1990) in demonstrating that there can be no Adjuncts in the (unextended) base.[46] Lebeaux (1988; 1990) had arrived at this conclusion and at a way around it: a generalized transformation he called "Adjoin alpha" that combines PMs. Speas accepts Lebeaux's proposal and (1990: 49) interprets Lebeaux to mean that "adjuncts are added to the phrase marker after D-structure." While this may be technically true, it is misleading; or, perhaps better, it points to some unremarked on issues in those architectures which lack the Extended Base.

The central point is that the mapping from D-structure to S-structure is mediated by – even defined as – Move Alpha. These are distinguished strata within the architecture. But what then is the relation of Adjoin Alpha to these strata? Lebeaux (1988: 150–1; 1990: 35) holds that as the domains of the two operations are distinct – Move is an intra-PM operation; Adjoin an inter-PM operation – it is natural to conclude that no ordering holds between them. He concludes (1988: 151; 1990: 35) that since Adjoin Alpha is "simply an operation joining phrase markers" it is available both before and after Move Alpha. This means that it can operate on both D-structures and S-structures. But now, if Move Alpha is the content of the mapping between D-structure and S-structure – that is, it takes D-structures as its input – then if Move Alpha is to apply after Adjoin Alpha, it follows that the output of such an application of Adjoin Alpha must itself be a D-structure, or else Move Alpha could not apply, contrary to the assumption. Lebeaux never draws out this entailment of his position. Notice, though, that it is just the basic idea of the Extended Base: the outputs of adjoining, being D-structures, must satisfy the conditions of the theory of the base.

But this is only half of Lebeaux's proposal. The other half is that Adjoin Alpha can apply *after* Move Alpha, to S-structures. What then are these results of Adjoin Alpha? Evidently, not D-structures. Presumably, they would be S-structures, as they would be inputs to the mapping to LF. If so, they would have to be subject to the conditions of the theory of S-structure. But what are these conditions? The content of S-structure is given by Move Alpha, so perhaps, for example, Structure Preservation or Binding Theory are among the conditions (though Lebeaux does not think so with respect to the latter). Regardless of what is among the conditions, it is crucial to notice what is not: (the remnants of) X-Bar Theory, the theory of phrase structure, or, more generally, the theory of PM well-formedness. These are the theory of the base. It is these conditions (on well-formed Projection Chains) that determine which post Adjoin Alpha structures are licensed and which are not. TPM argues that as these are conditions on D-structures, Move Alpha must be done after Adjuncts are added.

But perhaps this is not so. Suppose we take Structure Preservation to be a defining property of S-structure, and we understand it to mean that the only structures which are licit S-structures are those which are independently licensed as D-structures. Now, if the set of D-structures is extended by means of Adjoin Alpha, then, according to Structure Preservation, these (extended) base structures are now also possible S-structures. And they would be just those S-structures formed by Adjoin Alpha applying at S-structure. Notice that this way of understanding Structure Preservation requires taking it as a well-formedness condition on the set of S-structures, not as a condition on either the application or output of Move Alpha.

So, perhaps the theoretical argument in TPM is wrong. We do not have to take Adjunct placement as occurring prior to Move Alpha, given the two assumptions that it does so occur, enlarging the set of base structures and that Structure Preservation defines (in part?) the set of well-formed S-structures. In this case, then, Adjoin Alpha serves to enlarge the set of structures not just at D-structure, but at strata throughout the derivation. Indeed, it would now seem natural for it to take LFs as input as well – we should presumably be surprised if it did not on this view.

But there are at least a few questions we might ask of this view. One is whether Structure Preservation so construed is *true*. As it is a crucial piece of the argument, this is an important consideration. If we had reason to doubt it, then we would have no particular way to license S-structure Adjuncts. Another is whether it is even *desirable* to have S-structure Adjuncts be possible. Theoretically, we might say that it is: Adjunct adding is just a way of enlarging a set of structures by combining, subject to the well-formedness conditions on the original set, so whenever the architecture presents a distinguished set of structures with its attendant well-formedness conditions, the combining should be allowed. And the architecture presents three such distinguished sets. There are potential problems here, however. One is the "attendant well-formedness conditions", as just noted with respect to Structure Preservation: are there any that do the required work? A second is what happens when the possible becomes actual? What are S-structure Adjuncts? How, if at all, are they different from D-structure Adjuncts? If they are different, does the theory explicate the difference satisfactorily? If they are not different, then it is a mystery why some are added at D-structure and others later in the derivation. Putting the point slightly differently, is there some problem which this degree of theoretical freedom helps to solve? If not, should the theory not be without this freedom? The theory should not countenance possibilities that need not be realized. We examine these issues now.

We begin with the second sort of issue, whether there is any work for non-D-structure Adjuncts to do. In this regard, we recall Speas (1990: 52–4) having discovered two sorts of Adjuncts, one present at D-structure, the other not. Speas suggests that only the second sort are added by generalized transformation.[47] But let us introduce the data which motivate this suggestion before we continue the theoretical discussion. The examples in (13)–(14) are from Lebeaux (1988: 146; 1990: 31; also in Speas 1990: 49). The statement in (15) is from Speas (1990: 50, her (54)).

(13)   a.   *He$_i$ believes the claim that John$_i$ is nice.
      b.   *He$_i$ likes the story that John$_i$ wrote.
      c.   *Whose claim that John$_i$ is nice did he$_i$ believe?
      d.   Which story that John$_i$ wrote did he$_i$ like?

(14) a. *He$_i$ destroyed those pictures of John$_i$.
     b. *He$_i$ destroyed those pictures near John$_i$.
     c. *Which pictures of John$_i$ did he$_i$ destroy?
     d. Which pictures near John$_i$ did he$_i$ destroy?

(15) *Lebeaux's Generalization*:
     Coreference is OK if the R-expression is in a fronted Adjunct (the relative clause or the **near**-phrase [in (13) and (14)]), but is not OK if the R-expression is in a fronted argument.

Now, the assumption that Adjuncts are (or can be) added after movement allows for an account of these so-called *antireconstruction effects* (van Riemsdijk and Williams 1981), viz, the unexpected well-formedness of (13d) and (14d).[48] So, in the terms of Speas (1990), Adjuncts added after D-structure show anti-reconstruction effects. But, as (11) (repeated here as (18)) showed, not all Adjuncts behave alike. In particular, not all Adjuncts show antireconstruction effects. Therefore, some Adjuncts must be present before movement (since it is being added after movement that gives rise to the effects). Thus, these Adjuncts must be present at D-structure (Speas 1990: 51–2, ((59)–(62))).

(16) **Temporal location** vs. **locative**
     a. In Ben$_i$'s office, he$_i$ is an absolute dictator.
     b. *In Ben$_i$'s office, he$_i$ lay on his desk.

(17) **Rationale** vs. **benefactive**
     a. For Mary$_i$'s valor, she$_i$ was awarded a purple heart.
     b. *For Mary$_i$'s brother, she$_i$ was given some old clothes.

(18) **Temporal** vs. **locative**
     a. On Rosa$_i$'s birthday, she$_i$ took it easy.
     b. *On Rosa$_i$'s lawn, she$_i$ took it easy.

(19) **Temporal** vs. **instrumental**
     a. With John$_i$'s novel finished, he$_i$ began to write a book of poetry.
     b. *With John$_i$'s computer, he$_i$ began to write a book of poetry.

In TPM (116–18), where all Adjuncts are held to be part of the Extended Base, such examples are argued to simply counter-exemplify Lebeaux's Generalization, and no suggestion is made as to how to account for antireconstruction effects. This was a reasonable position, as Lebeaux's account, which predicted the effects in (13)–(14), was falsified by the counter examples in (16)–(19), while Speas made what seemed a theoretically unworkable, even incoherent, suggestion with respect to D-structure Adjuncts versus non-D-structure Adjuncts. TPM made no prediction with respect to (13)–(14), hence was not falsified by (16)–(19), and did not suggest an unworkable bifurcation of the class of Adjuncts. The theoretical situation is apparently different now, however, as we are considering the possibility of generalizing the notion of the Extended Base to cover all distinguished strata.

The obvious suggestion is that the D-structure Adjuncts, which do not show antireconstruction effects, are added in forming the Extended Base, while the non-D-structure Adjuncts, which show the effects, are added in forming "Extended S-structure". But the same objection recurs that was raised to the original version of this proposal by Speas: how are these classes to be independently identified? Speas is required to claim, for example, that locative PPs, but not temporal PPs, are in a thematic relation to a verb, and this is, I think, a somewhat surprising claim.[49] She writes (1990: 52) of "theta-marked Adjuncts" that "[a]lthough such phrases are not part of a particular verb's theta grid, they behave as though they are governed by the verb and bear a thematic relation to the verb." But is this not merely a statement of the problem? Or is there nothing more to be said: Adjuncts either are or are not "theta-marked", and it is only their behavior that tells us which are which; there is no independent analysis, either semantic or syntactic, of the Adjuncts or the verbs, that can tell us this. While I confess that this is not a situation I find particularly attractive, it is not incoherent or impossible, and it apparently would provide an approach to the antireconstruction effects.[50]

There are other considerations, however. From within TPM, there is the theory of Islands. Notice that S-structure Adjuncts would have to be Islands because they are added after Move Alpha has applied. We would now have two distinct routes to the Island status of Adjuncts, depending on when in the derivation they are added, presumably an unattractive situation. We might suggest that if all Adjuncts are Islands, then all Adjuncts are S-structure Adjuncts, as this gives a fairly simple account of their Island status – but this flies in the face of the antireconstruction facts which motivated this exploration. In any case, we seem to lose the general approach to Islands developed in TPM, as neither Subjects (presumably still D-structure entities) nor PS rule licensed structures (some CNPs) are accounted for. It might be argued that the TPM claim that all these structures are Periphery (because rule-licensed) carries over, and therefore so too does the identification of these structures as noncharacteristic, hence frozen, structures. They no longer form a single entity, the Extended Base, but, on this view, that does not matter. The Extended Base is then an artifact with respect to explaining Islands, the true taxonomy being in terms of rule-licensed versus non rule-licensed structure, regardless of where in the derivation the rule applies. But this means that not only do we have two possible ways in which Adjuncts are given Island status – either as S-structures or as rule-licensed structures – but also that some Adjuncts are Islands for both reasons (viz., S-structure Adjuncts). If TPM is on the right track with respect to Islands, then having Adjuncts added at more than one stratum in the derivation is theoretically undesirable.

We can also take note of an argument made by Speas (1991: 252–5).[51] She argues that examples such as (20) show the antireconstruction effect, if (and only if) *pictures* is given focus intonation. If it is not given such intonation, then it is ungrammatical.

(20)   Pictures of John$_i$, he$_i$ likes.

The argument Speas makes here relies on two crucial assumptions. First, focus is a type of quantification. Second, quantification is represented at LF with an adjunction structure, but is not represented at D-structure. With these assumptions, her proposals can get the correct results: given focus and the adjunction structure, coreference is allowed; if there is no focus, hence no adjunction structure, coreference is correctly disallowed. Speas's point is that on Lebeaux's analysis the focussed and unfocussed versions of (20) would have to have different D-structures because the referring expression *John* would have to be inserted after D-structure in the focussed variant and be present at D-structure in the unfocussed variant. But, she objects (1991: 254), if D-structure "is a pure representation of GF-Theta, it is difficult to see how focus intonation could change the D-structure of a sentence." We can grant the point, but draw a different conclusion.

Crucially here, Speas has run together *Adjuncts* and *adjunction*. Her analysis of focus relies on the latter, not the former; but it is the former, not the latter, that Lebeaux's analysis deals with. Therefore, if her analysis is correct, then the conclusion to draw, I believe, is that the best theory of Adjunct placement should not immediately lead to an account of antireconstruction effects, because something other than Adjunct structure, namely an adjunction structure, can apparently give rise to the effect. Notice, too, that this dovetails with the fact that not all Adjuncts give rise to the effect, the conclusion which Speas's other data (16)–(19) led us to. We now see that not all and not only Adjuncts give rise to antireconstruction effects. It may be that the sort of configuration which Adjuncts and adjunctions are generally assumed to share is necessary (though not sufficient) for the effect, but no one believes that these structures are derived in the same way. Therefore, having the effect as an immediate consequence of one of these derivations would evidently require some other way to account for the presence of the effect given the other sort of derivation.[52] All of which ultimately supports the TPM account of Adjunct adding which does not predict the antireconstruction effects over any alternative that does. And, recall, it was exactly the possibility of predicting these facts which set us off examining this alternative to TPM.

Let us recap where we are. We have been considering an alternative to TPM that generalizes Adjunct adding from a strictly base extending operation to an operation that may extend any distinguished stratum in the derivation. There seem to be both theoretical and empirical considerations in favor of this move. Theoretically, generalization is typically thought to be favored over restriction, as the latter is assumed to require special statements that the former does not. Empirically, the antireconstruction effect data suggest that a distinction between D-structure and non-D-structure Adjuncts is motivated.

There are also considerations that weigh against the alternative. Theoretically, we seem unable to distinguish the D-structure Adjuncts from the non-D-structure Adjuncts except in these terms, so it is a mystery why any particular Adjunct should be added where it is. Internal to TPM, we lose the explanation of Islands in terms of a syntactic kind, noncanonical phrase structure, explicated as rule-licensed phrase structure. Empirically, the focus datum and analysis of Speas (1991) argues that point of placement of Adjuncts should not lead immediately to an explanation of the antireconstruction effect, because something other than an Adjunct can show the effect. At this point, then, the case for neither position seems overwhelming, though, unsurprisingly, no doubt, I incline toward TPM. However, we can turn now to examination of the crucial premise in the alternative theory, viz., that Structure Preservation should be understood as a condition on S-structure representations such that the only licit structures at S-structure are ones which have already been licensed as D-structures. In doing this, we move from Adjuncts to adjunctions within TPM.

TPM argues that the new mother node in an adjunction structure need not be labelled. TPM also holds that all D-structure nodes are labelled. It therefore follows that if TPM is correct with respect to adjunction, then Structure Preservation cannot be understood as the alternative account of Adjuncts requires, and so the alternative cannot be correct. TPM, moreover, also puts forward a different understanding of Structure Preservation in keeping with the general argument.

TPM (89–106) argues against the usual approach to adjunction in terms of a rule of C(homsky)-adjunction. Central to the argument is an investigation of the conditions on node labelling. The issue is whether there are general principles at work, and, if so, at which stratum or strata such principles hold. Note that if there are no such principles, or if they do not hold at post D-structure strata, then the usual C-adjunction structures must be an ad hoc stipulation.

Within the MPST, there are two mechanisms for node labelling: projection and selection. The first licenses the Projection Chain of a Head and is governed by Project Alpha. Nonheads are not determined by Project Alpha. They are determined by selection and "are present only in virtue of the licensing relation that they bear to a node in the projection [chain]" (Speas 1990: 45). Given that Heads select syntactic categories, and that labelled nodes are the structural realization of syntactic categories, it follows that the labels of nonheads are licensed due to selection by the Head.[53] Thus, Heads and nonadjunct nonheads are licensed as labelled nodes at D-structure by means of either projection or selection. In each case, the particular labels are determined by the properties of particular lexical items. We note, too, that every node in (unextended) D-structure will be labelled, because nodes must be licensed and these are the two modes of licensing.[54] And finally, it should be emphasized that these mechanisms are part of the theory of the base, the theory of well-formed D-structures. We are now in a position to inquire into node label licensing at strata other than D-structure.

For nodes that have been licensed (hence labelled) at D-structure, we assume that nothing more need be said; they bear the labels which licensed them in the base. In adjunction, however, it is precisely the case that we have a node which was not licensed at D-structure, for the simple reason that it did not there exist. Instead, it comes into being at another stratum, either S-structure or LF. How, if at all, is a label to be determined and licensed for such a node?

The conventional answer, that there is a transformational rule of C-adjunction which labels this node with the label of its unmoved "Host" daughter, is unacceptable. Within the MPST, we have just seen that labels in general are mandated by individual lexical requirements of Heads. Transformations, however, do not enforce individual lexical requirements. Therefore, there can be no transformationally mandated labelling of nodes – if, that is, we want to maintain that labelling is a theoretical kind.

Nonetheless, while it should be agreed that a transformation cannot label, this does not entail that the node created in adjunction remains unlabelled, if there are any general principles that would require such a node to be labelled. And, indeed, there is such a principle: the Projection Principle. On any of its various versions, this requires that the structural representations of the lexical requirements of a lexical item be identical at every stratum in a derivation.

Thus, suppose we had a D-structure such as (21a), in which some Head Z selects XP as a subcategorizing complement, thus licensing the sub-PM rooted in XP. Now, if there were an adjunction which created a new node mother to host XP and the moved YP, then this new mother would also have to be labelled XP, or else Z would no longer be sister to a node labelled XP, as its lexical entry requires.[55]

(21)   a.   b.

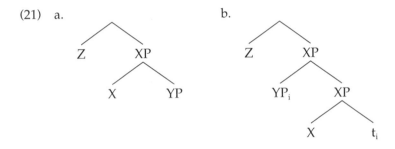

We see, then, that not only are there theoretical grounds for denying the possibility of a transformationally mandated label, but also there is no analytic need to suggest it. This is as it should be. We like to show that what is analytically unnecessary is also theoretically impossible (or at least unmotivated), as then we can claim to have explained its supernumerary status.

Let us take stock of our position. We are examining adjunctions in hopes of undermining the understanding of Structure Preservation which supports the alternative architecture for Adjunct adding. Specifically, TPM proposes that the new mother in an adjunction can be an unlabelled node, but such nodes cannot exist at D-structure, so there are, then, S-structures which are not "Structure Preserving" in the required sense. This is so because, as we have argued, all nodes in D-structure are labelled. We have further argued that there are no transformationally mandated labels, hence no C-adjunction rule that labels the new mother. However, we have just seen that the Projection Principle does require this mother to be labelled. Therefore, if we are to achieve our desired result, we must now either undermine the Projection Principle or alter it so that it no longer has this consequence. In fact, TPM (100–2) does both, first undermining and then altering the Projection Principle.

TPM (95–106) undermines the Projection Principle indirectly. The argument is directed against the analysis of C-adjunction found in May (1985; 1989) and Chomsky (1986a). This ultimately tells against the Projection Principle as commonly understood because these analyses are crucially concerned with explicating the nature of the new labelled mother node whose existence we now know depends on the Projection Principle. If examination of these explications reveals a theoretically flawed object – and this is indeed the conclusion TPM reaches – then this suggests that a principle which requires such an object is itself flawed. This leads, finally, to a new understanding of the Projection Principle (and to Structure Preservation) which new understanding does not license a label on the new mother, and therefore does not support the alternative architecture for Adjunct adding.

The gist of May's (1985; 1989: 91–2 (15)) analysis is a definition (22) that, when combined with the usual C-adjunction structure (stipulated by May by means of a C-adjunction transformation), leads to his "primary theorem" (23) (1989: 92 (16)).

(22)   Theory of Adjunction
    (i)   A Category $C = \{n_1, \ldots, n_n\}$
    (ii)   C dominates $\alpha =_{def} \forall n \in C$ (n dominates α)

(23)   Adjuncts are not dominated by the categories to which they are adjoined.

The intent of the definition is that "categories are sets of nodes, and to be dominated by a category is to be dominated by every member node" (May 1989: 92). Chomsky (1986a: 7 (12)) endorses May's proposals, and offers his own statement (24).[56]

(24) β is dominated by α only if it is dominated by every segment of α.

May and Chomsky, then, are developing new conceptions of two concepts basic to PS syntax: *dominates* and *category*. Chomsky also goes on to define a new concept *exclusion* in these terms, and then reformulates *government* in terms of exclusion. We might ask what motivates these moves, and what work they do for us. Crucially, the motivation and the work turn out to be identical: an analysis of adjunction structures. They are motivated by the label on the new mother node: because it is identical to one of its daughters, it is quite natural to try to revise or extend the concepts *dominates* and *category* to include this new configuration and account for its apparent idiosyncrasies. But suppose the apparent idiosyncrasies are true idiosyncrasies. That is, suppose these revisions and new notions have no application anywhere else in syntax. If this is so, if these are actually totally ad hoc revisions with no generality or further applicability, should we revise basic syntactic concepts to accommodate them? Does this not merely lend a spurious appearance of generality and depth? If there is idiosyncrasy, should not the grammar display this fact, rather than burying it in a series of definitions that extend and apply to nothing else?

Now, Chomsky himself admits with respect to "exclusion" (1986a: 9) that there is no application outside of adjunction. And May's revisions in (22) serve only to allow the derivation of the "primary theorem" of (23) – again, they apply nowhere else.[57] So the situation is exactly as suggested in the previous paragraph. There simply is not enough work done by these new conceptions and concepts to warrant our accepting them. They mislead us into supposing there is generality when in fact there is only stipulation. Still, as also noted above, the moves are natural ones, given the label on the new mother node. But this means we should understand the label as a problem, something to be eliminated, rather than as a discovery or an insight, as its existence leads to obfuscations of the sort promoted by May and Chomsky. Recall, however, that the label is required by the Projection Principle as generally understood. This, then, is our argument that there is something wrong with how the Projection Principle is generally understood. A deep principle of grammar should not lead to ad hoc revisions of basic concepts, let alone to making such revisions seem natural.

TPM (101) suggests revising our understanding of the Projection Principle in the following way: different syntactic strata do not represent different lexical requirements of the same lexical item. Overall, this gives the same result as conventional conceptions; in the case of adjunction structures, however, they can differ. This is so because the adjunction rule simply creates a new mother node for the moved element and the host. The new mother is not labelled by any rule, nor required to bear a label by any principle. Recall that Heads select or project syntactic categories, and that labelled nodes are the structural realization of syntactic categories. It therefore follows that no Head selects or projects an unlabelled node. But this means that in general an unlabelled node cannot satisfy the lexical requirements of any lexical item. It is thus the case that in particular no unlabelled node introduced at one stratum could represent a lexical requirement not represented at another stratum. So the revised understanding of the Projection Principle would allow the new node to be unlabelled, and no other rule or principle requires it to be labelled. Thus we rule out the ad hoc revisions and definitions of May and Chomsky.[58]

Basically, our revised conception of the Projection Principle says that all lexical requirement satisfaction represented at post-D-structure strata must also be represented at D-structure; or, no new lexical satisfaction is introduced in the course of the derivation. It may be objected that this is too weak. It does not require strict identity and preservation of lexical satisfaction throughout the course of the derivation. But that requirement is too strong. All that is actually required, in theory and in practice, is unambiguous recoverability of (D-structure) lexical satisfaction. One might understand this as one of the main insights of trace theory; it is, for example, a Chain that satisfies Theta requirements.

Where are we now? C-adjunction structures should not be licensed because the presence of a new labelled mother node leads to ad hoc and obfuscatory revisions of basic PS concepts, with only illusory gains. Traditional approaches which stipulate these structures as the result of a transformation are, for that reason, theoretically unsound. Usual conceptions of the Projection Principle give rise to the structures without stipulation, but it is plausible that any such conception is stronger than is independently necessary, and a weaker conception does not require a label on the mother. Were a stronger conception an error, we would expect to discover undesirable consequences of it. And that, of course, is exactly what we have discovered. So, the weaker conception both gives us everything we need elsewhere and does not give us what we do not want with respect to adjunction.

Adjunctions, then, give rise to structures containing unlabelled nodes. D-structures, however, do not contain unlabelled nodes. Therefore, the conception of Structure Preservation under consideration is undermined.[59] But without that conception, we lack any principles to form a set of "extended S-structures", so the suggestion that Adjunct adding applies at any distinguished stratum and extends that stratum in terms of such principles is undermined. We previously saw that there was no obvious general theoretical advantage to this alternative, and we now see specific theoretical problems with it, once the idea is pursued. Again, we should expect such "problems of execution" to arise when "leading ideas" are flawed.

Having both outlined TPM's approach to (C-)adjunction and argued against the alternative architecture for Adjunct adding, we now return and say farewell to TPM on Adjuncts. Adjuncts are placed by generalized transformation, a joining of PMs, which consists of sharing a single label (token). The operation is called Adjunct Adding in TPM. It extends the base, so that both its inputs and outputs must meet the (syntactic) requirements of the MPST. TPM thus does not offer any account of the antireconstruction facts. TPM shows by cases that the adjunction must take the form of C-adjunction (without the trace, of course) and must be to a Maximal Projection.[60] The upshot is simply that any other structure results in a violation of some sort, typically an ill-formed Projection Chain.

The account provides insight into the structural peculiarities of Adjuncts, and does so in a principled way. Joining PMs by (token) label sharing flows from the bases of PS theory generally, and quite specifically from the TPM version of the MPST. PMs are collocations of nodes and labels ordered by (immediate) dominance, and this is one of the two ways to combine two such collocations, the result itself a PM. TPM allows nodes and labels to be in a many-many relation, so two nodes sharing a label (token) is licit. There is an asymmetry with respect to nodes and labels, however. There can be labelless nodes, but no nodeless labels. For there to be a distinct operation based on label joining, there must also be new node creation.[61] TPM also explains why coordination is node sharing and Adjunct Adding is label sharing, and not conversely.

There are two possible situations in PM joining, both in terms of syntax and structuralization. The two syntactic situations are label or node joining, as noted. With respect to structuralization, the possibilities are that there needs to be a new licensing relation or that there does not. These correspond to Adjuncts and coordinate structures, respectively. So, our question becomes: why does a new relation require label sharing, while no new relation requires node sharing? Recall that nodes are all labelled in D-structure, and that these labelled nodes are the structuralizations of the various relations. Therefore, sharing a node will mean sharing a labelled node, which means that whatever relations these structuralized are simply carried over; no new relation can be structuralized, as nothing new is involved – a central entailment of the set-union approach to coordination, recall. Correspondingly, if there needs to be a new relation – in the case of Adjuncts, this is typically modification – then there must be something new to structuralize this relation. Sharing a label indirectly does the work required on account of the asymmetry pointed out above: there cannot be labels without nodes, though there may be nodes without labels. In order to have label joining, a new node must also exist to bear the label.[62] This new configuration must structuralize some relation, and, as it is a new configuration, it structuralizes a new relation.[63] Thus, within the theory the operations line up as they do inevitably.

This leads us to an issue not discussed in TPM: why are there Adjuncts anyway?[64] To sharpen the question a bit: why should there be anything with the particular syntactic properties of Adjuncts?[65] I think we can now get some insight into this generally unasked question. The starting point for the present architecture is that syntax is, in the first instance, the structuralization of lexical requirements of Heads. On the unavoidable view that Heads enter into relations other than required ones, there then has to be something more than just the first instance of syntax. However, as we have now seen, such non-first instances of structuralization will be, of necessity, not just different from those first instances, but different exactly in giving rise to typical adjunct(ion) structures. In other words, if the architecture is to allow for any sort of Head relations other than the required ones – and surely it must – then whatever those relations, they are going to end up structuralized as Adjuncts, and so should show the peculiarities of Adjunct syntax (e.g., stacking, indeterminacy of order with respect to one another). TPM does rather well with adjunct(ion)s, from which we now take our leave. We move on to Heads.

3.0 Heads and exocentricity

TPM has little new to say with respect to Heads. However, we can develop a new and insightful approach to exocentric constructions within the TPM theory. This latter is not something that is found either in TPM or in Speas (1990).

3.1 *Heads*

The general position in TPM on Heads is that elaborated by Speas (1990). On this view, Heads are lexical items which "found" Projection Chains and are, thus, fundamental to PS syntax. Endocentricity is a basic postulate, enforced by the definition of a Projection Chain. Structure exists because of "the requirement that all lexical properties of the head be instantiated in syntax . . . The head continues to project until all of the positions in its theta grid have been discharged" Speas (1990: 45).[66] It is this conception of the role of lexical Heads that creates the need for the Extended Base. If the theory of well-formed PMs is the theory of base structures (D-structures), defined as structuralizations of theta grid requirements of Heads, then if there are to be Adjuncts or coordinate structures, then there must be some way to enlarge the set of PMs. Given this approach to D-structures, either there are **no** structural realizations of the Adjunct and coordinate relations, or there is an Extended Base.

The analysis of coordinates has one aspect worthy of comment in this context. Though a Projection Chain has a unique Head, a given node may be a member of more than one Projection Chain, if it is a node that is joined in a coordinate structure. Such a node marks a "splitting point" in that there is one Projection Chain above it (or at it, if it is a Maximal Projection), but more than one below it (or at it, if it is a Minimal Projection). But there remains, for each Chain, a unique lexical Head.[67] We move now to the hinted at new approach to exocentricity.

3.2   *Exocentricity: the gerund*

Because endocentricity is assumed, no discussion or analysis of certain potentially problematic phenomena can be found in TPM (or in Speas (1990)), e.g., gerunds. We shall focus on gerunds, the most widely discussed and, presumably, a characteristic, exocentric construction.

Abney (1987: 231f) articulated one approach to gerunds within P & P.[68] It makes use both of his proposals for Functional Elements and of innovations which are no less problematic, perhaps. In particular, Abney takes "bar-level" to be a multi-valued feature, with -*ing* being a nominalizing affix specified as [+N] but of no bar-level. Abney then proposes that morphological and syntactic licensing of structure are not distinct, and puts forward a specific revision with respect to morphological licensing that takes advantage of the specification of -*ing* as of no bar-level. The upshot is that -*ing* can appear in a syntactic structure as an affix which is sister to either a VP or an IP, and the mother of these sisters is the nominalized category corresponding, respectively, to VP or IP, viz., NP or DP. These are the *poss-ing* and *acc-ing* structures (respectively).[69] The details need not detain us. We are suspicious of this approach to Functional Elements. We do not accept that "bar-level" is a feature at all. The homogenization of syntax with morphology lacks antecedent plausibility. The specific revision of morphological licensing is seemingly ad hoc. But if this account is not acceptable, is there a better one?[70]

Pullum (1991) and Lapointe (1993a; 1993b), working outside the P & P tradition, but within X-Bar theory (they employ versions of GPSG), have each suggested ways to accommodate gerunds. Lapointe (1993b: 201–2) offers theoretically compelling criticisms of Pullum (1991), whose proposals would in any event not integrate well with TPM (or most P & P work), so we shall not examine this work. Lapointe's ideas, however, provide the starting point for our TPM based proposal. Lapointe (1993b: 202) proposes what he calls *dual lexical categories*: (DLCs), elements in the lexicon specified as belonging to two major categories <X,Y>, one of which determines internal syntax, Y, the other external syntax, X. Importantly, a syntactic projection of such an element "can occur only when it is anchored by a lexical item to which an appropriate lexical-level operation has applied to create [a DLC]." I shall not discuss the details of Lapointe's work further, but the suggestion I want to make is inspired by Lapointe's ideas.

Let us adopt and adapt the idea that there are DLCs formed in the lexicon by specific lexical operations. Let us suppose that -*ing* affixation is such a lexical-level operation that creates from a V an element with dual specification, <N,V>. However, neither specification is stipulated to determine either internal or external syntax. Now, such an element (e.g., *noticing* in *Kim's noticing*) can only instantiate a node which is itself labelled with both N and V. But, of course, TPM allows for multiple labelling of nodes, so, unlike in other architectures, this is not a problem. The fact in need of explanation is that the gerund has the internal syntax of a VP, but the external syntax of an NP. Can this be derived without stipulation? Our theory requires that sufficient structure be licensed to satisfy the lexical properties of the Head within the Head's Projection Chain. In the case of a gerund, there are the specific requirements of the verb root and from the affix the general nominal allowance for a Specifier/Subject. But this means that the only internal syntactic properties are those of the verb root. In order to satisfy these requirements, other items (e.g., a direct object complement to *notice*) must be in particular, canonical structural relationships to the Head. This is why the Specifier/Subject allowed by the nominal affix is "higher" than all the verb's relata, and why the gerund itself has the external syntax of an NP, not a VP – having the Specifier/Subject lower (inside the VP, essentially) would break up the required structural relation between the verb and some relatum or other. Both the V and the N are part of the Projection Chain up until the point at which the requirements of the V are structurally realized; after that node, the Chain becomes an N Chain only, as the V no longer has requirements to structuralize, while the N does. In principle, the N member of the Chain could be Maximal at any point, but if in fact it is Maximal while internal to the VP, then the presence of a daughter that is licensed as nominal Specifier would break up a required structural relation between V and one of its relata, as noted, so the in principle possibility cannot be realized. So, the characteristics of the gerund can be straightforwardly derived.[71]

This sketch of an account of a construction that has typically had only ad hoc and unprincipled analyses is something of an advance, I believe. It follows from general properties of the theory – the approach to structuralization and the related notion of Projection Chain – from a particular and well-motivated aspect of TPM – the allowance for multiple labelling of nodes – and from the assumption that there can be specific lexical-level operations that create DLCs. Notice that this last flows naturally from TPM, since given a syntax that independently allows multiple labelling of nodes, we are not surprised to discover lexical operations that create items to fit such structures. Indeed, it should be counted against the theory were there no such lexical items at all, given that the theory is "lexical-entry driven" and allows for multiple labelling; without DLCs, there would be an unused degree of freedom within the architecture. Instead, however, the architecture is further confirmed.[72]

TPM thus has relatively little to say that is new or original in the matter of Heads, though the general family of approaches makes of Heads a central notion for understanding why PS is what it is. Further, though the general approach takes endocentricity as a foundational notion, so leaving apparently exocentric constructions such as the gerund without analysis, in fact TPM affords new and much needed insight into gerunds (and, by assumption, into exocentricity more generally) by providing theoretic space for assimilating them as actually endocentric and thus falling under general principles. Because TPM allows for multiple labelling of nodes, apparent exocentricity is just that, apparent. Such constructions are headed, and singly headed at that; the single Head, however, is itself of a dual lexical categorization, and this leads directly to the otherwise anomalous properties of the gerund. We move now to Functional Categories and the generalization of X-Bar Theory.

4.0   Functional Categories

TPM says virtually nothing about Functional Categories.[73] Given the discussion in Chapter One, section 3, this might seem an advantage of TPM. However, as with argument alignment,[74] so too, here: if this is a central area of PS theory, then supporting no counterfactuals may be counted a theoretical weakness at least as easily as a strength. We now take up the nature of X-Bar Theory in TPM.

5.0   X-Bar Theory

There are two topics here. One is the status of PS rules. The other is branching.

5.1   PS rules

TPM places itself in the tradition of "X-Bar reduction" of which Speas (1990) is the zenith. PS Rules and schema are entirely eliminated as statements in the grammar.

> However, rather than increasing the restrictions encoded in the X-Bar schema, I have proposed a theory of projection from the lexicon in which the only restriction imposed by X-Bar theory is the restriction that sentences have hierarchical structure, and that all structure is projected from a head. All other restrictions on domination relations are to be captured in other modules of the grammar. (Speas 1990: 55)

A number of the details of this program have already been presented.[75] The program has also had its critics, most notably Pullum (1985) and Kornai and Pullum (1990).[76]

TPM (21) points out four areas of convergence between Speas (1990) and Kornai and Pullum (1990): (1) Head is the central notion in X-Bar theory (2) "bar-level" is not a required concept[77] (3) adjunct(ion) structures are not licensed by (the pristine version of) the theory and (4) Maximal and Minimal Projection are definable concepts in the theory. Given these convergences and the response by Speas to Pullum's objections, TPM concludes that there is no principled theoretical problem with the elimination program.[78] That said, it is important to note that TPM proposes (re)introducing schema for explicit PS rules.

TPM (134–5) gives the schema in (25). These are to be interpreted as node admissibility conditions (McCawley 1968; Speas 1990: 19–24), with the variable X ranging over members of unextended Projection Chains: the Maximal Projection, the Minimal Projection, any intermediate link, but not the new distinguished label.[79]

(25)   a. $X \rightarrow \ldots X' \ldots$
      b. $X' \rightarrow \ldots X \ldots$

If PS rules are to license anything new, it must be an "intermediate label"; there is simply nothing else for such a rule to do.[80] The "bar notation", recall, is used simply for familiarity. It has no content other than "new and theoretically potent", and this will result in it being intermediate. Recall, too, that the existence of such schema is virtually a corollary in the theory, as it flows from (1) the MPST positions on how unextended base structures are licensed and what those structures consist of and (2) the Core versus Periphery distinction in terms of no rules versus rules. Given (1), an instance of (2) is essentially limited to something like (25).

The basic idea here is that UG makes available for grammars of particular languages the possibility of incorporating a theoretically potent intermediate node label in any category, but there is no requirement that such a possibility be realized for any category in any language. Again, the MPST does not enjoin such intermediate labels, it simply does not itself license them.[81]

We should note the following theoretical point. Insofar as TPM offers theoretical justification for PSRs, it is liable if there should be no reason to have PSRs. TPM uses PSRs to license a theoretically potent intermediate label. So, if there should be no reason to have such a label, then the case for the PSRs in TPM would be undermined, and the degree of freedom which allows PSRs and which is claimed to be natural to TPM would also be undermined. The empirical considerations which TPM alludes to in support of the theoretically potent intermediate label are the analysis of restrictive relative clauses as sisters of N' and the possibility of reconstructing as V' Adjuncts the VP-internal Adjunct (versus VP Adjuncts) Speas refers to in her discussion of "theta-marked" Adjuncts. Neither of these suggestions is entirely worked out or uncontroversial, so if the TPM theoretical argument for PSRs is a good one, this could end up being a solution in search of a problem, a weakness rather than a strength. We move now to branching.

5.2   Branching

TPM argues for the nonexistence of less than binary branching, and acknowledges that there might be justification for a limitation to no more than binary branching. The former, however, is given theoretical discussion, while the latter is treated as a possible empirical generalization.

TPM (14–15, 27–8) follows Richardson and Chametzky (1985) in its discussion of the four types of nonbranching domination represented in the literature.[82] The two most plausible types are theoretically reconstrued within TPM. One is the relation between a lexical item and a terminal node, which is not the part-whole relation of syntactic constituency, but is rather the exemplification relation called *instantiation*.[83] The other type is nonbranching within the Projection Chain of Head. This is rejected in favor of multiple labelling of nodes.[84] In fact, TPM argues (28) that we do not need to reject nonbranching domination as such. Instead, formally we allow both of two very general conditions for PMs: (1) we allow nonbranching domination and (2) we allow multiple labelling of nodes. The possibility of the latter reduces the need for the former to zero. This might seem to allow an undesirable degree of freedom in the theory, as it seems there is an option available in principle that is unneeded in practice. While true, this is not the sort of problem alluded to at the end of the previous subsection. That is because here we are dealing with formal conditions for specifying PMs, while there we were dealing with substantive considerations of theoretical architecture. With respect to the formal considerations, we can accept more general conditions, even if these are not fully realized. Indeed, we prefer the more general conditions, if the lack of full realization can be independently explicated in the theory. In this way we avoid stipulative purely formal prohibitions. With respect to substantive theory construction and architecture, however, the situation is different, as typically the reason some degree of freedom is unutilized is simply that some phenomenon or other does not occur. And this is not an acceptable theoretical situation.

In any event, TPM does not consider there to be any cases of nonbranching domination, and argues that this can be explained in part by allowing for multiple labelling of nodes. There is a technical question that arises with respect to interpreting the PSRs.[85] The issue is this. In cases where other views would have a nonbranching Projection Chain, TPM will license a multiply labelled node. But PSRs are typically interpreted as licensing direct/immediate dominance relations between a mother and daughters. How then can one interpret PSRs with respect to multiply labelled nodes? TPM (186, fn. 7) suggests that MPST PSRs will have to license both direct/immediate dominance and reflexive (i.e., self-) dominance. As dominance is understood to be a reflexive and transitive relation, this just means that the two most local instances of dominance are licensed by PSRs, while only "dominance at a distance", the transitive portion of the relation, as it were, is not. While this is nonstandard, I do not find this interpretation of PSRs objectionable.

More than binary branching is scarcely addressed in TPM. Kayne's (1981) *unambiguous path* concept, which motivates no more than binary branching, is considered and rejected as a basic theoretical concept (TPM: 32–6). However, it is allowed that for empirical reasons, unambiguous paths might be required, and that this would then result in no more than binary branching. And, in fact, in the analysis of Adjunct adding (TPM: 112–13), it is suggested that if there were more than binary branching, then the MPST could not immediately rule

out daughter-adjunction as an option. It is thus noted that if there were independent empirical reasons to impose the unambiguous paths condition, this
would, on account of the no more than binary branching consequence, aid the
MPST account of Adjunct adding. This evidently equivocal endorsement is
such discussion as there is in TPM.

So, TPM is vocal on an issue on which most are nearly silent (less than
binary branching), and nearly silent on an issue on which most speak in agreement, if not loudly (no more than binary branching). We turn to our final
issue, the ordering relations of dominance and precedence.

6.0 PM ordering

TPM develops a novel argument against precedence as a basic ordering relation
in the specification of PMs.[86] Very often works in P & P assume or state that
the X-Bar conditions or rule schema that license bases structures are "order
free" or "parameterized" with respect to order (e.g., Stowell 1981; Chomsky
1986a; Speas 1990), but rarely if ever is an explicit argument given against having a formal ordering relation of precedence for PM specification. I therefore
here summarize that in TPM.

The argument begins with two observations. First, that McCawley (1982)
strongly suggests that it is an empirical issue whether or not languages have
discontinuous constituents, i.e., syntactic units which are not wholly contiguous
in the sentence string. Second, standard formalizations for PMs rule out the
possibility of such discontinuous constituents.[87] Insofar as the issue is an empirical, substantive one, TPM argues that it is wrong to use a formalization
that essentially stipulates an answer before the investigation has even begun.
Thus, some alternative formalization for PMs, one that does not rule out the
possibility of discontinuous constituents, is called for.

Three such alternatives are examined: McCawley (1982), Huck (1985), and
Higginbotham (1982). It is shown that the alternatives no longer treat dominance and precedence as on a par as formal ordering relations for specifying
PMs, unlike the standard formalization, and these authors' apparent intentions
notwithstanding. In the case of Huck (1985), precedence relations depend on
"Head of" relations, a substantive relation explicated within particular syntactic
theories. In the cases of McCawley (1982) and Higginbotham (1982), many
precedence relations are determined by means of dominance relations. Indeed,
only precedence relations among *terminal elements* are determined without
recourse to dominance. Terminal elements (elements which dominate only
themselves) are instantiated by lexical items, *formatives* (Higginbotham 1982),
and it is over these items that precedence is defined. By way of explication,
Higginbotham (1982: 150–1) writes:

> [t]he notion of precedence is to reflect the ordering of formatives in speech . . . [and]
> [t]hat they will be so ordered is a consequence of the application of the laws of
> physics to the human mouth . . . reflecting the physics of speech.

Notice that this means that an object cannot be a *formally* licit PM unless it is instantiated by lexical items, because without these formatives, no precedence relations can be determined. This means PMs are formally licit only as the PMs of particular sentences. But this cannot be correct. The well-formedness of a PM as a *formal* object cannot depend on a particular sentence of which it may be the PM. A PM can be complete *as a formal object* without being instantiated by formatives, though it is not then the PM of any particular sentence.

We further note that precedence obtains only on account of "the physics of speech" and "the human mouth". But how can this be *syntax*? Only by inter-polating the formatives into the syntactic objects, because nodes bearing labels are not themselves subject to the physics of speech and the human mouth. Precedence, then, is not grounded in the conceptions of category (word class labels) and structure (immediate constituent node) of PS-based syntax.

There are, then, no basic syntactic precedence relations left. Some are deter-mined by means of dominance. The others pertain just to terminal elements, but these obtain only on account of formatives' properties which have no status in PS conceptions of the fundamental syntactic concepts. But if there are no basic precedence relations, then precedence is a derivative syntactic relation, and thus not a basic formal ordering relation for specifying PMs. In section 1.2 above we have already presented some consequences (and nonconsequences) of this conclusion.

This concludes the discussion of TPM. It is a work in and of P & P PS theory, so it has much to say about our various topics, and our topics bear directly on much of it. It would be unseemly for me to say more than (the not small amount) I have already.

Notes

1   Though published subsequent to them, it was written prior to the appearance of Chomsky (1995), or Kayne (1994) (TPM: 171, fn. 1); sometimes you can't tell a book by its title page, either.

2   This is the novel argument against precedence as a formal ordering relation for specifying phrase markers alluded to in section 5 of Chapter One. The argument is available not only in TPM, but also in Chametzky (1995); I give a brief third performance of it below in section 6.

3   This "rule" is more aptly called a "principle", I believe. This is more than just a terminological quibble; see section 1.5 below.

4   See Chametzky (1995) for fuller discussion.

5   *Exclusivity*: any two nodes are related either by dominance or by precedence, but not by both. *Nontangling*: if two nodes in a precedence relation each have descend-ants, then those descendants are also in precedence relation, and the descendant of the preceding ancestor is the preceding descendant.

6   See Chapter One, section 4.2 generally, Chametzky (1987: 51f) for analysis and formalization of *instantiation*, and Higginbotham (1985) and McCawley (1988) for recognition of the fact of instantiation, if not the term.

7   See section 1.5 below.

8   See Chapter One, section 1.2.

9   We build on the analysis of C-command found in Richardson and Chametzky (1985).

10 There are two technical issues here. One concerns nonbranching domination, the other graphs with "loops". See TPM (175, fns. 3 and 5) for discussion and resolution.

11 A *factorization* is just an exhaustive, nonoverlapping constituent analysis of a PM, as in the structural descriptions of the Standard Theory transformational formalism. This set is called the *minimal string* in R/C.

12 We do not consider any incomplete analyses, as we would have to explain why the particular nodes left out were left out. And we do not consider redundant analyses for reasons already canvassed in the text.

13 All of this is demonstrated, with formalization, in TPM (chapter 2).

14 See TPM (chapter 2) for discussion of how other frameworks obfuscate the explanatory inquiry.

15 See Lebeaux (1988; 1990), Speas (1990, 1991) for revival of generalized transformations.

16 This is the term used in TPM.

17 This is demonstrated in TPM (chapters 3 and 4). It is also shown in TPM (150–2) that the joining operations line up as they do – labels with Adjuncts, nodes with coordinate structures – not arbitrarily, but necessarily, within the theory as constructed. See the discussion at the end of section 2.3 below.

18 Given that the MPST allows for multiple labelling of nodes, it might seem that the shared node in a coordinate structure could therefore bear more than one distinct label. Indeed, it can. However, the parallel Projection Chains will typically have to stand in the same syntactic relations to the same other elements in the sentence, and this generally will fail to be the case when differently labelled nodes are joined. For discussion of situations where this does not fail to be the case, and so we have licit coordination of unlike categories, see Chametzky (1985; 1987: ch. 2).

19 Consisting of the set of nodes, the set of labels, the relation between them, and the (immediate/direct) dominance relation on the set of nodes.

20 See TPM (56f) for discussion of D*-sets.

21 Virtually: somewhat more is needed, in fact; see TPM (65–9).

22 This is defended – at length – in Chametzky (1987).

23 WH-Islands are not Islands in the TPM theory. See TPM (145–8) for discussion.

24 Subjects have Adjunct PS in TPM. See section 2.2 below.

25 This follows the analysis in Fodor (1989).

26 "Something like" because the strict FP is part of the Wexler and Culicover (1980) theory.

27 Fodor here is analyzing various scattered remarks by Chomsky with respect to Core versus Periphery.

28 Actually, PS rule schema are proposed. Different grammars may instantiate these as they "choose".

29 The proposal is not without problems. Its greatest theoretical strength – that Islands arise from the interaction of the syntactic architecture with Learnability considerations – also leads to its greatest potential empirical weakness: it has apparently no degrees of freedom. It is thus difficult to see immediately how the well-known variability of Island effects, both cross-linguistically and within a language, can be accounted for. See TPM (pp. 141–2; p. 186, fn. 10).

30 There are differences between Speas and Lebeaux. For example, Speas adopts a version of the theta-grid hypothesis (due originally to Timothy Stowell's unpublished 1981 MIT dissertation) concerning lexical information and the interface between the lexicon and structural syntax, while, as briefly discussed in section 3.5 of Chapter One, Lebeaux (1988: 68–70) argues for trees, rather than grids. TPM

takes no overt position on this issue, though Speas is generally adverted to and followed. If, however, the arguments in sections 3.4 and 3.5 of Chapter One are correct, this may require something more like Lebeaux's position.

31   As we have noted, TPM does not build explicitly on this rationale, but given the arguments in Chapter One, sections 3.4 and 3.5, it may be important for a theory to be at least consistent with Lebeaux's Conjecture.

32   Instead, it (largely tacitly) follows Speas (1990) and, to some extent, Lebeaux (1988).

33   TPM also takes no explicit position with respect to argument alignment; and, again, in context its silence can plausibly be read as following the positions of Speas (1990) (see Chapter One, section 1.0). However, it is not clear that TPM is in any significant way committed to the views of Speas (1990), or any views, on this matter. As noted in the text, this is not clearly a theoretical plus.

34   See Chapter One, section 1.1.

35   Well, adumbrated, anyway, in section 1.5 above.

36   Though if no objections or alternatives exist, this need not be so. Sadly, such is not the case here.

37   This is still true on the TPM redefinitions and reconstruals.

38   See Chapter One, section 1.2.

39   See section 2.3, below for further discussion.

40   She suggests (54) that "thematic Adjuncts" may be "equivalent to the class which has traditionally been called VP-internal Adjuncts." Again, I do not see that this distinguishes the cases in (11).

41   As was noted in Chapter One, section 1.1.

42   It is for this reason that Speas (1990: 109) rejects Predication Theory.

43   This means, of course, that thematic Subject placement is Periphery, not Core grammar. This might be thought problematic, but it is not. See TPM (128, 134). Notice that both the Saturation Requirement, mandating a Subject, and the LCH, requiring arguments to be internal to the projection headed by their verb, are Core. It is only the *placement* of the thematic subject that is Periphery.

44   This account is explored in some more detail in section 2.3 below.

45   We might also note this statement of the LCH by Speas (1990: 102): "all of the arguments of the predicate are in some sense internal to a projection of the predicate." TPM makes clear what *in some sense* means in this quote: Subjects are internal, but not in the same way as other arguments, in that they are placed in Adjunct structure as both a sister and a daughter to a Maximal Projection.

46   The demonstration proceeds by cases and is unedifying, so I do not repeat it (TPM: 106–7).

47   In the alternative considered below, all Adjuncts are added by generalized transformation, but at different points in the derivation – to different strata.

48   In fact, it takes somewhat more than just this. See TPM (109), Lebeaux (1988: 154–5; 1990: 37–9).

49   The examples (i) and (ii) illustrate a well-known fact about these phrases – either can appear closer to the verb than the other – that might be hard to accommodate with this suggestion:

(i)   Kim ate at noon in the lunchroom.
(ii) Kim ate in the lunchroom at noon.

50   In part – recall that other assumptions are necessary (note 48). These are criticized in TPM (116).

51   Speas is here arguing against Lebeaux's "derivational" approach in which Adjuncts are added to a PM and in favor of a "representational" analysis in which Adjuncts

are always present in a PM. See TPM (183–4, fn. 25) for why the argument does not tell against the TPM theory. The discussion in the text closely follows TPM here.

52 Though she does not distinguish Adjuncts from adjunctions there, this does support Speas's (1991) idea that antireconstruction effects should be given a "representational" rather than "derivational" analysis.

53 Despite terminology, this remains true even for Chomsky (1986b: 86–92) and those who follow him. According to Chomsky, there is only "s(emantic)-selection" and no "c(ategorial) selection" among the listed properties of lexical items. S-selection, however, implies the "canonical structural realization" of that category (CSR(C)) as well. This is misleading. It is not **structure**, but rather **syntactic category** that is implied by the CSR(C); so, for example, Chomsky (1986b: 87) takes "CSR(patient) and CSR(agent) to be NP . . ." and NP is a category (name), not a determinate piece of structure. It turns out, then, that ultimately selection by a Head is cashed out in terms of syntactic category here too – as, presumably, it must be in any PS-based syntactic system.

54 Extended Base structures will also have only labelled nodes because Extended structures must also be licensed by the MPST and it does not license unlabelled nodes. Notice that it will not be the interface aspects of the MPST – e.g., selection and projection – that do the work here, but rather the purely syntactic aspects – e.g., definitions of Maximal and Minimal Projections.

55 As William Davies pointed out, adjunction to the root node would not require a label on the new mother under this analysis, because the root node is not selected by a Head. To my mind, this just suggests that no adjunction mothers should be labelled, as this eliminates an otherwise somewhat puzzling asymmetry.

56 There are formal problems with these statements (Pullum 1989). These are fixed in TPM (97), Chametzky (1994: 254), and Stabler (1992: 252).

57 May (1985: 57–8) makes a brief suggestion for using his redefinitions for analyzing coordinate structures. This is a nonstarter, however. See TPM (179–81, fn. 10) for argument.

58 We note, too, that May's "primary theorem" is now a trivial consequence, with no revisions of *category* or *dominates* needed.

59 TPM (104) suggests that "structure preserving" be taken literally, at least in part. "Structure preservation" in something like the original sense of Emonds (1976) is about the (im)possibility of mismatches between labels on moved elements and on the positions to which they move; we might call this *label preservation*. Now, as adjunctions build structure, they are not "structure preserving" in the strongest literal sense (though perhaps they are on some weaker sense). Label preservation is a property of all and only literal structure preserving operations. Non-structure preserving operations – adjunctions – do not preserve labels because there is no label on the newly created node.

60 See TPM (112–13). As with the demonstration of the impossibility of having Adjuncts in the MPST without the Extended Base (see note 46), the demonstration is largely unedifying, so not repeated here. Largely, but not entirely; there are two interesting points. First, it appears that daughter-adjunction can only be ruled out if all branching is binary. Second, adjunction to the theoretically potent intermediate label is also possible; see TPM (186, fn. 8).

61 See TPM (188–9, fn. 1).

62 It might be thought that the label in question could simply be associated both with the host node and the root node of the Adjunct PM, as the MPST allows multiple labelling. However, this would give rise to an ill-formed Projection Chain on the Adjunct PM. Further, it would not join the PMs.

63   Actually, Adjunct Adding places Subjects as well as modifiers. Such indeterminacy of structure is evidently undesirable. However, (for at least the core cases) Subjects are NPs/DPs, while Adjuncts are not, so if there is a structural indeterminacy, there seems to be a categorial differentiation.

64   This is raised in Chapter One, note 34.

65   Notice that this question arises because we are giving the originally DT concept "Adjunct" a PS conception. Whether there is a corresponding issue about the peculiarities of the syntax of Adjuncts within DT I do not know.

66   There is disagreement between TPM (17–19) and Speas (1990). Speas (1990: 46) takes all structure to be "projected from the lexical items . . .", whereas TPM prefers to take lexical items as licensing structure. Speas (1990: 43) here "collapses the labelling function of X-bar theory with the implicit free generation of hierarchical structures." TPM separates these, arguing that this allows for the discovery of convergences between the independent theories.

67   Heads are unique because Projection Chains are licensed to satisfy the requirements of a lexical item (the Head). Sisters of items in a Chain would have to satisfy the differing requirements of the distinct Heads if there were multiple Heads. But in such a situation the results would be ill-formed, e.g., as a violation of the Theta-criterion.

68   See Chapter One, section 3.3.

69   Jackendoff's (1977: 221ff) "deverbalizing rules" are one, more general, precursor.

70   I should note that most P & P work assumes that some sort of "syntactic affixation" is possible, perhaps even desirable. Williams (1994: 2–3, 8f, 163ff) is a notable, and powerful, dissenter. I see very little reason to grant the usual assumptions, and shall do without such a process.

71   This is not to say there would be no problems. It is not immediately clear, for example, how to account for the differences among the poss-ing, acc-ing and ing-of constructions.

72   There remains a question: why are there so few DLCs and exocentric constructions? Unlike all other approaches, I think pursuing the TPM view could be enlightening on this question, though I have nothing currently to propose.

73   They are mentioned on 181–2, fn. 16.

74   See section 2.1 above.

75   See section 1.2 above.

76   TPM (20) summarizes these criticisms as "the program to 'eliminate phrase structure rules' . . . is largely a shell game." The central argument is that X-Bar restrictions on PS rules do nothing to the class of languages which a PSG can generate, and that the same can be said for their elimination. Speas (1990: 35–8, 56–60) has responded to these charges.

77   Speas (1990: 35) also notices this agreement.

78   TPM (22) also points out an apparent misunderstanding by Kornai and Pullum (1990) that vitiates some of their more formal objections.

79   There is a technical issue with respect to the interpretation of these rules and the nature of *dominance*. I return to this in section 5.2 below.

80   See section 1.5 above.

81   We note here the comment by Lapointe (1993a: 14): "While there may well be a universally specified set of PS rule schemas and general conditions governing the use of those schemas in individual languages, it is far from clear that that means we can abandon the use of explicitly stated PS rules in individual grammars." The TPM proposal can be seen as both agreeing with this comment from a P & P

perspective and offering theoretically motivated restrictions on the range of choices individual grammars can make.

82 See Chapter One, section 4.2.
83 See Chapter One, section 4.2 and section 1.2 above.
84 See Chapter One, section 4.2.
85 Noted in note 79 above.
86 See Chapter One, section 5 and section 1.2 above.
87 See, for example, Partee, ter Meulen, and Wall (1990: 443–4).

Chapter three

View of Toledo

The work

In Chapter Two I proposed the characterization *Late Classical GB* for the book, TPM, which we there examined. In this chapter we examine another book, *The antisymmetry of syntax* (Kayne 1994, hereafter AS). AS provides an idiosyncratic vantage point on syntactic theory and problems, taking a particular aspect of syntax and accentuating – some might say exaggerating – its importance and centrality well beyond what had previously been attempted or suggested, affording in the process a series of insights and analyses otherwise unavailable, even unimaginable. For this reason, it is not inappropriate, I think, to propose calling it a *Mannerist* work in the P & P tradition – hence this chapter's title. We begin with exposition of the general goals and results of the work, and then turn to examination of our PS concepts and issues.

AS has one basic idea, which it tries to justify theoretically and empirically. That idea is that precedence in the linguistic string implies asymmetric C-command in syntactic structure. More generally, AS (xv) "attribute[es] certain properties of linear order to hierarchical structure, in effect taking linear order to be of more fundamental importance to the human language faculty than is generally assumed. One of these properties is *antisymmetry* . . ."

1.0   The antisymmetry of syntax

1.1   *The Linear Correspondence Axiom (LCA)*

The central thesis of AS is given in (1) (AS: 6 (3)):

(1)   Linear Correspondence Axiom
      d(*A*) is a linear ordering of *T*.

There is evidently much that requires explication in (1). A *linear ordering* is a relatively familiar notion. A linear ordering is a relation on a set with the following three properties (AS: 4 (1)) (x, y, z range over elements of a set and L is a relation on it):

(2) a.   It is transitive; that is xLy and yLz → xLz
     b.   It is total; that is, it must cover all the members of the set: for all
          distinct x,y, either xLy or yLx.
     c.   It is antisymmetric; that is, not(xLy and yLx).[1]

A and T in (1) are sets made up of elements from phrase markers (PMs). T is
the set of all terminal elements in a given phrase marker, and A is the set of all
ordered pairs of nonterminals in that same PM such that the first member in
each pair asymmetrically C-commands the second member of the pair. We
return to asymmetric C-command below. d(A) is the *image* of A under d, where
the image of a single nonterminal, d(X), is the set of terminals which that
nonterminal dominates. For pairs of nonterminals <X,Y>, "d<X,Y> (= the
image under d of <X,Y>) is the set of ordered pairs {<a,b>} such that a is a
member of d(X) and b is a member of d(Y)" (AS: 5). The image of a set of such
ordered pairs, such as A, "is just the set formed by taking the union of the
images of each ordered pair in the original set" (AS: 5). An example may help
make this clearer.

(3)

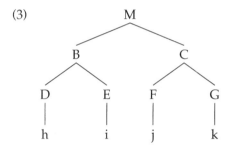

In (3), B asymmetrically C-commands F and G, and C asymmetrically
C-commands D and E, and these are the only asymmetrical C-command relations, so A is {<B,F>, <B,G>, <C,D>, <C,E>}. d(B) is {h,i}, d(C) is {j,k}, d(F) is {j},
d(G) is {k}, d(D) is {h}, and d(E) is {i}; these are the images under d for the
relevant nonterminals. In order to find d(A), we first find each of d<B,F>,
d<B,G>, d<C,D>, and d<C,E>, where each of these images is a set of pairs of
terminals in which the first member of each pair is dominated by the first
member of the corresponding pair of nonterminals, and the second member
terminal by the corresponding second nonterminal; we then union these sets.
The input sets are given in (4), and their union, d(A), in (5).

(4)   d<B,F> = {<h,j>, <i,j>}
      d<B,G> = {<h,k>, <i,k>}
      d<C,D> = {<j,h>, <k,h>}
      d<C,E> = {<j,i>, <k,i>}

(5)   d(A) = {<h,j>, <i,j>, <h,k>, <i,k>, <j,h>, <k,h>, <j,i>, <k,i>}

We can now ask whether the LCA is true of (3); that is, whether (5) is a
linear ordering on the set of terminals T of (3) (given in (6)). The answer is

"no". In fact, (5) fails to meet all three of the conditions required of a linear ordering on T.

(6) $T = \{h,i,j,k\}$

It fails to be transitive because, for example, it contains $\langle h,j \rangle$ and $\langle j,i \rangle$, but not $\langle h,i \rangle$. It fails to be total because, for example, it does not contain either $\langle h,i \rangle$ or $\langle i,h \rangle$. And it fails to be antisymmetric because, for example, it contains both $\langle h,j \rangle$ and $\langle j,h \rangle$. The significance of this failure is the following. All legitimate PMs must satisfy the LCA. Therefore, no legitimate PM can have the structure represented in (3). Thus, any syntactic analysis that posits such a structure for any construction in any language is an incorrect analysis. But we have gotten somewhat ahead of ourselves. We need to return to asymmetric C-command.

C-command is not asymmetric, since two distinct nodes may mutually C-command one another (as, for example, sisters do). AS (4 (2)) gives a straight-forward definition for asymmetric C-command.

(7)   X asymmetrically C-commands Y iff X C-commands Y and Y does not C-command X.

The obvious question, of course, is why bother with stipulating this defini-tion? The answer grows out of ". . . the intuition that a parsimonious UG would not have linear order and hierarchical structure be as independent of one another as syntactic theory normally assumes . . ." (AS: 131). If this intuition is a good one, then linear order and hierarchical structure ought to be "closer" to one another – in some way that can be made precise – than has ordinarily been believed. One way to precisely investigate "closeness" is formally, in terms of the properties of the relations which mediate linear order and hierarchical structure. Linear order, as mediated by the *precedence* relation, is, unsurprisingly, a linear ordering.[2] That is, precedence on terminals is transitive, total, and antisymmetric.[3] If hierarchical structure is formally "close" to linear order, then this "closeness" would be revealed by finding some relation which mediates hierarchical structure which is itself a linear order.

The obvious candidate is the *dominance* relation. This is so because, as we have discussed already at some length, *everyone* agrees that (immediate/direct) domin-ance is the basic relation ordering hierarchical structure. Within the standard formalizations of PMs, as we know, dominance is to hierarchical structure as precedence is to linear order; so, if the intuition behind AS is sound, this seems like the place to look. Sadly for that intuition, dominance is not a linear ordering. It is not total (though it is transitive and antisymmetric).[4]

In order to salvage something from the abrupt wrecking of its guiding intui-tion, AS (4) makes the following observation. Dominance with respect to a particular nonterminal node *is* a linear ordering. That is, for a given nonterminal node X, the set of all nodes which dominate X is linearly ordered by dominance – for any two nodes Y and Z which dominate X, either Y dominates Z or Z dominates Y.[5] AS calls such a relation – one founded on and restricted to a specific node – *locally total*, and further calls it *locally linear*, if it is also (locally) transitive and antisymmetric. Dominance, then, is a locally linear ordering, if not a linear ordering *simpliciter*. AS then goes on to consider C-command. C-command is neither total nor antisymmetric. This brings us back, finally, to (7), repeated here, the definition for asymmetric C-command:

(7)   X asymmetrically C-commands Y iff X C-commands Y and Y does not C-command X.

This is still not enough for even a locally linear relation, however. A further restriction to binary branching PMs is also required. With these restrictions, a locally linear version of C-command is available. In a binary branching PM, if Y and Z each asymmetrically C-command X, then either Y asymmetrically C-commands Z or Z asymmetrically C-commands Y.[6]

AS (5) suggests that there are now two viable candidates for fleshing out the intuition "that there should be a very close match between the linear ordering relation on the set of terminals and some comparable relation on nonterminals." The notion "comparable" is explicated as locally linear. Asymmetric C-command is anointed, with the following sentence the entire justificatory discussion provided:

> Of the two locally linear relations at issue, it is natural to take asymmetric c-command to be one that is closely matched to the linear ordering of the set of terminals. (AS: 5)

This is weak. Indeed, given (1) that there is no discussion of C-command – why it should be considered relevant at all, for example[7], (2) that asymmetric C-command is specially stipulated apparently just in order to create a locally linear ordering, (3) that a further restriction to binary branching PMs is required, and (4) that the locally linear orderings themselves are neither general (in the sense pointed out in notes 5 and 6) nor, for that matter, obviously "comparable" to the true linear order precedence, "weak" may even somewhat exaggerate the theoretical strength of this proposal. We might wonder whether *anything* is allowed in pursuit of a central intuition, and whether *nothing* is required that might give such pursuits antecedent plausibility.

Fortunately, something can be done. We shall reexamine a topic we have looked at previously, viz., the nature of C-command.[8] Though the analysis developed in Chapter Two supposes that there is no basic syntactic relation of precedence ordering PMs, we can nonetheless use the underlying insights into C-command of Richardson and Chametzky (1985; R/C hereafter) to give some much needed motivation to the otherwise aggressively free-floating proposals in AS.

Let us recall the central properties of C-command from Chapter Two. It is a relation between a single node X and a set of nodes, the set of nodes which C-command X. C-command is a generalization of the sister relation: the nodes which C-command X are the nodes which are sisters of the nodes which dominate X (dominance reflexive). C-command and dominance are, therefore, disjoint: not (YdomX and YCcmX). C-command is parasitic on dominance

– given just the dominance relation, C-command is definable – and entirely formal – no substantively linguistic predicates or relations are needed to define it. C-command is the basic command relation. And in a PM P, the set of C-commanders of X is the *minimal factorization* of P with respect to X.

For present purposes, we should notice that C-command itself is already *local* in the favored sense. We are looking at a specific node and determining which nodes C-command it. If what is required for AS is a relation that is local in this sense, then some version of C-command immediately seems a more likely candidate than does a version of dominance. In looking at a particular node and the dominance relation, there just is no reason independent of the guiding intuition of AS to look at the nodes which dominate X as opposed to those which X dominates (or both). We must go out of our way and restrict dominance in an arbitrary fashion. C-command, conversely, is given to us independently as exactly the right sort of relation. This is significant because one of our current desiderata is precisely to find some reason to ignore the basic ordering relation for hierarchical structure (viz., dominance) while looking for a way to make linear order and hierarchical structure "closer" than had been thought.

There is still more we can do. The R/C analysis assumes there is a precedence relation ordering PMs, and assumes as well the usual Exclusivity Condition on PMs whereby any two nodes must be related by either of dominance or precedence, but may not be related by both. This means that C-command holds only of nodes which are already in a precedence relation (given Exclusivity and the disjointness of C-command and dominance). Within such a setting we can make the following argument. We are looking to find a "closeness" between hierarchical structure and linear order. But the two basic relations, dominance and precedence, are governed by Exclusivity. If the intuition about "closeness" is also correct, we should, then, expect to find some other, third relation to mediate between the exclusive pair. The mediation such a relation must perform could be expected to have the following form: it should be constructible from one of the pair in such a way as to include only members of the other. But this is how C-command works: constructible from dominance, it includes only precedence pairs.[9]

We see, therefore, that the central intuition of AS can be used within standard assumptions to explain the existence and linguistic importance of C-command. C-command is the mediating formal relation required to bridge the gap between the basic ordering relations for PMs. Or, almost so. It is *asymmetric* C-command (in binary branching PMs) that AS requires, as C-command is otherwise not locally linear. However, this is a relatively minor point, easily and not unnaturally accommodated.

The important point is that the central intuition can motivate C-command as analyzed in R/C. The central intuition tells us to look for similarity between hierarchical structure and linear order. However, the basic ordering relations for these respective dimensions of PMs are, in the event, not relevantly similar and governed by Exclusivity. This suggests that if the intuition is sound, there should be some third mediating relation. The R/C conception of C-command appears to be just such a relation: constructible from dominance, yet including only precedence related nodes. This helps explain the linguistic significance of

C-command (and other command relations based on it). However, C-command itself is not formally as "close" to precedence as we might hope and expect. But, R/C's conception of C-command does have the crucially relevant property of being *local*. Indeed, we have motivation for the crucial relevance of this property: unlike dominance, C-command as characterized is intrinsically local, so if C-command, and not dominance, is the relevant relation, locality should be implicated – and, conversely, insofar as locality is implicated, this supports C-command (so characterized) over dominance. Moreover, it is simple enough to construct an asymmetric, hence locally linear, relation from C-command: merely remove any sister(s) of the node X (the node whose C-commanders the set contains). Asymmetric C-command is rather less odd than local dominance, it seems.

I think that the theoretical underpinnings of the LCA have been rendered rather more perspicuous by our discussion. AS here also raises issues with respect to the precise nature of the relations dominance and precedence which will be taken up in section 6 below. We move now to how the LCA is deployed with respect to a central aspect of PS theory, viz., X-Bar Theory.

1.2 X-Bar derived

As pointed out above, the LCA (1) disallows the structure (3).

(1) Linear Correspondence Axiom
     d(A) is a linear ordering of T.

(3)

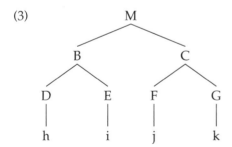

The fact that the LCA rules out a variety of structures can be used to derive a number of consequences, some of which explain central aspects of X-Bar structures. The derivation uses a definition of Head (AS: 11): a *Head* is a nonterminal that dominates no other nonterminal. Correspondingly, a *Nonhead* is a nonterminal that dominates at least one other nonterminal. The consequences of the LCA can now be stated as in (8) (AS: 11).

(8) For all nonterminal sister pairs, a PM P:
     a. is inadmissible if
         i.   both sisters are Heads, or
         ii. both sisters are Nonheads
     b. is admissible if one sister is a Head and one sister is a Nonhead.

These results are demonstrated by cases, as we shall presently see. From (8), "follow familiar X-bar-theoretic properties" such as (AS: 131):

(9)   a.   the need for a phrase to have a Head
      b.   the impossibility for a phrase to have more than one Head
      c.   the limitation to one specifier per phrase
      d.   the limitation to one sister complement per Head
      e.   the requirement that a complement not be a bare Head.

We shall discuss these in more detail below in sections 2, 3, and 5. We turn now to the derivation of the results in (8).

   Crucial to these derivations are the following: (1) the particular conception of C-command used in AS and (2) nonbranching domination. AS adopts a nonstandard conception of C-command, and requires that there be nonbranching domination. The version of C-command is given in (10); we discuss nonbranching domination further in section 4 below.[10] This conception of C-command is stated "in terms of 'first node up' and not in terms of 'first branching node up'" (AS: 7).

(10)   X C-commands Y iff neither X dominates Y nor Y dominates X and the first distinct node dominating X also dominates Y.

   Given our discussion in the previous section, which silently assumed a standard conception in terms of "branching nodes", this might seem to pose a problem. However, there is no significant problem. The difference between the two conceptions is realized with respect to nonbranching domination – it is only if there is any nonbranching domination that there can be any difference between them. Although the R/C conception assumes that there is no nonbranching domination, it can be straightforwardly generalized to include such cases.[11] The arguments made in the previous section are unaffected.

   Returning to our main thread, the derivation of the results in (8), we compare the PMs (11) and (12) (AS: 7,8 (1) & (2)). The only difference between them is that (12) lacks *N*, and the concomitant nonbranching domination relation between *N* and *P*. The LCA rules (12) inadmissible, while admitting (11).

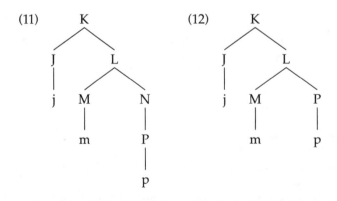

The LCA rules (12) out as follows. The set *A* for (12) – the set of pairs of nonterminals where the first asymmetrically C-commands the second – is {<J,M>, <J,P>}. This means that d(*A*) is {<j,m>, <j,p>}. This set is not a linear ordering on the set of terminals for (12) (viz., {j,m,p}), because it is not total: there is no pair that contains *m* and *p*.

The LCA allows (11) as follows. The set *A* is {<J,M>, <J,N>, <J,P>, <M,P>}. The set of terminals for (11) is the same as that for (12): { j,m,p }. However, the presence of the pair <M,P> in *A* for (11) crucially changes the set d(*A*). This pair of nonterminals means that d(*A*) for (11) is {<j,m>, <j,p>, <m,p>}.[12] The presence of <m,p> in this set makes it total with respect to the set of terminals. As it is also asymmetric and transitive, d(*A*) is a linear ordering on the set of terminals, as required.

The problem with (12) is that *m* and *p* and M and P "are in too symmetric a relation to one another" (AS: 9). As (12) is an arbitrary PM, and M and P have no particular properties other than the fact that they both meet the definition for a Head (neither dominates any nonterminal distinct from itself), we see that (8ai) holds.[13] And (11) shows us that (8b) holds, as M is a Head and N is a Nonhead.

(8) For all nonterminal sister pairs, a PM P
    a. is inadmissible if
        i. both sisters are Heads, or
        ii. both sisters are Nonheads
    b. is admissible if one sister is a Head and one sister is a Nonhead.

That this conclusion has substantive syntactic implications is illustrated by (13) and (14): the former is an instance of the admissible (11), and the latter of the inadmissible (12) (AS: 10 (4), (5)). Thus, the LCA chooses between potentially conflicting syntactic analyses.

(13)   (14)

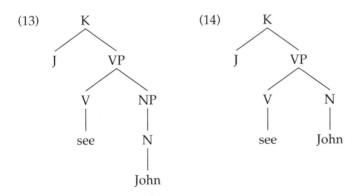

We have one case left from (8), (8aii), where both sisters are Nonheads, and the structure is not admitted. The relevant structure is (15) (AS: 10 (6)).

(15)

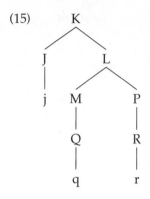

The set of nonterminals for (15) is {j,q,r}. The set A, of asymmetric C-command pairs, is {<J,M>, <J,P>, <J,Q>, <J,R>, <M,R>, <P,Q>}. The crucial fact about d(A) is that it contains both <q,r> – which is d<M,R> – and <r,q> – which is d<P,Q> – and thus fails to be antisymmetric and consequently also fails to be a linear order on {j,q,r}, violating the LCA. As (15) is an arbitrary PM and M and P have no properties other than meeting the definition for Nonhead (each dominates at least one other nonterminal), (8aii) is established. Our example (3), repeated here, is another instance of this, one in which neither of the Nonheads B and C is nonbranching, showing the irrelevance of branching for this conclusion.[14]

(3)

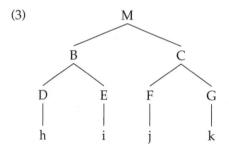

In addition to the X-Bar consequences listed in (9) above, and discussed in subsequent sections, AS (11–12) suggests that (8) provides the means to explain the existence of coordinate conjunctions. That is, it is suggested that examples such as (16) (AS: 11 (8)) do not have a coordinate interpretation on account of the LCA. A constituent [[the boy] [the girl]] would be exactly an instance of two Nonhead sisters, as in (3), hence illicit. So, it is suggested, if there are to be structures with a coordinate interpretation, then there must be another Head present – the coordinate conjunction – and the structure cannot be a "flat" one, but is rather [[the girl] [and [the boy]]] (AS: 12). We return to the topic of coordination in section 1.6.

(16) a.   *I saw the boy the girl
      b.   *The girl the boy were discussing linguistics.

Obsessively careful readers may be somewhat puzzled at this point, as it might seem that "... specifiers and adjoined phrases appear to have no place in theory being elaborated here" (AS: 15). How AS seeks to relieve this puzzlement is the subject to which we now turn our attention.

1.3 Specifiers and adjunction

The LCA-based theory "appears to rule out sentences such as [(17)], in which the subject clearly must have a sister constituent that is not a head" (AS: 16).

(17) The girl saw John.

In order to accommodate such examples, and more generally, to accommodate Specifiers, AS makes the following proposal: Specifiers are a species of adjunction in AS. This reduces the problem of Specifiers to that of adjunctions, but does not solve the problem. In order to solve the problem, theoretical space must be provided for adjunctions. To this end, two technical adjustments are required.[15]

The first is to adopt the *segment/category* distinction of May (1985; 1989) and Chomsky (1986a).[16] In (18) and (19) we give May's (1989: 92 (16)) "Theory of Adjunction" and the statement of his "Primary Theorem".[17]

(18) Theory of Adjunction
  (i)   A Category $C = \{n_1, \ldots, n_n\}$
  (ii) C dominates $\alpha =_{def} \forall n \in C$ (n dominates α)

(19) Adjuncts are not dominated by the categories to which they are adjoined.

The intent of the definitions in (18) is that "categories are sets of nodes, and to be dominated by a category is to be dominated by every member node" (May 1989: 92). *Segment* is the name given to a member node of a Category.

The second adjustment is to the definition of C-command, and makes use of this first one. The idea is that "a segment cannot enter into a c-command relation" (AS: 16). This is enshrined in (20) (AS 16 (3)) (italic in original).

(20) X c-commands Y iff *X and Y are categories* and X excludes Y and every category that dominates X dominates Y.

Exclusion is from Chomsky (1986a: 9 (17)):[18]

(21) α excludes β iff no segment of α dominates β.

With these revisions in place, we can now license adjunctions (and, of course, Specifiers) as follows (AS: 15–16 (2), (4)). In (22b), otherwise identical to (22a), we have an adjunction structure on account of replacing the root L with P. This permits the LCA now to admit (22b), while still disallowing (22a).

(22)   a.   b.

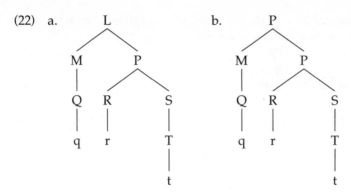

The LCA rules out (22a) because *A* contains both <M,R> and <P,Q>, and the images of these are, respectively, <q,r> and <r,q>. But this means that (22a) fails to be antisymmetric. For (22b), however, <P,Q> is no longer a member of *A*. This is because the lower *P*-labelled node is not a Category, merely a Segment, and so cannot C-command *Q* (or anything else) given the italicized portion of (20). And the entire Category *P*, comprising both *P*-labelled nodes, cannot C-command *Q* because it does not exclude *Q* (the higher *P* Segment dominates *Q*).

Having here outlined the basic technical aspects of the approach to adjunction, we return to some of its specific and strong consequences in section 2.3 below. We move now to word order.

1.4   *Subsequence, precedence, word order*

There is both a substantive and a theoretical/conceptual topic here. The substantive area concerns the relative order of Heads, Complements, and Specifiers with respect to one another universally. We return to this below. The other, theoretical/conceptual topic is whether the relation which orders the string of terminals is *precedence* or *subsequence,* and whether a principled basis can be given for choosing one over the other. We begin with this discussion.

1.4.1   *Theoretical considerations*

The ultimate conclusion is that precedence, not subsequence, orders the string of terminals. The argument for this conclusion is fairly complex and indirect (AS: 36–7). First, we are asked to reconsider asymmetric C-command and dominance. It is remarked that these relations are "significantly similar" in both being locally linear. A difference between them is then noted. All PMs are *rooted*: they each have a single node which properly dominates all other nodes in the PM.[19] With asymmetric C-command, there is no corresponding "root node" – no node which asymmetrically C-commands all other nodes in the PM. The suggestion is then made that these relations can be made yet more similar if such a "root node" for asymmetric C-command is postulated. For every PM, then, there is postulated an "abstract node *A*" which is "adjoined to the root node" and which, therefore, asymmetrically C-commands all other nodes in the PM[20] (AS: 36).

Next, a corresponding terminal is suggested for A. This is because all other nonterminals dominate "at least one (perhaps empty) terminal element" (AS: 37). In fact, a question is now raised: should A dominate an abstract terminal *a*, which precedes all other terminals, or an abstract terminal *z*, which follows all other terminals? The abstract terminal *a* is argued for. We reproduce the entire argument:

> The intuitive motivation for taking $d(A) = a$ rather than $d(A) = z$ is that *a* and *z* are not quite as symmetric as they might seem, in a way that favors *a*. Let us think of the string of terminals as being associated with a string of time slots. That by itself is not sufficient to induce an asymmetry between *a* and *z*. Let me then make the further claim that what is paired with each time slot is not simply the corresponding terminal, but the substring of terminals ending with that terminal (i.e., the substring produced up to that time).
>
> In other words, a string of terminals abcdz (with a and z abstract) is mapped to a set of substrings.
>
> (5) a, ab, abc, abcd, abcdz
> An asymmetry between *a* and *z* has now appeared: *a* precedes every terminal in every substring, but *z* does not follow every terminal in every substring (since *z* figures in only one substring). If the abstract root node for asymmetric c-command needs to be mapped by *d* to a corresponding abstract "root node" for terminals, and if that root node for terminals must be in some fixed relation to every terminal in every substring, then that abstract terminal must be *a* and the fixed relation must be "precedes". (AS: 37)

There is much that needs to be chewed on here before it can all be swallowed, but we shall keep our bits in just a while longer, because this argument and conclusion are themselves merely a way station in AS. The further destination to be reached is ordering of the terminal string: is it by precedence or by subsequence? The choice is made for precedence, again with an argument, again reproduced.

> Now by hypothesis the abstract node A asymmetrically c-commands Y, for all Y, so that <A,Y> is in A, for any phrase marker containing Y. Since d(A) = a, it follows that <a,y> is in d(A) (for all y dominated by Y). So that if <x,y> is "x follows y", we conclude that "a follows y" for all y. But a is the abstract beginning terminal. Thus, we have a contradiction. Therefore, <x,y> cannot be "x follows y" but must rather be "x precedes y". (AS: 37)

Now we can see the argument whole. The terminal string is ordered by precedence

(23) 1. If there is an abstract A which asymmetrically C-commands all other nonterminals and
     2. If the abstract nonterminal A dominates an abstract terminal a and
     3. If the terminal string is associated with a string of time slots and

4.   If the string of time slots is mapped to a set of substrings of terminals, not a set of single terminals and

5.   If the substrings are strings of all the terminals up to and including the current terminal and

6.   If the abstract terminal a dominated by abstract A is in a fixed relation to every other terminal in all the substrings.

The percentage of assumptions to conclusions could seem on the high side here, which could give rise to our earlier worry, viz., "We might wonder whether *anything* is allowed in pursuit of a central intuition, and whether *nothing* is required that might give such pursuits antecedent plausibility". Let us see what we can do.

The central intuition, recall, is that formally the hierarchical structure and the terminal string in syntax are more like one another than has been supposed. The basic relation ordering hierarchical structure is dominance. The basic relation ordering the terminal string is what is now in question: is it precedence or is it subsequence? The relation mediating between dominance-ordered hierarchical structure and the terminal string is asymmetric C-command, through the LCA. In this context, then, we can sharpen our question: can the choice between precedence and subsequence for ordering the terminal string be resolved by pushing the central intuition? That is, can a new or unremarked on formal closeness between dominance-ordered hierarchical structure and the terminal string be discovered or established which would decide for one of the relations as *the* relation? Further, this new closeness would need to be mediated by asymmetric C-command, if it were to appropriately fit into this context.

From this starting point, we are led to examine hierarchical structure in terms of its basic ordering relation of dominance. We do this because we are aiming to determine what the basic ordering relation for the terminal string is, and we are aiming to do this by relating the terminal string to hierarchical structure. It is thus natural to look at the basic ordering relation for hierarchical structure. We have already made dominance more like precedence/subsequence by rendering it locally linear. Now, if we examine PMs in terms of dominance, we immediately notice that PMs are *rooted*; that is, there is a single node which dominates all other nodes, and which no other node dominates. While it may not be the only property we might so notice, it is an extremely obvious and basic one. It is, more significantly, perhaps the only "global" property involving dominance and the PM, in the sense that it involves *every* node.[21]

Given that rootedness is both global and basic with respect to dominance in the PM, it becomes antecedentally plausible to use it in pursuing the central intuition. We now seek a *root terminal* in the terminal string, in the sense of a terminal that precedes/follows all other terminals. But, beyond that, we seek it by means of asymmetric C-command and the LCA, the mediators between structure and string. If there is to be a root terminal, it must be the image of some nonterminal in the PM. More exactly, the root terminal must precede/follow every other terminal, and therefore it must be the image of a nonterminal which asymmetrically C-commands every other nonterminal, as it is the members of A, the set of asymmetrical C-command nonterminal pairs, which are mapped into pairs of terminals by d, the image relation.

But there is no node which asymmetrically C-commands every other node. Either, then, our inquiry is over, or we must postulate one. Suppose the latter. It will have the properties ascribed to it in AS: (1) it is abstract (2) it is adjoined to the root and (3) it dominates an abstract terminal.[22] We have now returned to where we left ourselves chomping at the bit: to the issue of whether the abstract root terminal is a or z, one which, respectively, precedes or follows all other terminals. We are, however, somewhat better off than before, in that our route has been made less arbitrary.

There is surely nothing objectionable about associating the terminal string with time slots; insofar as one is translating syntax into speech (and not, say, writing or signing), this presumably has to be done in some way or another. Potentially more controversial is the association of the time slots with substrings of terminals. Each such substring is identified in AS (37) as "the substring produced up to that time":

> In other words, a string of terminals abcdz (with a and z abstract) is mapped to a set of substrings.

(5) a, ab, abc, abcd, abcdz (AS: 37)

The argument seems to depend on the following. Consider a string of five terminals (two abstract) and the translation of this object into speech by means of association with time slots. Some terminal must be the first one associated, some must be the second, some must be the third, some the fourth, and some the fifth. Call the second one "b", the third one "c" and the fourth one "d". Now, what AS has also done is identify the first one with "a", the abstract terminal that precedes all other terminals, and the fifth one with "z", the abstract terminal that follows all other terminals. Is this necessary? Could we, for example, identify the first one with "z" and the fifth with "a"? The result would be (5′), rather than (5) from AS. Is there something wrong with (5′)?

(24) (5′) z, bz, bcz, bcdz, abcdz

In (5′) z follows all other terminals and a, once it appears, precedes all other terminals – just as in (5), z, once it appears, follows all other terminals. There is nothing wrong with (5′), and other alternatives are imaginable. However, no such alternative allows what (5) does: a simple and entirely straightforward way to identify a substring and a terminal. With (5) we can use "the substring of terminals ending with that terminal" (AS: 37). No similar statement is possible with (5′) – notice that we could not even make reference to the substring of terminals ending with the terminal immediately preceding z, as this would not work for the final substring and a.[23] Thus, we see that the AS conclusion is, again, better supported than the text lets on.

It is, no doubt, helpful to be clear about what is and is not going on here. The fact that a string of time slots is ordered by temporal precedence does not by itself imply that precedence rather than subsequence orders the syntactic terminal string, even when the string of time slots and the syntactic string of terminals are associated. Crucial for understanding this is the role of asymmetric C-command and the image relation d. The issue concerns arbitrary pairs of terminals, where these pairs are given by d as applied to nonterminal pairs in the asymmetric C-command relation (i.e., members of the set A). The question is: for an arbitrary pair of nonterminals <X,Y> in A (that is, X asymmetrically C-commands Y), in the terminal string does the image of X precede the image of Y, or does the image of X follow the image of Y? The associating of the terminal string to a string of time slots does not answer this question. Nor does simply mapping the string of terminals to a set of substrings. Thus, the conclusion for precedence over subsequence is not *merely* the result of importing into syntax the temporal ordering of speech (though, to be sure, it is in part such a result). Rather, that conclusion is arrived at by means of theoretical syntactic inquiry: we sought a root terminal as analogue to the root node in a PM, using asymmetric C-command and the LCA to mediate the relation between structure and string, in keeping with the overall project of pursuing the central intuition.

We can take note here of comments by Chomsky (1995a: 437, fn. 32; 1995: 390–1, fn. 108). Chomsky suggests that he differs from AS in taking the ordering relation "to be literal precedence, not simply a transitive, asymmetric, total ordering among terminals." But as we have seen, this is incorrect. AS in fact *argues* that the ordering relation is "literal precedence". Indeed, in this regard, AS may be at an advantage when compared to Chomsky's own practice, which merely *assumes* "literal precedence" as the ordering relation.

Chomsky's further claim, that "any interchange" of sisters which satisfy the LCA will also satisfy it, is also incorrect. Indeed, it seems to rest on a serious confusion or misapprehension. It obviously presupposes that there is some sense in which sisters can be "interchanged", but there is no sense to this idea in AS. No precedence relations are defined on the nonterminal nodes in a syntactic tree in AS. Precedence relations are defined *only* for the terminals, the leaves, of the tree. The tree itself is ordered by (immediate) dominance and, derivatively, (asymmetric) C-command, which relations are mapped to precedence relations in the string of terminals. While nothing explicit is said in AS about precedence relations among nonterminals, this very silence implies that precedence relations only hold among those elements (terminals) for which they are explicitly defined. So, the notion of "interchange" of sisters on which Chomsky's criticism is based is literally meaningless in AS.[24]

This is significant for the following reason. We have seen that the laconic presentation in AS can leave the project open to doubts and objections of a quite basic sort. We have now seen, however, that elaborating and expanding on that presentation can meet such doubts and objections. The various moves and proposals in AS, while they have not been shown to be inevitable, can be seen in fact to be rather natural ones in context, a context that is a theoretically syntactic one. We turn now to the substantive argument and conclusions.

1.4.2   *Substantive considerations*

As we noted above, the issue here is about the relative order of Heads, Specifiers, and complements.[25] It is concluded that universally the relative order is Specifier-Head-complement. This conclusion dovetails with and supports the conclusion that the basic relation ordering the terminal string is precedence, and not subsequence. We now examine how these conclusions are reached.

Consider a PM for a Head with Specifier and complement (AS: 34 (3)). In (25), R is the Head, M the Specifier (note that it is adjoined to P) and S is the complement.

(25)

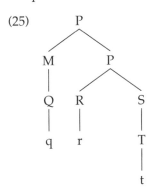

As M asymmetrically C-commands R and R asymmetrically C-commands T, <q,r> and <r,t> are in d(A). This, in turn, implies that regardless of whether the basic relation ordering the terminal string were precedence or subsequence, q and t would be on opposite sides of r – that is, the Specifier and complement are on opposite sides of the Head. This holds no matter how internally complex a Specifier or complement might be (AS: 34–5). From this it follows that the only two possible orders are Specifier-Head-complement and complement-Head-Specifier. Typological/universal evidence is then cited to support the former as "the only one available..." (AS: 36). If this is correct, then the relation interpreting pairs such as <q,r> and <r,t> from (25) must be precedence, not subsequence. If it were subsequence, then q would follow r and r would follow t, but that would be the unavailable complement-Head-Specifier order, rather than the available Specifier-Head-complement.

We can now see how the theoretical and substantive inquiries dovetail with and support one another. If the substantive observations are correct, and Specifier-Head-complement order is overwhelmingly more common universally, then we should want to know why this is so. The theoretical inquiry gives us this explanation, in two steps. First, the LCA licenses only Specifier-Head-complement or complement-Head-Specifier. Second, the argument examined in section 1.4.1 above motivates precedence, rather than subsequence, thus choosing between the two possible orders in a way that explains the observed phenomena. And conversely, the theoretical position is buttressed by the observations. In general, as important as it may be for basic assumptions to illuminate the phenomena, it is perhaps even more important for internally natural elaborations and extensions of basic assumptions to do so. Otherwise it is hardly a theoretical inquiry at all. AS succeeds rather well here, motivating precedence as the basic ordering relation internally, in terms of the central intuition and the specific means of pursuing it (asymmetric C-command and the LCA).

We move now to some further implications of what has just been established.

1.5   Et seq.

We have here a congeries of consequences of the finding that "UG unfailingly imposes S-H-C order . . ." (AS: 47). The first consequence concerns cross-linguistic word order variation. All such variation must be the result of "different combinations of movements" (AS: 47). This is because, given the rigidity of UG with respect to Specifier-Head-complement order, there can be no "directionality parameter in the standard sense of the term" (AS: 47). And, further, all the movements will be leftward movement.[26] Therefore, most analyses of word orders other than the allowed Specifier-Head-complement order will have to be redone in terms of movement.

A second consequence is that the LCA holds of all syntactic strata (AS: 48–9). The argument here is the following. (1) The LCA replaces X-Bar theory as the underpinning for properties of phrase structure. (2) If the LCA does not hold of a particular syntactic stratum, then the phrase structural properties alluded to in (1) would be "inapplicable to" that stratum.[27] (3) But, taking the LCA to hold of all strata is the more restrictive alternative. (4) Given (3), the *prima facie* conclusion to draw is that the LCA holds of all strata. (5) Moreover, there is no compelling evidence (presumably of the sort which (2) suggests) against (4). (6) Therefore, the LCA holds of every stratum, and every stratum "is automatically associated with a fixed linear ordering of its terminal symbols" (AS: 49).[28]

We note two further "further consequences". One is that if agreement is always mediated by a Specifier-Head construction, then an asymmetry in agreement between adpositions and their complements can be explained (AS: 49–50). The asymmetry is that there are languages with obligatory agreement between postpositions and their lexical complements, while no prepositional phrases in SVO languages show such agreement.[29] This is explained because the complement to a postposition must either be in or have moved through a Specifier position, while the complement to a preposition need not ever be in a Specifier position.

The final consequence is that Head movement is always leftward. This follows from the fact that Heads must precede their complements. Given this, a lower Head that moves out of a complement to a higher Head and into the higher Head's position must be moving leftward.[30]

1.6   And, *again*

The claim made about coordination, recall, concerned examples such as (16) (repeated here).[31] The claim is that the ill-formedness of such examples with a coordinate interpretation (this interpretation would obviate any theta violation) is accounted for by the LCA, because the structures for such examples would have Nonhead sisters, which the LCA rules out. For such examples to have coordinate interpretations, there must be a Head present as sister to one or another of the Nonheads, thus creating the necessary asymmetrical structure. So, the LCA explains the existence of coordinate conjunctions by requiring them as Heads for phrases containing the conjuncts.

(16)   a.   *I saw the boy the girl
       b.   *The girl the boy were discussing linguistics.

AS makes further proposals with respect to the placement of conjunction words, coordination of Heads, coordination with *with*, and Right Node Raising.

With respect to conjunct placement, the problem is posed by examples such as in (26) – why is (26a) good, while (26b) is bad (AS: 58)?

(26)   a.   I saw Kim, Pat, and Dale.
       b.   *I saw Kim and Pat, Dale.

The proposal is that in (26a) there is a second conjunction Head, phonetically unrealized in English, which takes the phrase headed by *and* as its complement and *Kim* as its Specifier. If, however, the same analysis is attempted for (26b), then *Dale* would be the Specifier to the new phonetically unrealized Head, and *Dale* would have to be adjoined to the right of this Head (Specifiers, recall, are structurally adjunctions). But Specifiers must always precede their Heads in the AS theory, so (26b) is out.

There is, however, an alternative derivation for (26b), one in which the two Heads are interchanged with respect to their positions in (26a). Under this analysis, the phonetically unrealized Head takes *Dale* as its complement and *Pat* as its Specifier, while *and* takes that entire phrase as its complement and *Kim* as its Specifier. The proposal for ruling this out is that (1) *and* raises at LF and (2) a phonetically unrealized conjunction is licensed by a raised realized conjunction.[32] In this alternative derivation for (26b), with the phonetically unrealized conjunction below *and* in the tree, the claim is that *and* raising would not license the phonetically unrealized conjunction, thus ruling (26b) out.[33]

Before considering other claims made in AS for its approach to coordination, we should note something that it does not do. It is generally taken to be the central empirical fact about coordinate structures that only like syntactic categories conjoin.[34] If this is the central empirical fact, then the central theoretical desideratum should be to derive this fact. AS makes no mention of this fact, and, indeed, does not do well theoretically when confronted with it, as we now demonstrate.

AS claims that conjunction lexical items head phrases, with the conjuncts as complement and as Specifier. What this conspicuously fails to do is relate the categories of the conjuncts, the complement and Specifier, in any way. One might imagine stipulating that for conjunction lexical items complement and

Specifier must be of the same category. That this simply restates the central fact while affording no insight into it should be obvious. Moreover, it is not even true, on the AS analysis, that complement and Specifier are of the same category. This is because any conjunction lexical item other than the last one takes a phrase headed by another conjunction lexical item as its complement. Thus, for example, in (27), the lower *and* has the NP/DP *Dale* as its complement and the NP/DP *Pat* as its Specifier, while the higher *and* has the CONJP(?) phrase headed by the lower *and* as its complement and NP/DP *Kim* as its Specifier.[35]

(27)   I saw Kim and Pat and Dale.

We see, then, that the AS approach to coordination not only does not offer any insight into or derivation of the central empirical fact about coordinate structures, but also that its analysis is inconsistent with that fact. An AS proponent might conclude so much the worse for the central empirical fact; and, indeed, while central, it is not without its problems and exceptions. However, if the AS position would be that the central fact is actually an epiphenomenon or artifact, about which the best theory should say nothing, this itself needs to be said, and argued. Saying nothing is not the same as arguing that nothing should be said.

There can be no coordination of Heads under AS assumptions (AS: 59), Heads being defined as nonterminals which dominate no other nonterminal. This is because there would have to be a constituent made up of both one of the conjunct Heads and the conjunction Head. But such a constituent would thereby have two Head sisters, something we have already seen the theory disallows (recall (8) in section 1.2 above). As is noted (AS: 59), this is an unusual conclusion. It requires that examples such as (28a) have a structure as indicated in (28b) (AS: 61). This is an instance of Right Node Raising, for which AS must adopt a deletion analysis (following Wexler and Culicover 1980: 298–303) (AS: 67–8), rather than either a discontinuous constituent analysis (McCawley 1982) or the more common rightward movement analysis, neither of which is consistent with AS assumptions. Thus, coordination is of full VPs (or V's, perhaps – in any event, not merely of Vs). It is argued that examples such as (29) independently show that (28a) need not be V conjunction.

(28)   a.   Kim noticed and criticized the children's mismatched shoelaces.
      b.   Kim noticed [e]$_i$ . . . [the children's mismatched shoelaces]$_i$

(29)   Kim noticed and then criticized the children's mismatched shoelaces.

Similarly, an example like (30a), in which the coordinated constituent denotes a single individual, cannot be analyzed as N conjunction. Instead, it is noted that a single individual is also denoted by the coordinated constituent in (30b), wherein N conjunction is presumably not an option (AS: 61).

(30)   a.   my friend and colleague Pat Jones
      b.   my friend from high school and beloved colleague Pat Jones

It is also argued that in general clitics in Romance do not conjoin, and that this follows immediately if clitics are Heads.

Finally, the suggestion by Lakoff and Peters (1969) that (31) and (32) be related is taken up. AS does not require that these be related. However, if the evidence supports relating them, it is possible to do so in a way that is consistent with the constraints of the AS theory (AS: 63–6).

(31)   Dale and Dana collided.

(32)   Dale collided with Dana.

This concludes the account of coordination. There are both some unusual and some unfortunate implications of the AS theory in this domain. We turn now to our PS concepts and issues, and how they fare in the context of AS.

2.0   Syntactic structure and argument structure

Our three subtopics in this section are the familiar ones of (1) structuralization and argument alignment, (2) the position of Subjects, and (3) adjunct(ion)s. We take them up each in turn.

2.1   *Structuralization and argument alignment*

AS places some constraints on structuralization. For example, no Head may have more than one complement (AS: 69). When we recall that a complement must be sister to its Head, we see immediately why this conclusion follows. It is simply a case of the general consequence that two sisters cannot both be Nonheads ((8) above); in this case, it would be the multiple complements themselves that offend. From this and the impossibility of right adjunction structures, AS "derives the small clause analysis of [(33)] (i.e., [(34)]) '[gave [a book to the child]]'), plus the fact that the small clause must have a head (if it did not, the antisymmetry requirement would again be violated)" (AS: 69). However, "the theory does not automatically tell us whether to take the head to be *to* or rather to be a V position . . ." (AS: 147, fn. 1).

(33)   Kim gave a book to the child.

(34)   Kim [gave [a book to the child]]

The conclusion that Specifier-Head-complement is the only allowed order (section 1.4.2 above) also restricts structuralization possibilities. It also implies that there may be a far greater number of Heads (hence Specifiers) than would otherwise be expected, so as to derive those word orders that appear to violate the allowed order. We return to this in sections 3 and 4 below.

However, AS does not take, and does not seem committed to, any specific positions on the more general issues of structuralization and argument alignment (e.g., there is no mention of U(T)AH). Thus, though the LCA is taken to hold of all syntactic strata, whether or not one of those strata represents canonical structuralizations is not discussed nor, it seems, is any conclusion implied. Similarly, no particular conclusion seems to follow about the details of argument alignment in examples such as (33).

Somewhat more concretely, we can say the following. Two alternatives for (33) are suggested as compatible with the theory. One has the small clause headed by *to*. The other has it headed by a V. In the former case, presumably, the complement would be *the child*, and *a book* the Specifier. If, conversely, the Head were a V, then it seems perfectly consistent that *a book* be the complement and *to the child* the Specifier. Similarly, with respect to (35a) a headed small clause analysis is required (35b), but with *Dale* "perhaps raising up to its surface position from a lower position that is within the small clause and below *a book*" (AS: 147, fn. 1).

(35) a.   The teacher gave Dale a book.
      b.   The teacher [gave [Dale a book]]

This is interesting for several reasons. First, it suggests that it might be desirable for *Dale* to be lower in the structure than *a book*, and that if this is desirable, it is consistent with the theory. The reasons making such a positioning desirable might be ones having to do with argument alignment – the theta goal/beneficiary (or whatever) being structuralized lower than the theta theme in this case. Second, however, we should note that no grounds are actually given or discussed for this positioning. Third, we should also note the *perhaps* that introduces the quote above. It is apparently not required by the theory that *Dale* originate as suggested; this is just a potential derivation consistent with both the theory and an unmentioned possible desideratum.

AS, then, does not explicitly have much to say about some of the central issues in structuralization and argument alignment. What one can conclude is the following. If there seems to be good reason to take a specific position on one or another of these general issues – e.g., accepting U(T)AH or some kind of thematic hierarchy mapping proposal – then the restricted set of structural options AS makes available may yet be consistent with such commitments, but requiring structures and derivations that might otherwise not seem particularly well motivated or plausible.

2.2   Subjects

Little is said directly in AS about the position of Subjects, and the little that there is is mostly said in passing (AS: 118; 141, fn. 16; 149–50, fn. 11). From these remarks it is clear that the theory is (intended to be) consistent with the

VP internal positioning of Subjects, and may even assume it: "this analysis [of extraposition] assumes crucially that subjects can move up into Spec,IP from a lower position" (AS: 118). If this is assumed, then, in combination with the general restrictions of the theory, (thematic) Subjects are typically in Specifier position, hence have Adjunct structure.[36] This means that AS is most likely in basic agreement with TPM, for example, on the position of Subjects – VP internal, with Adjunct structure – though the details of the structure are not discussed. However, it is not clear that anything in AS requires such an analysis, as the VP internal structure seems to have no necessary connection to the theory.

This is a consequence of the more general agnosticism with respect to the larger questions of structuralization and argument alignment pointed out in the previous subsection. As we noted previously, this is not necessarily good. If our concern is PS theory, then compatibility with just about any position on such central topics and problems in PS theory is less than one might hope for – or require – in a restrictive theory.

On the other hand, one might argue alternatively that this represents a desirable *modularity* in theoretical architecture. Questions of structuralization and argument alignment are, properly speaking, interface questions mediating the relation between lexicon and syntax. The best theory of this interface is, on this view, whatever it is, but it is not, strictly, something the best theory of syntactic structure as such need address.

What this best theory of syntactic structure as such must do is offer as constrained a space of options as possible on its side of the interface, determined by whatever properly syntactic principles are discoverable. The theory in AS, moreover, is a theory of syntactic structure as such, and it does offer a highly constrained space of options determined, so it seems, by properly syntactic principles. Whether it is the best such theory is, of course, an open question. But on this view, it is the right *kind* of theory, hence a viable candidate for best theory status. And that it does not address the interface questions is therefore nothing to fault it over. Indeed, one might go further, and argue that, as AS is not, after all, (intended to be) a work of or about PS theory directly, it would be a mark against it were it to require positions on interface questions and issues. Perhaps this goes too far, and theoretical restrictiveness should be welcomed whenever and wherever it can be discovered. Regardless of how this issue might be resolved, the general argument for modular theoretical architecture is a powerful one, and it is not clear that one can – or should try to – disarm it.

2.3 Adjunct(ion)s

There are a number of immediate consequences of the approach to adjunction in AS. We should note first of all that because the consequences hold in virtue of the structural peculiarity shared by Adjuncts and adjunctions, viz., a Category made of more than one Segment, they hold in both cases. These consequences include:

(36) a. No adjunction of a Nonhead to a Head.
      b. No iterated adjunction of multiple Heads to a single Head.
      c. No iterated adjunction of multiple Nonheads to a single Nonhead.
      d. No adjunction of a Head to a Nonhead.

What is allowed are the following:

(37) a. Adjunction of a Head to a Head.
      b. Adjunction of a Nonhead to a Nonhead.

Because Specifiers have Adjunct structure two further consequences follow immediately. From (36c) it follows "that a given phrase can have only one specifier" (AS: 22). And it follows from (36d) "that specifiers cannot be heads" (AS: 32). These are strong and interesting results, with some substantive implications as well. We shall turn our attention, however, to the underlying theoretical assumptions and arguments.

Let us begin with the assimilation of Specifiers to Adjuncts. What does this assimilation mean? More precisely, in a PS-based system, for Specifiers and Adjuncts to have the same phrase structure, structure different from all other (unmoved) structure, must mean *something*. And what it must mean is that these two form a *syntactic kind*. This is an unusual, even unique, conclusion. Typically, Specifiers are thought to be part of a Head's "center" while Adjuncts are "on the margin". But AS requires a new taxonomy, one that opposes complements, on the one hand, to both Specifiers and Adjuncts, on the other – perhaps as a class of Noncomplements. At least, this is so if Adjuncts do, in fact, have Adjunct structure; but because "in [(38)] '[a book on Sunday]' must be a headed constituent . . . postcomplement adjuncts . . . are themselves in a complement position with respect to some head."

(38) Kim bought a book on Sunday.

As well, because relative clauses, typically analyzed as Adjuncts in the N projection, are given a raising analysis in AS, with the raised nominal landing "in Spec,CP as the result of movement. . . ." (AS: 87), relative clauses are perhaps more like adjunctions than like Adjuncts. In (39), *picture* is in Specifier position, but it gets there by movement, unlike a typical Specifier (or Adjunct?).

(39) the [[picture]$_i$ [that Kim saw [e]$_i$]]

So we may be faced with a quite remarkable situation. Specifiers have an Adjunct structure, but Adjuncts do not. There then would be no new structural kind comprising Specifiers and Adjuncts, but there would be one comprising complements and Adjuncts. We should also notice the following. The four common diagnostics for Adjuncts are given here in (40).[37] Now, within usual PS-based approaches to Adjuncts, their particular phrase structure illuminates these properties. The first two emerge specifically from the contrast between the phrase structure for Adjuncts and that for complements (arguments). The last two emerge from the specifics of Adjunct phrase structure, viz., the identity of the labels on the host and mother nodes. What is crucial to understand is that in the AS analysis, none of these properties are any longer illuminated by the specific phrase structure of Adjuncts, given that Adjuncts have complement phrase structure (or undergo movement). This is unexpected, at best, in a PS-based approach to syntax.

(40) (1) they are not mandatory
(2) they appear farther from the Head than do arguments
(3) they iterate
(4) they do not appear in a specific order with respect to one another.

The pivotal issue is one familiar from our discussions of Dependency Theory and Grimshaw (1991).[38] *Adjunct* is a relational/dependency concept. In order to coherently make use of it in a PS-based syntax, it needs a unique and consistent phrase structural "implementation". In AS, *relational* Adjuncts are *structural* complements, while *relational* Specifiers are *structural* Adjuncts. Phrase structure no longer distinguishes elements in Adjunct relations from those in complement relations. And those elements in adjoined phrase structure apparently have disparate relations: some are Specifiers, others are simply moved elements of one sort or another. But if relational/dependency concepts pick out true syntactic kinds, then a PS-based syntax must reconstruct them in phrase structure terms. This is simply part of what it is to be a PS-based approach to syntax.

These considerations bring us back to the central theoretical fact with respect to adjunct(ion)s: these are noncanonical structures.[39] AS implicitly recognizes this status by making moves necessary only in order to accommodate adjunct(ion)s, viz., importing the Segment/Category distinction and "exclusion" and then reformulating C-command in these terms. But given that this is noncanonical structure, what does it encode here? We now move back again to the issue raised in the previous subsection: general problems and proposals in structuralization. Though the force of the argument for modular theoretic architecture may be granted, ultimately, a PS-based syntax *must* take positions on issues of structuralization if any sense is to be made of the notions "canonical" and "noncanonical" structure. And if a PS-based approach is to reconstruct the relational/dependency contrast between "Adjunct" and "complement" – as well as account for "displacement" phenomena (Chomsky 1995: 222) – then it *must* make sense of "canonical" and "noncanonical" structure (terminological differences notwithstanding). The resources available in PS-based syntax, to repeat, are word class labels (category) and immediate constituent nodes (structure), along with whatever can be built up from these beginnings. If a PS-based syntax cannot or does not use these resources in its theoretical sense making tasks, then it cannot be correct.

What we have begun to see by way of our examination of AS are two potential problems of great seriousness in theory construction. One is a general concern, the other is particular to our inquiry.

The general concern is one with respect to highly modularized theory construction and architecture. If subdomain theories are constructed entirely independent of one another, it is possible that the subtheories arrived at will not fit together into a coherent and consistent whole. This "lack of fit" can then itself become a subject of inquiry and theory, perhaps in terms of another subdomain and theory, that of "(possible) interfaces". There is surely nothing in principle wrong with such a course of inquiry. The potential problem, of course, is that much of it could be artifactual, the result only of the assumption of extreme modularity in architecture. It is surely possible that subdomains more directly influence one another, without the mediation of an interface subject to its own principles. However, there is no way to resolve such issues when they are pitched at such a high level of abstraction. It is only by pursuing variously modular architectures that clarifications can be attained.

Particular to our inquiry is the following. By ignoring some foundational issues in PS-based syntax, theorists may be led to deeply problematic proposals. I have in mind both the sort of considerations raised several paragraphs ago – what the basic building blocks of PS-based syntax are and the requirement to use these and concepts constructed from them in theorizing – and also the fundamental idea of PS syntax itself:[40]

> The guiding idea here is that there must be some systematic relation between individual lexical requirements (i.e., argument structure) and syntactic structure – lexical items cannot appear in arbitrary places in a well-formed sentence – and that characterizing this relation is to some large degree what the theory of PS is about and for.

Now, these two sorts of potential problems may interact. It is possible that highly modularized theorizing could lead one more easily to ignore foundational issues, if it seems that these lie outside the subdomain. I suggest that this may be true with respect to AS, in that the fundamental idea of PS syntax may seem somewhat too "interfacey", hence not strictly relevant to properly syntactic theorizing. That this is not so, and that it must be relevant to PS-based approaches, is, I hope, clear by now.

Despite their analytic ubiquity in AS, then, adjunct(ion)s actually constitute a serious theoretical problem for the project, if the reconstruction of concepts, and not just the importation of terms, from relational/dependency syntax remains a goal.

3.0   Heads

Heads are defined in AS (11) as in (41a), with Nonheads correspondingly defined as in (41b).[41]

(41)   a.   A Head is a nonterminal that dominates no other nonterminal
     b.   A Nonhead is a nonterminal that dominates at least one other nonterminal.

This is both perfectly straightforward in itself and also theoretically sound. It offers a reconstruction in entirely phrase structure terms of the relational/dependency concept *Head*, which is exactly what any PS-based syntax should aim for. We have also seen that a number of consequences follow from the interaction of these definitions with the LCA ((8) and (9) above, repeated here).

(8)   For all nonterminal sister pairs, a PM P
      a.   is inadmissible if
          i.   both sisters are Heads, or
          ii.   both sisters are Nonheads
      b.   is admissible if one sister is a Head and one sister is a Nonhead.

(9)   a.   the need for a phrase to have a Head
      b.   the impossibility for a phrase to have more than one Head
      c.   the limitation to one specifier per phrase
      d.   the limitation to one sister complement per Head
      e.   the requirement that a complement not be a bare Head

What we have to make note of is that nothing in the discussion in AS actually serves to tie its defined PS concept of Head to the relational/dependency concept of Head. To focus the point a bit, consider (9a) and (9b). They appear to derive a strong form of the central idea of endocentricity. However, there is nothing in the notion of Head as defined in (41) that requires of a phrase and its Head that they be categorically related to one another. We return to this in some detail in section 5.0 below. For now, the point is simply that if *endocentricity* is to mean merely Headed, then, indeed, AS assures endocentricity. But if there is something more required or desired, then AS could be found wanting. Of course, it may be replied that further desiderata are by no means ruled out by the theory and should properly be localized elsewhere, and that providing a PS definition of Head with such immediate, strong implications is *prima facie* evidence in favor of the AS approach. Good points all, all taken and granted; we move on to Functional Categories.

4.0   Functional Categories

Functional Categories occupy a niche in AS that one might be tempted to characterize as "paradoxical". On the one hand, the nature of Functional Categories receives no discussion at all in AS. On the other, they are crucial to many of the analyses which are allowed or required by the theory. Indeed, the theory forces one "to posit numerous abstract functional heads . . ." (AS: 132) and claims to offer "at least a partial answer to . . . the more fundamental question: why are there so many functional heads?" (AS: 29). The answer to this question is worth giving in full:

Assuming that phrases of various kinds must move out of their base position at some point in the derivation, the answer is that functional heads make landing sites available. Spec-head configurations are used for licensing for a principled and simple reason: there is no other possibility. Given that double adjunction to the same projection is prohibited, there must, for every moved phrase, be a distinct head to whose projection it can adjoin as a specifier. (AS: 30)

The reasoning here is fairly straightforward. It depends on (1) there being only two licensing PS positions: (a) complement of a Head and (b) Specifier of a Head and (2) the disallowance of iterated adjunctions ((36b and c), repeated here).

(36)   a.   No adjunction of a Nonhead to a Head.
       b.   No iterated adjunction of multiple Heads to a single Head.
       c.   No iterated adjunction of multiple Nonheads to a single Nonhead.
       d.   No adjunction of a Head to a Nonhead.

As movement to a complement position is impossible, movement must be to a Specifier position.[42] If movement is necessary, but there is no (apparent) Head to provide the needed Specifier landing-site, then a (non-apparent) Head must be posited. And because iterated adjunctions are illicit, it may be necessary to posit further (non-apparent) Heads to provide further Specifier positions as landing-sites for further movements. Hence the proliferation of abstract Functional Heads.

We should note that AS manifestly notices something that is at best latently observed in much other work, viz., that the usual taxonomy of Heads into *Lexical* or *Functional* is itself crosscut by another distinction. This is a distinction between Heads that "are intrinsically contentful, such as Lexical Heads and Functional Heads like Tense and Aspect . . ." on the one hand, and Heads "lacking intrinsic content . . ." on the other (AS: 30). These latter are the "numerous abstract functional heads" (AS: 132) which are ". . . imposed upon phrase markers by the paucity of available adjunctions sites, with this paucity following from the present theory" (AS: 30). Nothing is made of this alternative taxonomy in AS.

Suppose we try to make something of it. Following Lebeaux (1988), we have suggested a different way to think about Functional Categories.[43] A central idea is that "open class elements license semantically, closed class elements license syntactically . . ." Another is that, following the analysis of Grimshaw (1991), *selection* is not relevant to Functional Categories; arguing against Grimshaw, we also rejected her favored alternative to selection, viz., *projection*. These considerations combine to suggest that Functional Categories need some new licensing mechanism, one that is purely syntactic.[44] The general point is the following:[45]

> Functional elements and their structuralizations provide the syntactic licensing which lexical elements require. . . . This means that analysts should posit functional elements and their structuralizations only if it can be plausibly argued that there is an independent syntactic licensing relation which can both legitimate that functional element and spread to a lexical element that requires such licensing.

Now, the alternative taxonomy mentioned, but not used, in AS seems to fit rather nicely into this theoretical picture. The "intrinsically contentful" Heads are semantic licensers and engage in interface relations – both with the lexicon and with the wider cognitive/conceptual system. The Heads which lack "intrinsic content" are syntactic licensers, and are entirely internal to the syntactic component – both in how they arise and in all their relations. We may not be able to identify these "abstract functional heads" entirely with Lebeaux's "closed class elements" – with some real potential loss here – but the actual losses, gains, and range of identification remain to be worked out.

We can say this. We have independent theoretical argument that some sort of taxonomy like that adverted to in AS is desirable and that the traditional approach to Functional Categories is theoretically unsound. AS (implicitly) suggests that we should not group what it calls "abstract functional heads" with Functional Categories that have "intrinsic content"; this further suggests that the *Functional Category* may not be a true syntactic kind at all. Using this single term for these apparently quite different sorts of elements may obscure more than it illumines. Instead, in the spirit of Lebeaux (1988) and Chapter One, section 3.5, we might take the following line. Phrase structure is, in the first instance, determined by those elements which engage in semantic licensing, those with "intrinsic content" and which have interface roles to play (and by the LCA). It is augmented by elements which engage in purely syntactic licensing, and which have no "intrinsic content" and no interface roles (though still regulated, of course, by the LCA). On this view, in a sense, one of the principal properties of syntax is to introduce material that, from all other perspectives, is irrelevant and invisible. All this material does is support a purely phrase structural object in terms of purely phrase structural relations. The suggestion being made is that the "abstract functional heads" are neither themselves objects found in and drawn from, nor related to elements in, the lexicon. It might be wondered whether such objects are possible, and where they originate. Recall the definition of Head in this regard. It specifies merely that a Head is a Nonterminal that dominates no other Nonterminal. This does not require that a Head have any relation to any other element (viz., an element from the lexicon), nor that it be itself drawn from the lexicon. Heads are defined in purely PS syntactic terms, and we could understand "abstract functional heads" as objects which meet this definition, but have no other (significant) properties.

Now, to be sure, this is a tentative and sketchy proposal, and one that AS does not, of course, make itself. If the argument and analysis in Chapter One, section 3.5 with respect to Functional Categories is found wanting, AS is not thereby undermined. But given that argument and analysis, it is especially noteworthy to find this convergence with AS. AS, for reasons entirely internal to itself, does make available a route for reconstructing the distinctions from Chapter One, section 3.5 in terms of its taxonomy using "abstract functional head" and its definition of Head. Given the complete independence of these inquiries, this convergence suggests quite strikingly, I think, that there is something to the analysis in Chapter One, section 3.5. It also suggests that AS may be the vehicle for pursuing that analysis.

5.0   X-Bar Theory

There are two subtopics here. The first is the derivation of results which X-Bar Theory stipulates. The second is branching.

5.1   *Derive and Concur*

AS claims that the "familiar X-bar-theoretic properties" in (9) (repeated here) are consequences of the theory.[46] From this derivation the further claim is made ". . . that X-bar theory, although largely accurate in its standard form, should not be considered to be a primitive part of syntactic theory (i.e., of UG)" (AS: 131). It is now time to examine these claims.

(9)   a.   the need for a phrase to have a Head
      b.   the impossibility for a phrase to have more than one Head
      c.   the limitation to one specifier per phrase
      d.   the limitation to one sister complement per Head
      e.   the requirement that a complement not be a bare Head

Eliminating phrase structure rules is a common desideratum of P & P theorizing.[47] Within P & P, this comes down, effectively, to some sort of attempt to "derive X-Bar Theory", so AS is quite squarely in the tradition both in its acceptance of X-Bar as "descriptively accurate" and in its eliminativist goal.

Now, we have already noticed that nothing in the AS notion of Head requires any categorial connection between a (syntactically defined) Head and the phrase of which it is the (relationally defined) Head.[48] That is, there is nothing which requires, or even suggests, that, for example, a Noun is the Head of Noun Phrase. Exactly this problem had been pointed out with respect to PSGs prior to X-Bar Theory, and X-Bar Theory provided a solution to the problem.[49] AS, it seems, has here moved us backwards.

What AS needs, evidently, is some notion of "projection" in order to insure that there is the desired connection between the syntactically defined Head and the phrase of which it is the Head. But this is essentially all that is left of X-Bar Theory in the "X-Bar Reduction" program of Speas (1990: 55): "I have proposed a theory of projection from the lexicon in which the only restriction imposed by X-bar theory is that sentences have hierarchical structure, and that all structure is projected from a head. All other restrictions on domination relations are to be captured in other modules of grammar."

We see here, then, another convergence. Everyone wants to eliminate X-Bar statements. In AS, you get a number of purely structural results and restrictions, but you still need some notion of "projection". In Speas (1990), you get a theory of projection, but you still need some "other modules of grammar" to give you structural results and restrictions. The two inquiries can meet at the concept *Head*, which both require every phrase to have. AS defines Head purely structurally, while Speas gives us an explication in terms of a theory of structuralization, a theory of the lexicon-syntax interface. As we have seen, this is something AS needs anyway. These two approaches to X-Bar elimination complement one another, each providing something that the other needs. This is an impressive result, one that strongly supports the sort of highly modularized theorizing we have discussed.[50] The two inquiries have been pursued entirely independently,[51] in the attempt to construct best theories in their respective domains. The results of these inquiries are neither irrelevant to each other nor conflicting, but rather have a meeting point and each reinforce the other.

5.2   *Branching*

Binarity is the issue, and it has, fittingly enough, two aspects. We begin with no more than binary branching, then move on to less than binary branching.

AS needs branching to be no more than binary in order for asymmetric C-command to be locally linear.[52] However, if asymmetric C-command is taken to be the relation which mediates between structure and string by way of the LCA, then, as we have seen, branching must be no more than binary, given the consequences summed up in (8) and (9) (repeated here).

(8)   For all nonterminal sister pairs, a PM P
     a.   is inadmissible if
        i.   both sisters are Heads, or
        ii.   both sisters are Nonheads
     b.   is admissible if one sister is a Head and one sister is a Nonhead.

(9)   a.   the need for a phrase to have a Head
     b.   the impossibility for a phrase to have more than one Head
     c.   the limitation to one specifier per phrase
     d.   the limitation to one sister complement per Head
     e.   the requirement that a complement not be a bare Head.

This suggests that stipulation of binary branching in order to make asymmetric C-command locally linear is not necessary. The argument is as follows. Our goal – driven by the guiding intuition of AS – is to make C-command formally more like precedence by making the former locally linear. Most centrally, C-command already is *local* in the favored sense. This property is both crucial in achieving the goal and it gives motivation for C-command (and not dominance) as the mediating relation for the LCA.[53] To be locally linear, any relation must be *asymmetric*; so C-command is made asymmetric. We have then done what we can and must do to C-command in order to meet our formal goal – there are no further manipulations of C-command itself that could help achieve the goal of local linearity. This (asymmetric, local) version of C-command, which has as much of local linearity built into it as can be, is locally linear in the context of (no more than) binary branching phrase markers. But given this version of C-command, motivated independently in terms of the guiding intuition of AS, phrase markers allowed by the LCA must be (no more than) binary branching. So, the formal goal is established.

It is important to see that this result is neither circular nor particularly gerrymandered. The guiding intuition of AS is independent of branching. So too is the argument in favor of (some version of) C-command as the mediating relation. Whatever the mediating relation, it would have to be asymmetric, so that is the version of C-command needed. But asymmetric C-command guarantees that branching is no more than binary, and this provides the context required for asymmetric C-command to be locally linear. We do not have circularity or special pleading; rather, we have a most remarkable meshing of independent strands of theorizing.

No more than binary branching, then, is not stipulated in AS. Rather, it follows from its guiding intuition and an independently motivated way of realizing that intuition. In this way, AS is more like Kayne (1981), in which (no more than) binary branching is also an effect, not a cause, than like many who purport to follow this work, but in fact merely stipulate a limit on branching. We turn now to less than binary branching.

AS requires that there be less than binary branching. Crucial cases were given in section 1.2, (11)–(14), repeated here. The examples without less than binary branching, (12) and (14), are ruled out by the LCA, while the alternatives with less than binary branching, (11) and (13), are allowed.

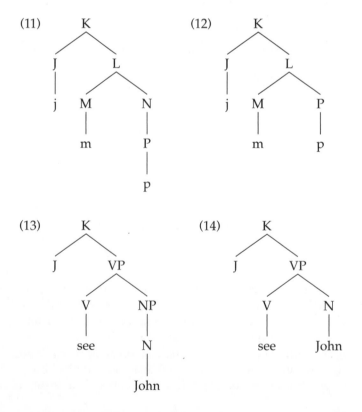

There is not, so far as I can determine, any alternative to this result. While no discussion is typically given of this sort of analysis, it is also typically not a requirement, as it is in AS. As the conceptual grounding of nonbranching domination in the part/whole relation of constituency is less than obvious, it may be taken as something of a theoretical advance that AS motivates this relation so strongly and in the way that it does, in terms of its central concept, the LCA.[54]

Both the prohibition on no more than binary branching and the requirement for less than binary branching grow out of the trunk of AS, so to speak. These branching positions are ones to which the theory is fully committed, which cannot be sawed off.

6.0 PM ordering

We have already argued that AS does not order PMs by means of both dominance and precedence.[55] Precedence, it was argued, orders the terminal string, and dominance (and, derivatively, C-command) orders Nonterminals in the PM. No mention is made in AS of any precedence relations among Nonterminals. As we noted, this very silence is crucial in a work devoted entirely to working out a way to relate the ordering of the string to the ordering of the structure. AS (4) explicitly says "[a]t least in the PF wing of the grammar, the terminal symbols must be linearly ordered." Nothing more is said about the domain of precedence.

But we can say more. The guiding intuition of AS (131) is that "linear order and hierarchical structure [are not] as independent of one another as syntactic theory normally assumes." The entire project is based on relating precedence relations among Terminals to hierarchical relations among Nonterminals. If Nonterminals were already related to one another by precedence, it is not clear what the point of the inquiry would be. Indeed, having Nonterminals related by precedence already requires that linear order and hierarchical structure not be so independent of one another: in some formalizations (e.g., McCawley 1982; Higginbotham 1982), precedence relations among Nonterminals are projected from those among Terminals; in more standard formalizations (e.g., Partee, ter Meulen, and Wall 1990), a pair of Nonterminals is in a precedence relation if and only if it is not in a dominance relation. In such standard formalizations, then, precedence relations are determined with respect to dominance as the "elsewhere" case for Nonterminals. Further, standard formalizations also include a "Nontangling" condition on PMs, which also regulates PM well-formedness by inter-relating dominance and precedence.[56]

It is exclusively in the context of independent domains for the ordering relations that the AS project makes sense. The UG problem of how to relate linear precedence to hierarchical structure only arises once the two are entirely separate.

This concludes the discussion of AS. It is an intricate work, perhaps overly terse in some of its presentation. We have suggested some ways to expand or improve the argument, and shown how interwoven the various parts often turn out to be. We have seen a few weaknesses from our particular PS perspective, but also some perhaps unanticipated strengths and convergences with more strictly PS research. AS is not a long book, but I think it has well repaid the close attention we have given it, and would continue to repay further inquiries along the lines we have opened.

Notes

1   Strictly, an antisymmetric relation allows xLy & yLx just in case x = y. If this case, too, is ruled out, then the relation is *asymmetric*. All asymmetric relations are antisymmetric, but not vice versa (see, e.g., Wall 1972: 112; Partee, ter Meulen, and Wall 1990: 40–1).

2   In fact, whether linear order is mediated by precedence (and not *subsequence*) has not at this point been established. This is discussed in chapter 4 of AS and below in section 1.4.

3   Strictly, it is asymmetric, as it is *irreflexive* (i.e., it contains no pairs of the form $<x,x>$)

4   Actually, this depends on whether you take dominance to be reflexive or not. If it is reflexive, then dominance is antisymmetric; if not, then it is asymmetric. Standardly, dominance is taken to be reflexive.

5   Note that this cannot be generalized to the set of all nodes with which X is in a dominance relation. That is, we cannot include those nodes which X dominates as well as those which dominate X. This is because two nodes which X dominates need not be in a dominance relation to one another – as, for example, when X is the mother of two daughters Y and Z. Sisters are not in a dominance relation to one another.

6   As with dominance, so with asymmetrical C-command: the relation cannot be generalized to those nodes which X asymmetrically C-commands and remain a locally linear ordering. Again, the case where Y and Z are sisters shows this. If X asymmetrically C-commands such Y and Z, neither of this latter pair of sisters asymmetrically C-commands the other.

7   It is noted that the relation is a "familiar" one (AS: 4).

8   See section 1.3 of Chapter Two.

9   A slight modification is required in the AS context. AS need not assume Exclusivity, because it does not assume that nonterminal nodes are ordered by precedence as well as dominance. In AS, dominance and precedence are exclusive in the stronger sense of having distinct domains (viz., terminals for precedence, nonterminals for dominance). This means that there cannot be any such relation as is characterized in the text: constructed from one of the basic ordering relations and containing only pairs from the other basic ordering relation. In this context, we should instead look for a new relation constructible, yet disjoint, from one of the basic ordering relations; disjointness is desirable because that makes it "new" in the strongest possible way. As well, since the new relation is to mediate between two strongly exclusive relations, this disjointness tracks, as far as possible, that exclusivity. For the reasons given in Chapter Two and summarized in the text above, C-command is the new relation when dominance is the basic ordering relation used. So, though the letter of the text argument may not apply, its spirit does.

10   AS does not actually include a statement corresponding to (10), but only implies one. The first definition of C-command given is a revision of such an implied statement. It appears in Chapter Three (AS: 16 (3)), and is discussed below in section 1.3.

11 This is pointed out in TPM (175: fn. 3). Note that C-command is then no longer a generalization of the sister relation.

12 It is of no significance that "<j,p> corresponds to both d<J,N> and d<J,P>" (AS: 133 fn. 1).

13 AS shows that it holds even if there were a third, Nonhead sister to M and P in (12). However, given that binary branching must be assumed in order for asymmetric C-command to be locally total, it is not clear why this demonstration is required, so we omit it here.

14 AS (11 (7)) gives an example in which only *P* is a branching node.

15 AS (134: fn. 4) notes that the justification for these revisions is empirical: "we know" that adjunctions and Specifiers are needed, so, given the LCA, there must be a Segment/Category distinction. However, one might imagine the converse conclusion: that since the pristine LCA does not allow for them, there are no adjunctions. Specifiers, presumably, would then require reanalysis in accord with the admissible Head/Nonhead configuration – perhaps with the Specifier as Head, for example (see AS (17)).

16 See Chapter Two, section 2.3, Chametzky (1994) and TPM (95–106) for critical discussion of this distinction.

17 These are repeated from Chapter Two, section 2.3

18 I have changed the original's *if* to *iff*.

19 AS (36), apparently assuming dominance to be irreflexive, takes the root node simply to dominate all other nodes in the PM.

20 Because *A* is adjoined to the root node, there are no Categories dominating *A*. This means that it vacuously satisfies the definition for C-command (20). See AS (132: fn. 3).

21 Recall, in this regard, it was exactly the failure of dominance to be a *total* relation that led to the restriction to local dominance when originally pursuing the central intuition.

22 Notice that if (3) were not true, then this node would have no image, and so there could be no root terminal, contrary to our assumption.

23 An alternative that associated a and z as the first two terminals could use such a statement, but the statement itself is still less simple and straightforward than that in AS.

24 As we noted in Chapter One, section 4.2, on this interpretation AS departs here from standard assumptions about PMs. We return to this issue in section 5.2 below.

25 AS also argues that the LCA applies "below the word level" (38f). The extension of phrase structure concepts to subword level is tendentious at best, and, in any event, not strictly relevant to our narrow topic of phrase structure concepts in syntax, so we shall not pursue these matters.

26 This is so because all movement is to a (n asymmetrical) C-commanding position. Since asymmetrical C-command is mapped into precedence, all movement up the tree is also movement leftward in the string.

27 There is some unclarity in the formulation here. If the LCA did not hold of a given stratum, all that could be concluded would be that the phrase structure properties which follow from the LCA were not *required* to hold of that stratum. This is consistent with, for example, a "default and override" situation, in which the properties would generally hold, but could be overridden by specific statements or procedures of some sort. This is basically the view in TPM, for example, wherein X-Bar considerations are taken to define and hold of the base only; in this case the range of possible deviations from the base would evidently require inquiry.

28   When we directly examine the treatment of X-Bar theory in AS in section 5 below, we shall return to this argument as well.

29   Kenneth Hale is cited as the source of this information (AS: 49).

30   Evidently, Head-to-Head movement is assumed not to be to an asymmetrical C-commanding position, since, if it were, this argument would be redundant.

31   See section 1.2 above.

32   Munn (1993) is cited as the source for *and* raising (AS: 58).

33   Presumably, *and* raising (somehow) licenses the phonetically unrealized conjunction by moving through the latter's position, though nothing explicit is said in AS.

34   See section 1.4 of Chapter Two.

35   Similar considerations hold for phonetically unrealized conjunction lexical items as well.

36   Subjects of unaccusative verbs would originate as complements (AS: 117–18).

37   Repeated from Chapter One, section 1.2.

38   See Introduction, section 2.1 and Chapter One, section 3.4, respectively.

39   See Chapter One, section 1.2.

40   Quoted from Chapter One, section 1.0.

41   See section 1.2 above.

42   Movement, recall, is always leftward up the tree. This means there cannot be movement to be the complement position of a Head that lacks a complement, as this would have to be rightward movement. It cannot be leftward movement because a leftward move would have to originate from within the complement that, by hypothesis, does not exist. If a Head already has a complement, then there can be no movement to a second complement position to that Head, as Heads may have only one complement (sections 1.2, 2.1). As this exhausts the possibilities, there can be no movement to complement position.

43   See Chapter One, section 3.5.

44   Though selection might be purely syntactic, it was noted in Chapter One, section 1.0 that Grimshaw (1979, 1981) and Rothstein (1991a, 1991b) have contested this proposal. Projection is an interface concept, hence not purely syntactic.

45   Quoted from Chapter One, section 3.5.

46   See section 1.2 above.

47   See Chapter One, section 4.1.

48   See section 3.0 above.

49   See Introduction, section 3.0.

50   See section 2.3 above.

51   This is perhaps slightly strong. They have both accepted as a constraint on theorizing both that there should be no explicit X-Bar theoretical statements and that such statements did encode something real.

52   See section 1.1 above.

53   See section 1.1 above.

54   AS also supposes that the relation between Heads and Terminals is nonbranching dominance. Nothing, however, rides on this – indeed, AS (5) itself separates the dominance relation among Nonterminals from the "dominance" between Heads and Terminals. The various definitions and statements can be reformulated in terms of, say, *instantiation*, with no loss (and, perhaps, some gain in perspicuity).

55   See section 1.4.1 above.

56   *Nontangling* prohibits "crossed branches". McCawley (1982) and Higginbotham (1982) do not contain such a condition. AS does not either, but the theory rules out crossed branches (AS: 169, fn. 4).

Chapter four

Less is More

The work

To begin each of Chapters Two and Three, a "stylistic" characterization was offered of the work discussed therein. *Late classical GB* was proposed for Chapter Two and *Mannerist P & P* for Chapter Three. The book discussed in this chapter, *The minimalist program* (Chomsky 1995; MP hereafter), offers to do this bit of work for us. It provides its own name for its style – *Minimalist*. This may not seem like much, but I am more than willing to accept whatever gifts – however small – authors offer us for understanding and analyzing their works, so I propose to accept this self description without ungratefully looking very closely at it. Presented with an *eohippus*, you would have, basically, a gift horse.

MP offers a new theoretical architecture for generative grammar, one that is both "unistratal" and also derivational. The goal is to limit the architecture to what is required by "virtual conceptual necessity" (MP: 169, 171) – this is what is "minimalist" about the project. A leading idea is to give up all distinguished syntactic strata other than one that corresponds, more or less, to what has been called LF in previous P & P work (see Hornstein 1996). So, there is no D-structure and no S-structure. These lie outside virtual conceptual necessity because they do not function as interfaces with nonlinguistic systems; virtual conceptual necessity requires such interfaces, so there must be representations to subserve these functions (viz., LF and PF, more or less).

A related, though separate, desideratum is to limit syntactic operations to what virtual conceptual necessity requires. The position developed is strongly derivational: the single PM is constructed from items drawn from the lexicon, with partial structures being licit insofar as they are the result of the "minimalist" operations sanctioned by virtual conceptual necessity.

It is important to keep the representational requirements of virtual conceptual necessity distinct from the derivational requirements of virtual conceptual necessity. Indeed, we shall see that these two sorts of "minimalism" need not cohere, and may at times conflict.

1.0 The minimalist program

We shall not examine all of MP; instead, its chapter 4 ("Categories and transformations") is our focus, though we shall have occasional recourse to chapter 3 as well. We shall explicitly discuss only sections 4.2.1 and 4.3 (see (1)); all other discussion is "thematic", taking up either the concepts necessary for understanding MP or the questions and concepts in PS theory that structure our inquiry.

(1)   Sections of MP, chapter 4 specifically discussed, are:
   4.2.1   The computational component
   4.3   Phrase structure theory in a minimalist framework

1.1   *The computational component*[1]

As noted above, MP provides a strongly derivational approach to syntax (as opposed to a "representational" approach; see MP: 223–4). The derivation is the business of the *computational component*. A derivation maps a *numeration* to a completed LF PM. A numeration is a set of pairs (L, i), where L is a lexical item and i is its index, indicating the number of times L is used in the derivation.[2] A derivation which terminates in an acceptable LF PM *converges* (at LF). Among the conditions which must be met for convergence is that all indices must be "reduced to zero" (MP: 225). Necessary for there to be derivations at all is (at least) an operation that removes lexical items from the numeration. This operation is called *Select*, and it both removes a lexical item from the numeration, making of a lexical item a *syntactic object* (if only because it is now in the syntax), and reduces the item's index by one (MP: 226). A derivation, then, comprises a set of syntactic objects.

   Further, it is held that for purposes of interpretation, an LF representation must be "a single syntactic object" (MP: 226). It therefore follows that in addition to Select, there must be some operation for forming new syntactic objects by recursively combining syntactic objects already formed. This operation is called *Merge*. Select and Merge, it is argued, satisfy virtual conceptual necessity, as without them there could be no derivations.

   We note two other desiderata for derivations (MP: 225). First is the property of *inclusiveness*: "outputs consist of nothing beyond properties of items of the lexicon (lexical features) – in other words, that the interface levels consist of nothing more than arrangements of lexical features." Second is a property we can call *potency* (it has no name in MP): "the principles of UG involve only elements that function at the interface levels; nothing else can be 'seen' in the course of the computation. . . ."

   Two violations of inclusiveness are countenanced in MP. One results from the need to distinguish "the syntactic objects formed by distinct applications of Select" to a single member of the numeration. Some way is needed to mark "as distinct" two syntactic objects "if they are formed by distinct applications of Select accessing the same lexical item" in the numeration (MP: 227). Whatever the form of the "mark", this is information introduced in the derivation, not present in the lexical items originally. We discuss this violation below in section 1.2.

   The second violation "involves the deletion operation (Delete alpha). Let us assume that this operation marks some object as 'invisible at the interface'".

Thus, again, information is introduced in the derivation that is not originally present in the lexical items. We shall not discuss deletion further.

A final operation is Move.[3] Move furthers the derivation by copying an already existing syntactic object and performing Merge on it, forming a *Chain* that comprises the copy and the original syntactic object (the "trace") (MP: 251). We shall now critically examine Move.

1.2 Against Move

Select and Merge are argued to hold on account of virtual conceptual necessity. What about Move? The answer is "no" – at least, it is never claimed that the answer is "yes" when the question "Why Move?" is raised (MP: 316). Instead, the following justification for Move is given. It is taken as an obvious fact about human language that "items commonly appear 'displaced' from the position in which the interpretation they receive is otherwise represented at the LF interface" (MP: 316; see also 221–2). It is therefore necessary that there be "an indication at LF of the position in which the displaced item is interpreted; that is, chains are legitimate objects at LF." But, "[s]ince chains are not introduced by selection from the lexicon or by Merge, there must be another operation to form them: the operation Attract/Move" (MP: 316).

Now, the reason that Chains can arise only through Move, and not Select and Merge, is because the elements in a Chain are identical and "we distinguish among distinct selections of a single item from the lexicon . . ." (MP: 251). This means that it is the violation of inclusiveness noted above – the creation of a "mark" on distinct selections of a single lexical item – that makes Move necessary. From the minimalist point of view, then, we have discovered a reason we might be suspicious of Move, as it is a desideratum of the approach that there be no violations of inclusiveness. On the other hand, it has been said of this particular violation of inclusiveness that it is "one that seems indispensable: it is rooted in the nature of language . . ." (MP: 227). But why, exactly? What problem does the violation solve, and is there truly no other way to solve it?

The claim is that "the syntactic objects formed by distinct applications of Select to LI [a particular lexical item] must be distinguished; two occurrences of the pronoun *he*, for example, may have entirely different properties at LF" (MP: 227). Let us grant the claim. But why does this require introducing a "mark"? Consider the following: "we want to distinguish the two elements [identical syntactic objects] of the chain CH. . . . The natural way to do so is by inspection of the context in which the term appears. Given the way syntactic objects are formed, it suffices to consider the co-constituent (sister) of a term . . ." (MP: 251–2). But if considering the context suffices to distinguish the identical objects in a Chain, it can also distinguish the identical objects formed by distinct applications of Select and Merge on a single lexical item – without the inclusiveness violating mark. If it works in the one case of a Chain, context cannot fail to work in the other of Select and Merge. There is, then, no need for the "mark". But if not, then there is no need for Move, either, since, as we saw above, it is only the putative inability of Select and Merge to introduce Chains that makes Move necessary. And, within minimalist theorizing, that which is not necessary should not be possible.

It is, moreover, a very strong indication that Move is on the wrong track that a principle which it requires – contextual syntactic distinguishing of identical lexical items – undermines the very assumption that makes it necessary.

Strictly, the fact that no "mark" is in fact needed does not result in creation of a Chain. Rather, it allows for Select and Merge to introduce the syntactic objects which, under Move, comprise a Chain. However, no further object, a Chain, is now constituted. But so what? We should note that a Chain "meets several conditions . . ." (MP: 253). There are three of these. One is that of C-command: the "trace" is C-commanded by the moved object. But this stipulation in the definition of Move simply falls out if there is no Move, but only Select and Merge.[4] The other two, *uniformity* and Last Resort, if correct, seem no less (nor more) stipulative in the one approach than the other (MP: 253).[5] While we still do not have a Chain, we do have available the objects which make up a Chain, Merged into the positions in the PM which they would have occupied had there been Move. From the minimalist perspective, this is an advantage; if no new operation creating a new sort of object is required, this is all to the good. And it is not clear that there is any work for the Chain object to do that cannot be done by the objects which would have comprised the Chain sitting in the positions which the Chain would have required of them.

Arguably, what the Chain does is exactly provide an interpretable object at LF. Without the Chain as a discrete object, the claim would be, there is no way or reason to interpret the multiple syntactic occurrences of a single lexical item in precisely the way that a Chain requires. There are two possibilities here. One is that this claim is false. The other is that it is true.

Suppose the former. That is, suppose it is possible to get the desired interpretation of a Chain without there being such an object. Perhaps this would be so because it would be impossible to interpret the structure otherwise. In other words, a PM which would have had a Chain had there been Move can be given an interpretation only if the objects which would have been the members of that Chain are treated *as if* there were a Chain. If such an approach is workable, then Chains are, evidently, not needed, and, of course, Move too is otiose.

Suppose, on the other hand, that the claim is true – that the approach sketched immediately above is impossible, and Chains are, for whatever interpretive reasons, necessary. Then we shall have Chains. Recall that all syntactic objects needed are present, and in their appropriate positions. All we need do is stipulate that Chains are created from such objects in such positions, subject to (some version of) uniformity and Last Resort, should these be correct. We are still better off. Though both approaches now have a new operation which creates Chains, they differ in ways that disfavor Move. Move requires (1) copying and (2) the C-command stipulation, neither of which the alternative requires. And, of course, Move is based on the assumption that inclusiveness is violated by placing of a "mark", which the alternative also obviates. While this alternative is less desirable than that in the previous paragraph, it is still preferable to Move.

The conceptual point is the following. In minimalist theorizing, we seek the most direct path to our goal. In the case of Chains, that is doing without them as distinguished objects, just because they cannot be formed with only Select and Merge. If there must be Chains, then the most straightforward way to create them should be investigated first, and this way is not through Move.

We have seen that internal to MP there are minimalist grounds for rejecting Move. There are also yet more general, architectural minimalist reasons to reject it.

We want now to ask a "transcendental" question, viz., what assumptions must a theoretical architecture embody such that it *requires* movement? We are taking for granted the empirical fact of "displacement", and asking under what conditions a theory would have to account for this phenomenon by means of movement. There are two crucial assumptions; it is their combination that requires movement.

The two assumptions are the following. First, the theory must be exclusively a PS theory. That is, the "computational component", the mediation between the lexicon and LF (or its functional equivalent) is entirely phrase structural. The second is that there is, for every sentence, a distinguished representation which is entirely and exclusively *non*displaced – what, in TPM, are called "canonical structuralizations of lexical information" (TPM: 158–60) – an example being D-Structure in earlier P & P work. Given these, and the fact of displacement (TPM's "noncanonical structuralizations"), then there *must* be movement: all the theory can do is provide a means to relate the nondisplaced PS representation to one or more displaced other PS representations.

But suppose you give up the first assumption. Then, there is no longer any need for movement. Instead, one can have a rather different way to account for displacement, as, for example, in Lexical Functional Grammar, or in various versions of Categorial Grammar. But while the first assumption is necessary for requiring movement, it is not sufficient. The second assumption is also required.

If one no longer assumes there is a representation with the defining property of D-Structure, then it is no longer necessary to relate by movement displaced and nondisplaced positions. This is because it is this assumption that makes lexical items enter syntax, the computational component, only in nondisplaced, canonical positions. Once the assumption of such a distinguished representation is dropped, it is no longer *necessary* for lexical items to enter syntax only in nondisplaced positions.

Having dropped this assumption, it is still *possible* to require items to enter syntax canonically, but this becomes an extra requirement, an added stipulation, which serves the purpose only of "going proxy" for the dropped assumption, and thus making movement necessary. In minimalist theorizing, such an un-necessary requirement should be abandoned. Thus, in minimalist theorizing, while lexical items need to be either in or related to (as in a Chain) canonical/ nondisplaced positions in order to be interpretable at the interface, there is simply no justification for further stipulating that they must enter syntax only in such positions. If some items are uninterpretable – either because they are neither in nor relatable to nondisplaced positions – then the derivation fails to converge. If all items are interpretable, then the derivation converges. Evidently, then, convergence will come about just in case all lexical items are in fact Merged into interpretable positions (i.e., nondisplaced positions) or are Merged into positions relatable to such positions (i.e., from which Chains are (re)constructible).

What we see, then, is that if you drop either of these assumptions, then movement is no longer required. But, of course, MP both drops the second assumption and also still invokes movement. It is possible to do this if, as pointed out above, it is further stipulated that lexical items enter syntax only in nondisplaced positions. But, as argued above, this is now pure stipulation, losing whatever motivation it previously had once the assumption of a D-Structure(like) representation was dropped. On minimalist grounds, then, the stipulation should be abandoned, particularly if, as suggested above, it does not even do any analytic work.

We conclude, then, that Move is conceptually unsound, and should be dropped from minimalist theorizing.[6] From this perspective, it is interesting to consider an argument made in TPM (158–60), referring to an earlier version of minimalism (Chomsky 1993, now included as chapter 3 of MP). The argument there is that the architecture of MP (the earlier and later versions are relevantly the same) will fail when it comes to the goal of *explanatory adequacy* as this is explicated in Chomsky (1965: 36): "[a] theory of grammar may be descriptively adequate and yet leave unexpressed major features that are defining properties of natural language and that distinguish natural languages from arbitrary symbolic systems." The idea is the following.

"Displacement" is one of the "defining properties of natural language." In MP, as noted, we have a purely PS approach that has only one distinguished syntactic stratum. MP nonetheless requires lexical items to enter syntax in nondisplaced positions and derives nondisplaced structures by means of the operation Move. Moreover, "[w]hile Merge is costless for principled reasons, movement is not: the operation takes place only when forced . . ." (MP: 235). Quoting TPM (159):

> In such an architecture, should there be noncanonical structuralizations, [i.e., displacements] they must be realized in the single representation, along with the canonical [i.e., nondisplaced]. But in such an architecture noncanonical structuralizations should seem odd and surprising. Given the architecture with only one representation and the requirement of canonical structuralization, the most natural meshing would have just these. There is no natural locus for noncanonical structuralizations; they might exist, but they should be rare, because the grammar is forced to overlay them on the single representation. In this architecture, it should be "less costly" to have only canonical structuralizations . . . [w]ith such an architecture, we should expect to see many – or at least *some* – languages that only have canonical structuralizations. But we do not. And the architecture makes this seem to be an odd and accidental fact, rather than something fundamental.

Now, we have argued that the stipulation that lexical items must enter syntax in nondisplaced positions should be dropped from minimalist theorizing, and, concomitantly, the "costly" operation Move should be eliminated.

Therefore, it might seem that the argument from TPM just rehearsed no longer goes through. However, we must be careful. While it is true that nondisplacement no longer has a special status with respect to construction of the PM, it nonetheless remains the case that the displaced/nondisplaced distinction remains. It has merely been "kicked upstairs", so to speak: it is now part of the conditions imposed for successful interpretation at the interface. Recall that if a lexical item is not introduced in a nondisplaced position, then, to be interpretable, it must be *relatable* to such a position. And, while the costly operation Move is gone, it is not clear that whatever mechanism allows for the relating of displaced and nondisplaced positions will itself be "costless". So, while the revised minimalist architecture freely allows for items to be introduced in displaced positions, it does not explain why such positions should be interpretable, i.e., why they are licensed. Thus, it seems still to be the case that "we should expect to see many – or at least *some* – languages that only have canonical structuralizations."

But perhaps not. By having "kicked upstairs" the licensing of displaced positions, syntax – the computational system – is freed from having to say anything at all about whether and why they are licensed. That is, if displaced positions are universally licensed on account of some requirement of the interface with the cognitive/conceptual system, then it is incorrect to even *attempt* to explain this universality from within the syntax/computational system. All the syntax/computational system says is that displaced and nondisplaced positions are simply on a par.

My own view is that this does successfully defuse the objection in TPM, and that this provides a further argument for the proposed revisions in minimalist theorizing. Note, however, that it also appears to require rethinking the notion "explanatory adequacy". While it still seems plausible to consider displacement a "defining property" of natural languages, it is no longer the case that the theory of grammar, strictly construed, should account for this fact. Indeed, the grammar positively should not account for it. However, a broader notion of "theory of grammar", one that included the fact that there are properties of language that result from interpretive conditions imposed by requirements of the interface with cognition, would account for it. If this is the correct notion of "theory of grammar", then "explanatory adequacy" remains. Thus, dropping the stipulation that lexical items must enter syntax in nondisplaced positions, and concomitantly eliminating Move – ideas argued for on independent grounds here – provide the needed bases for countering TPM's objection to minimalism in terms of explanatory adequacy.

Having argued that it is conceptually unsound, we take our leave of Move, and proceed to another facet of the computational component, the *numeration*.

1.3   The numeration

"A numeration is a set of pairs (L, i), where L is a lexical item and *i* is its index, indicating the number of times L is used in the derivation."[7] Why is such an object required? It is worth noting that it is entirely *sui generis*: it is not a part of the lexicon; it is not an *inclusive* object – it goes "beyond properties of items of the lexicon" (MP: 225); and it is not a syntactic object.[8] It mediates the relation between the lexicon and syntax, but, apparently, is not an "interface" between the two (as was D-Structure) since there are, by definition (fiat?) only two "interfaces": (corresponding to) LF and PF.

It may be helpful to compare the numeration to D-Structure, as their functional roles are in some ways analogous, though D-Structure "is dubious on conceptual grounds . . . [and lacks] independent conceptual support" (MP: 187, 188). D-Structure is the interface between the lexicon and syntax: as the projection/structuralization of lexical items into syntax, it is where/how lexical items enter syntax. D-Structure is also a syntactic stratum, constrained by the theory of syntax and of syntactic objects, while at the same time it is constrained by the properties of the lexical items it structuralizes. The numeration not only is not, but should not be so constrained. If it were, this would require explanation, as it is explicitly neither a part of syntax nor an object sensitive to the properties of the lexical items it contains. Indeed, given the assumptions and architecture of MP, the numeration *must* be sui generis: for it to be continuous with either the lexicon or syntax, or to be a bona fide interface, would violate assumptions of MP. It seems obvious that virtual conceptual necessity could not require any such object, but that it is entirely for reasons internal to MP that it is postulated. Within more general minimalist theorizing, there is then prima facie a heavy burden to meet in justifying such a construction; it might even be thought that it "is dubious on conceptual grounds . . . [and lacks] independent conceptual support."

There are three justifications for the numeration in MP. One, barely mentioned, and not discussed, is the following. The syntactic and phonological sides of a computation "must be based on the same lexical choices" (MP: 225). This is because "it is not the case that any sound can mean anything" (MP: 225). So, in order to insure *compatibility*, "some array A of lexical choices" is required (MP: 225). The numeration is what this "array A" is taken to be. But this hardly seems required. If lexical items were selected directly from the lexicon, without "stopping" first in the numeration, what would be lost in terms of compatibility? Nothing, it seems, as Spell Out, which "strips all the phonological features . . . and initiates the phonological derivation" (Johnson and Lappin 1997: 279), is itself an operation applying in the syntactic derivation. "Stopping" in the numeration neither adds to nor subtracts from a lexical item with respect to anything effecting the application of Spell Out. In terms of compatibility, at least, the numeration is irrelevant.

The second and third justifications are different from the first, and resemble each other. They have to do with the nature of the derivation. In order for there to be a derivation, Select must "exhaust the numeration" (MP: 226). That is, every integer in every member of the numeration must be reduced to zero: each lexical item which is in a numeration member must undergo Select n times, where n is the integer index in that numeration member. If the numeration is not "exhausted", then "no derivation is generated and no questions of convergence or economy arise" (MP: 226). Obviously, this function cannot be subserved by directly Selecting lexical items from the lexicon one-by-one. The point here is the following. In the absence of a stratum such as D-Structure, it is the numeration that allows specification of the particular lexical items which *must* be included in a given derivation.

This leads to the final justification. The numeration is taken "to fix the *reference set* for determining whether a derivation . . . is optimal – that is, not blocked by a more economical derivation" (MP: 227). The idea here is that, in comparing derivations in terms of economy, only those derivations with the same "starting point" should be compared to one another. And again, in the absence of a stratum such as D-Structure, it is the numeration which provides the starting points.[9]

It should not be thought that the similarities between the functions of D-Structure and the numeration must count against the latter, even amongst those who accept the arguments against the former in MP. We might think, rather, that the numeration allows discovery of the required properties of whatever it is that mediates the relation between the lexicon and the computational component proper. In earlier theories, for various reasons, this was assumed to be a syntactic stratum; in minimalist theorizing, one could metaphorically imagine "squeezing out" all the extraneous properties, leaving only those absolutely necessary for constructing a derivation from lexical items. Compatibility, we have seen, does not require the numeration. Economy-of-derivation considerations might; note, however, that Johnson and Lappin have argued that this does not work in fact (see note 9), and that, more generally (285), "the economy-of-derivation model strikes us as strongly anti-minimalist, since global economy principles do not follow from 'virtual conceptual necessity' under any interpretation of that phrase that seems plausible." Put differently, this latter point seems to be that general minimalist theorizing does not appear to require that a theory be one involving economy-of-derivation considerations, which seems quite true. This justification, then, rests on the particular assumptions of MP, not minimalist theorizing more generally. In this respect, the numeration is hardly better off than was D-Structure in the earlier theories, each lacking "independent conceptual support" and depending on special assumptions and architecture of the favored approach.

The second justification remains, however. It seems to be true that any theory which includes a derivation requires some way to determine exactly which items must be in a specific derivation. And all theories seem to do this by "pulling out" from the lexicon some group of lexical items. Where earlier theories did this by "projecting" as D-Structure, MP does it by constructing the numeration. D-Structure had various other roles and properties; the numeration, perhaps, has "squeezed out" all of these, and is left with just this one role and property. If this is true, then we have (approached) virtual conceptual necessity with respect to the numeration: given a theory that is derivational and has a lexicon, then there will need to be something with this second property of the numeration. That it is sui generis, and has no other roles or properties, is, perhaps, keeping it as minimalist as possible.

We move now from the computational component to the account of phrase structure in MP.

2.0   PS in MP

In this section, we lay out the approach to PS given in MP. In subsequent sections, we return to the specific concepts and themes examined in previous chapters, to see in detail how they fare in MP. In earlier versions of minimalism (viz., earlier chapters of MP), "X-bar theory is presupposed, with specific stipulated properties" (MP: 242). The goal now is to see how many of the earlier stipulated properties can be derived from basic assumptions in minimalist theorizing.[10]

Basic assumptions are that requirements of the LF interface determine what must be present in the computational component (i.e., the syntax). Minimally, lexical items and their formal features must be available, as must "larger units constructed of lexical items . . . along with their types: noun phrases and verb phrases interpreted, but differently, in terms of their type, and so on" (MP: 242). These larger units are, by assumption, maximal projections. This means that "maximal projection" is part of minimalist theory, as is "minimal projection".

Because of inclusiveness, there should be no "special marking" that identifies maximality or minimality; instead, they must be structurally defined "relational properties of categories, not inherent properties of them" (MP: 242). "Maximal" is just a category that does not project any further; "minimal" is one that does not project at all. All others, with one exception, are "invisible at the interface and for computation." The exception is what, in earlier X-Bar theory, was labelled X^0. An item can be both Minimal and Maximal (MP: 390, fn. 95). We turn now to the mechanics.

2.1   *Minimal mechanics*

The pieces of PS mechanics in MP can be divided into two parts, which we may as well call *ontology* and *metaphysics*. We have already made mention of most of the ontology: Selected lexical items, complex objects constructed from Selected lexical items, and type indicators. These latter are called *labels* in MP (243). More precisely, we have (cf. MP: 243):

(2)   A syntactic object K is
    a.   A Selected lexical item (with lexical items sets of features) or
    b.   K = {g, {a,b}}, where a,b are syntactic objects, and g is the label of K.
    c.   Nothing else is a syntactic object.

(3)   A label g in {g, {a,b}} is one or another of a,b (MP: 244)

A further bit is required, the definition of what are called *Terms* in MP (247).

(4)   For a syntactic object K
    a.   K is a Term of K
    b.   If L is a Term of K, then the members of the members of L are Terms of K
    c.   Nothing else is a Term

We can begin the metaphysics with Terms, as these are unfamiliar. Terms "alone can be functioning elements" in a PM (at a given stage in its derivation) (MP: 247). That is, Terms define what, at any given point, may play an active role in the computation, or, when the computation is complete, in the interpretation. We return to this notion, and (4), below.

For two, related, reasons the label g in (3) must be either a or b. Recall that the need for labels stems from the need to identify the type of a nonminimal syntactic object, e.g., to distinguish noun phrases from verb phrases. Thus, if a syntactic object is a derived object (i.e., licensed by (2b) above, rather than by Select), it should be the case that it gets its type from one of its parts – this is just one of the original motivations for X-Bar Theory.[11] But, given inclusiveness, it must be the case that a derived object is not merely related to one of its parts, but is, in fact, identical to it.[12] Thus, we have, apparently, derived a version of one of the crucial aspects of PS theory, the existence of the "Projection Chain" in the terms of Speas (1990). Actually, the particular version does not follow so simply, but this leads us directly to (2), and then back again to (3).

In (2) (repeated here), we see that derived syntactic objects are sets constructed from other syntactic objects. This is what Merge does. The assumption is that Merge operates on two syntactic objects to create a new syntactic object. Further, Merge is held to apply "in the simplest possible form: at the root" (MP: 248). That is, at any given stage in the derivational construction of the PM, Merge always applies to the entire PM, never to a subpart of the PM, and to some element Selected from the numeration. The nature of the new object formed by Merge is at question. The choices are (A) it is constituted from the two parts (B) it is the same regardless of what the parts are or (C) it is random. Options (B) and (C) are rejected as "neither worth considering" (MP: 243). That leaves (A); the further claim is that "the simplest object" constructible from two distinct objects is the set containing those two objects (MP: 243).[13] The parts (a and b in (2b)) are the *constituents* of the new syntactic object (K in (2b)) (MP: 243). This returns us to (3) (repeated here).

(2)   A syntactic object K is
    a.   A Selected lexical item (with lexical items sets of features) or
    b. $K = \{g, \{a,b\}\}$, where a,b are syntactic objects, and g is the label of K.
    c.   Nothing else is a syntactic object.

(3)   A label g in $\{g, \{a,b\}\}$ is one or another of a,b (MP: 244)

Why is g one or another of a,b? We have seen that in order to function as a label, and given inclusiveness, it has to be related to, and not "more than", one of the constituents. MP (244) argues as follows. Given two lexical items as constituents, and that lexical items are sets of features, "the simplest assumption" (MP: 244) is that g is

(5)   a.   the intersection of a and b
    b.   the union of a and b
    c.   one or the other of a, b

It is asserted that (5a and b) "are immediately excluded" because they are each "generally irrelevant to output conditions" and, further, the intersection is "often null" while the union is "'contradictory'" if the constituents "differ in the value for some feature, the normal case."[14] This leaves (5c). Whichever one is the label is said to *project*, and is the *Head* of K (MP: 244). In fact, *Head* is restricted to *terminal elements*, where these latter items are "selected from the numeration, with no parts (other than features) relevant to [the computation system]" (MP: 245).

Having outlined the basic mechanics of the PS theory in MP, we turn now to an examination of those mechanics.

2.2   *Spanners in the works*

The basic idea in MP is that most all of what is wanted or needed for PS theory (as, for example, encoded in X-Bar Theory) simply falls out of the process of constructing syntactic objects from lexical items by means of Select and Merge, and that anything that does not fall out should be thrown out. But, questions arise.

2.2.1   *Merge*

To begin with, why should Merge be limited only to pairs?[15] From one point of view, this is minimal: any less is impossible (because there is no forming a new syntactic object from a single syntactic object), and any more is unnecessary (because a new object can be formed from two objects). But from another point of view, it lacks generality, and therefore is not minimal. That is, given an operation and a collection of potential operatees, why should it be limited to only pairs? More specifically, let the operation just take any number of operatees at all, and, should there be problems with some results, it would be the output conditions enforced at/by the interface that would do the sorting out. As there have to be output conditions anyway, why should they not do this sort of work, which would permit a more general operation?[16] Further, given that the operation here is Merge, and Merge is taken to be set formation, presumably something would have to be said to limit it so that it always forms doubletons, as nothing in set theory requires such a limitation. Indeed, given that the operation that works on Selected lexical items is one that forms sets, it is then not even true that pairs are the minimal possible inputs which deliver new objects, as singleton sets are objects distinct from their members.

This is an example of the tension between representational minimalism and operational minimalism.[17] The minimal operation does not stipulate restrictions on numbers of inputs or outputs, while a desire for a minimal representation leads to an operation with such stipulations. A related instance appears to lie in the idea noted above that Merge "applies in the simplest possible form: at the root" (MP: 248). Once more, we can ask why Merge could not simply apply freely, with no stipulated restriction on where it applies, and why this is not "simpler" than the alternative in MP.

However, this latter objection can be countered as follows. If syntactic objects are sets, and Merge simply takes such objects as inputs and forms as output another set with the input sets as its members, then not to apply "at the root" would require something that goes beyond simple set formation. Specifically, Merge would also have to remove something from a set (a member, or a member of a member, or a member of a member of a member, or . . .) in order not to apply "at the root", and this, evidently, is not just a more general application of the same operation. It seems, then, that the limitation to applying "at the root" is not mere stipulation, but follows rather clearly from the nature of syntactic objects as sets, and the minimalist desideratum of keeping the new object (set) forming operation Merge as pristine as possible.

Now we can ask whether the original objection to Merge as always operating on pairs and returning doubletons can be similarly countered. The restriction can be traced back to the operation of Select. If Select must always take a single lexical item from the numeration into syntax, then, perhaps, Merge will always work on pairs, if we assume (1) Merge is required to have more than one input element and (2) whenever it can apply it must apply. Both of these assumptions are necessary. If Merge can form new sets with only a single input, then, of course, it need not operate only on pairs; it seems impossible to avoid such a stipulation so long as Merge is understood to be set formation. And if in all situations where it could apply (e.g., two lexical items have been Selected) it does apply, then there will never be a situation in which more than two potential inputs are available in the syntax (computational component).

2.2.2 *Select*

But, evidently, all we have done now is moved the problem: why should Select be limited to one-at-a-time operation? Given a numeration, why should not more than one lexical item be Selected (viz., enter the computational component) at a time? In such a case, then, Merge could have available more than two potential inputs on which to operate. It might be argued that if, as there must be, there is some operation that takes lexical items from the numeration into syntax, then the "minimal" such operation – the "least" such operation that does the required work – is one that takes items one-at-a-time. This is not entirely implausible, but it is not entirely convincing, either. Why not an operation that simply takes all the items at once? It might work as follows. Given a numeration, for each member pair in the numeration, copy the lexical item member of such a pair n times, where n is the integer in the pair. The copies – not now part of any larger object – are now all in the computational system, available for Merge. It is not clear, at least to me, why such an operation is less "minimal" than the alternative. Perhaps it will be reasserted that one-at-a-time Select just *is* "simpler" and "more minimal". But this is at best just assertion, and perhaps not even that good.

In this regard it is important to recall two points. (1) "If Select does not exhaust the numeration, no derivation is generated and no questions of convergence or economy arise." And (2) that Select is " 'costless'; [it does] not fall within the domain of discussion of convergence and economy" (MP: 226). These are important because they indicate that there is no such operation as one-at-a-time Select. We have seen that given a lexicon and derivations, it is necessary that there be something like the numeration, with its sole property of identifying the lexical items in the derivation.[18] Given the numeration and syntactic derivations, it is also then necessary that the numeration be exhausted in the translation of lexical items into syntax (the quotes above). But "exhausting the numeration" is the sole property which the translation into syntax *must* have – and it is this limitation to what is necessary, to what is a matter of virtual conceptual necessity, which makes it "costless". To propose the one-at-a-time operation Select is then to go beyond what is required, beyond virtual conceptual necessity, in that properties are ascribed which are not necessary solely in order to achieve the necessary translation into syntax. It therefore follows that insofar as the translation into syntax is "costless", it is not done by one-at-a-time Select, which, perforce, does not then exist.

Instead, we have an "operation" – if it can be called such – which is rather more like the alternative sketched above. Call it "Translate" or "Exhaust", if you like. It does only, exactly, and directly what is required: it translates the numeration into syntax, entering into syntax the lexical item from each pair n times, where n is the index in that pair (assuming, for concreteness, the MP characterization of the numeration). Alternatively, one can conceptualize it in the following manner. Given a numeration, there are n syntactic objects corresponding to the lexical item in each pair in the numeration, where n is the index in the pair containing the lexical item. In this formulation, there is no "operation" at all, just a well-formedness condition. I see no reason not to prefer such an approach.

But now, if there is no Select, what happens to Merge? It might seem that the argument above, using "costlessness" against Select, should apply, *mutatis mutandis*, equally to Merge, as the quoted passages above are in fact about both Select **and** Merge (MP: 226). We now examine this issue.

One-at-a-time Select is illicit because it goes beyond what is strictly required by virtual conceptual necessity: the required translation of the numeration into syntax. It is this latter requirement that is basic. With respect to Merge, the basic requirement is that there be a derivation of a single syntactic object (the LF PM). But perhaps this is already tendentious; perhaps, instead of "a derivation of" we should say "construction of". That is, it is a matter of virtual conceptual necessity that, given the syntactic objects translated from the numeration, there be a single syntactic object constructed from them; whether this "construction" should be termed a "derivation" may, however, be a substantive, and not merely a terminological, point.

Notice that this is the same two-step pattern of analysis used with respect to Chains, the numeration, and one-at-a-time Select. We ask first what the essential, underlying property involved is, and then we accept only the most direct means of realizing that property. In this way, in both steps we cleave as closely as possible to virtual conceptual necessity, the primary desideratum in minimalist theorizing.

2.2.3   *Merge, again*

We now ask whether Merge meets the requirements of virtual conceptual necessity. Merge is set formation: "The simplest object constructed from [a] and [b] is the set {a,b} . . ." (MP: 243). But is this true? Why not the *concatenation* of *a* and *b*? Is this less "simple" than the set containing *a* and *b*? How so is not immediately obvious. Perhaps it fails to be an "object" in some desired sense. But no desired sense of "object" has been specified, nor, within minimalist theorizing, should one be. That is, the properties of the new object should, presumably, be whatever they turn out to be, given the "simplest" operation for forming new objects. Notice, further, that concatenation, unlike set formation, need not be stipulated to have more than one input. While set formation can take a single object and give a new object (the set containing the single input), concatenation is undefined for a single input. And, again unlike set formation, concatenation is typically defined as a binary operation (e.g., Wall 1972: 165). Thus, concatenation would appear to have inherently two of the properties stipulated of Merge-as-set-formation.

2.2.4   *Labels and terms*

However, the result of Merge-as-set-formation also includes the label for the new object, as a member of the new object, as in (2) and (3), repeated here.

(2)   A syntactic object K is
    a.   A Selected lexical item (with lexical items sets of features) or
    b.   K = {g, {a,b}}, where a,b are syntactic objects, and g is the label of K.
    c.   Nothing else is a syntactic object.

(3)   A label g in {g, {a,b}} is one or another of a,b (MP: 244)

    If labels are indeed required, then this suggests that concatenation is not the correct approach to new object formation. However, it is suggested in MP (244) that labels may be "uniquely determined" and that "[t]o the extent that such unique determination is possible, categories are representable in the more restricted form {[a], [b]}, with the label uniquely determined." The question of whether labels are in fact uniquely determined for Merge is left open in MP (244). But if they are, as is evidently desirable within minimalist theorizing, then concatenation, which has no obvious resources for representing them, is again favored over set formation.

    With respect to this question, it is helpful to examine Terms, (4), repeated here.

(4)   For a syntactic object K
    a.   K is a Term of K
    b.   If L is a Term of K, then the members of the members of L are Terms of K
    c.   Nothing else is a Term

The first thing to point out is that, given an object K = {g, {a,b}}, the label *g* is not a Term. This is because it is neither *K* nor a member of a member of *K*; rather, the label is simply a member of *K*. The Terms are *K*, *a*, and *b*. But, since "terms alone are functioning elements" (MP: 247), it follows that labels are not functioning elements. But if they are not "functioning elements", then, evidently, they cannot do the work they are required to do (e.g., distinguish noun phrases from verb phrases), and should not be present. If labels are uniquely determined, hence eliminable, this is no problem.

There are other oddities about (4), however. One, noted already in MP (383, fn. 27), is that if lexical items are sets of features, then the members of these sets – the features – are Terms "– an unwanted result, though it is unclear that it matters." But, within minimalist theorizing, it does matter if a result "does not matter". That is, if the definition overshoots the mark in this (or any) way, that suggests the notion is not the minimal one we desire. Consider, in this regard, exactly what (4b) *says*: "the members of the members of L" – precisely how is *this* minimal? Why the "members of the members"? Why not simply the members? This seems to be just the sort of contrived and stipulative definition that minimalist theorizing is intended to rid syntax of. It might be responded that (4b) is the minimal statement that gets the right results. But this is exactly the kind of justification that minimalist theorizing is meant to eliminate. And, as we have seen, it does not get the right results anyway: it is too strong (it includes the features), and perhaps too weak (it leaves out the labels). If a convoluted definition such as (4) both seems necessary and also does not work right, this suggests that something fundamental may be wrong, that the problem is not just one of finding the right wording. As we have seen and argued in earlier chapters, if one's theoretical/conceptual bases are wrong, then one should expect to find clunkers like (4b) turning up once one begins to work out the implications.

2.2.5   *Merge, one more time*

Let us briefly recap where we are. We are considering the issue of the construction of new syntactic objects. This means examining Merge-as-set-formation. There are two questions before us, one active, the other on hold. The active one is whether *concatenation* is a viable minimalist alternative to Merge-as-set-formation. The on-hold question is whether the construction of new objects should or must be conceptualized as a *derivation*. We return now to concatenation, then to derivation.

From the standpoint of minimalist theorizing, concatenation seems to do pretty well when compared to Merge-as-set-formation, as we have seen. The problem with concatenation is that it is, so to say, *too* minimal. That is, if concatenation is how new syntactic objects are built, we no longer have a PS theory; the resources of this theory do not allow the construction of the hierarchically structured objects that PS-based approaches to syntax assume sentences to be. We can reject concatenation only if we *assume* that syntax is PS-based. This is a nontrivial result because MP claims that "phrase structure theory is essentially 'given' on grounds of virtual conceptual necessity" following the "reasoning sketched so far" (MP: 249). But this is only so if one antecedentally assumes that syntax must construct hierarchically structured objects. While this assumption may be *true*, it is not required for or by minimalist theorizing.[19] Nonetheless, given that *our* starting point is that syntax is PS-based, we can feel comfortable rejecting concatenation, regardless of more general minimalist strictures. This allows us to retain Merge-as-set-formation.

We move now to the question of the derivation. If Merge applies always to two inputs, then the PM is built up derivationally, in that it is necessarily constructed step-by-step. We saw, however, that this *Noahistic* (two-at-a-time) Merge itself depends on one-at-a-time Select, and that this latter is not well-motivated. If more than two objects are available to be Merged, and Merge is set formation, then, as we have argued already, it seems an entirely arbitrary stipulation to limit Merge to Noahism. Now, however, we have a potential problem. If Merge is the most general (simplest?) form of set formation, then there is no evident reason or way to prevent it from forming a new object that has all the items from the numeration as its members. But such an item will not represent the hierarchical structure which, by assumption, sentences have.

The apparent problem, however, suggests its own solution. If, indeed, we do assume that sentences are hierarchically structured objects, then Merge evidently cannot be the most general form of set formation. But what form must it take instead? Note that it must apply equally appropriately regardless of how many items there might be in a numeration. From this it follows that it must be Noahistic; if it were not, then, for some sized numeration, it would (or could) fail to construct a hierarchically structured object, which, by assumption, it cannot do. Put somewhat differently, Noahistic Merge is the only version of Merge-as-set-formation that guarantees a hierarchically structured object regardless of the size of the numeration, and such a guarantee is precisely what is required.

Given Noahistic Merge, we seem to have answered our question about the derivation – we do have a derivation, not just the construction, of the PM. However, the basic property here is that syntax is PS-based, that sentences are hierarchically structured objects. So, the real question is whether a derivation is the most direct, the most minimal, way to realize this property. All we have shown so far is that given the need to have hierarchically structured objects, Noahistic Merge and a derivation stand and fall together. Be that as it may, the derivational/Noahistic theory does appear to have an insuperable advantage over a nonderivational "construction". Such a "construction" would have to guarantee hierarchical structure for any numeration, and it is not clear how it would do so in any general way, without collapsing into a derivation (hence Noahism).

The only real alternative, then, may be some sort of representational theory,[20] perhaps a version of something like that sketched in TPM (18–19). With respect to this issue, it is important that the derivation and Noahism stand and fall together, because this means that any insights or results that appear to follow simply from Noahistic Merge in fact already presuppose that syntax is derivational, and thus do not obviously count against a representational approach to

PS-based syntax without begging the question. So, the assumption "that the only relations that exist for [the computational system] are those established by the derivational process itself" (MP: 254) appears to cut no ice in this comparison. That is, the putative fact that something significant falls out from the derivational process seems to lose its significance because this finding itself depends on the background representational assumption that sentences are hierarchically structured objects. Without *that* assumption, the derivational process could be something entirely different (e.g., concatenation).

But the objections can be countered. The background representational assumption is itself a (relatively) minimal one: sentences are hierarchically structured objects. In particular, no substantive assumptions about the hierarchical structure are made. Instead, a minimal means of constructing such objects is deployed: a derivation with Noahistic Merge. Can a purely representational approach do as well? Specifically, if the only background assumption is the (weak) representational one, how, if at all, could such a theory restrict the form of syntactic objects? It seems that such a representational theory should have to countenance either (1) arbitrary restrictions on the form of syntactic objects or (2) arbitrary forms for syntactic objects. Given that syntactic objects do not, in fact, have arbitrary (though hierarchical) forms, the theory of grammar must provide some principled (minimal) way of accounting for this. The Noahistic derivational theory does this; a purely representational theory does not.

2.2.6 Conclusions

We can now sum up the results of this section. One-at-a-time Select is illicit. The definition for *Terms* cannot be correct. Labels do not fall under the definition for Terms, but likely should not be included as parts of syntactic objects. Noahistic Merge is vindicated.

Previously, we argued that Move was conceptually ill-founded. We also saw that the revisions this entailed provided the means to counter an argument in TPM based on explanatory adequacy. We found, as well, that two of the three justifications for the numeration were suspect, but that one, the need to determine exactly which lexical items must be in a specific derivation, is ineliminable.

This ends the direct exposition and examination of PS concepts directly analyzed in MP. We turn now to examination of the inquiry structuring PS concepts and questions laid out in the Introduction and examined in earlier chapters, seeing how they fare within the system developed in MP.

3.0 Syntactic structure and argument structure

As is usual, there are three subtopics in this section: (1) structuralization and argument alignment (2) Subjects and (3) adjunct(ion)s. We discuss each in turn.

3.1.0 *Structuralization: theta-relatedness*

MP (312–16) discusses these issues in the context of the notion of *theta-relatedness*: being "able to assign or receive a theta-role" (MP: 312). The basic idea is that "theta-relatedness is a property of the position of merger and its (very local) configuration" (MP: 313). The goal is to derive this last proposition by minimalist reasoning. The argument goes as follows. A "configurational approach to theta-theory" (MP: 312) is assumed: "[a] theta-role is assigned in a certain structural configuration; beta assigns that theta-role only in the sense that it is the head of the configuration. . . ." and a similar condition applies for theta-role receipt (MP: 313). Given this, Chains are not possible theta-role assigners or recipients, as Chains are "not in any configuration". What about the head of the Chain, the moved element? With respect to theta-role receipt, the moved element "is not an argument that can receive a theta-role." And, "it makes little sense to think of the head of a chain as assigning a theta-role" (MP: 313).

However, as this last indicates, the argument does **not** in fact *rule out* the moved element assigning a theta-role or, somewhat more weakly, *contributing* to theta-role assignment, in its new position (MP: 389, fn. 84; 314). Indeed, the argument against such *contributing* turns out to be entirely empirical: if the moved element can contribute to theta-assignment, then certain in fact ungrammatical strings would incorrectly be licensed. The desired result – that theta-relatedness is a property of the position of merger – is then **not** truly derived by minimalist reasoning at all. Instead, for at least one case it has to be *assumed*. "The *principle* that theta-relatedness is a 'base property', restricted to configurations of lexical insertion, *has to* be understood in an austere form" (MP: 314, emphases added). In other words, what had begun as a conclusion to be reached by minimalist reasoning has now become a "principle" with a stipulated interpretation it "has to" have – in order that it "get the facts right". These are precisely the sort of maneuvers that minimalist theorizing was intended to eliminate.

This is a particularly important result in the present context because we argued above (section 1.1) both that there is no Move and that once the assumption of a D-structure-like stratum was dropped, requiring lexical items to enter syntax always and only in nondisplaced positions became purely stipulative. If the MP derivation of the proposition that "theta-relatedness is a property of the position of merger" went through, then this would tell against our earlier argument. That it does not go through provides further evidence in favor of our revisionist minimalism.

Notice, moreover, that the MP discussion takes as a goal that "the position of merger" is always a nondisplaced position, and that the necessity of this was denied in section 1.2 independently of the question of whether lexical items in fact always enter syntax in nondisplaced positions. The issues here are somewhat subtle, so some further elaboration of the discussion in sections 1.2 and 2.2.2 and 2.2.4 may be in order.

It is crucial to clearly distinguish between *introducing* items into syntax and "the position of merger". The former is the translation of the numeration into syntax (Select in MP), while the latter is the construction of the PM (Merge in

MP). In earlier P & P theorizing, these were not distinguished, as D-structure was simultaneously both the "position of merger" and the locus of introduction of lexical items into syntax. It needs to be stressed that once these are separated, "theta-relatedness" is no longer of necessity a "base property".

The central question in section 1.2 was about the operation Select: when it operates more than once on a single lexical item in a numeration, must it introduce a "mark" to distinguish each instance in syntax? The answer we came up with was "no", because structural facts can do whatever syntactic distinguishing is needed, as is argued, apparently inadvertently, in MP (251–2). Given this, then, it is *in principle* possible to use Merge to place lexical items in displaced positions, because without the "mark" the fully identical lexical items necessary for Chain formation can all be introduced by Select. This also meant that Select need not violate inclusiveness.

But the argument went even further, in section 2.2.2, claiming that Select itself is an artifact. The claim made was that there just is nothing for an *operation* such as (one-at-a-time) Select to do. The crucial fact about the translation of a numeration (a collection of lexical items) into syntax is that it be exhaustive with respect to the numeration, and the alternative was put forward that this exhaustiveness be enforced by, for example, a well-formedness condition that directly required it. One-at-a-time Select is an operation that goes beyond what is required for no apparent reason, and with no apparent gain.

Finally, in 2.2.4, it was argued that Merge is Noahistic (operates always on pairs). But, given that there is no one-at-a-time "mark" introducing Select, this operation can – and therefore must – merge items in displaced positions.

Our conclusion is the following. Minimalist reasoning does not lead to the result that "theta-relatedness is a property of the position of merger." We reach this in two mutually supporting steps. First, within MP assumptions, to derive the conclusion it is necessary to flatly assume it is true for entirely empirical reasons. That is, to reach the desired goal in MP, other than minimalist reasoning is required. Second, when purely minimalist reasoning was pursued in earlier sections, MP assumptions were independently rejected and the conclusion was shown to be false given the revised assumptions. As already noted, the failure to derive the goal by minimalist reasoning within MP assumptions further supports these revisions.

Now, what this conclusion does not show is that the assertion that "theta-relatedness is a property of the position of merger" is *false*. It may well be true – it may be that the best syntactic theory requires this. But, if it is true, then so much the worse for minimalist reasoning, which, apparently, cannot, by itself, derive this conclusion.

3.1.1 Structuralization: argument alignment

The question of where arguments are structuralized, and why, is addressed somewhat obliquely in MP. More precisely, there are direct statements about where arguments appear, but no direct arguments for why. If a verb has more than one internal argument,[21] then the analysis is one involving a "Larsonian shell" with a "light verb v" to which the original verb raises (MP: 305, 315). The internal arguments are in the complement and Specifier positions of the original verb; if one is obligatory and one optional, then "it is likely" that the obligatory argument is in complement position and the optional argument is in Specifier position (MP: 305).

Not all verbs have more than one internal argument, of course. Some have one, some have none. For the former, transitive verbs, "it would be natural to extend" the analysis suggested for verbs with two internal arguments (MP: 315). The class of transitives is taken to include "intransitive (unergative) verbs" as "hidden transitives", leaving "only unaccusatives" as true intransitives. This means that all but these last are analyzed by means of the "double-VP structure" with a light verb. Only the unaccusatives have "simple VP structures" (MP: 315–16). This entire set of analyses, it is claimed, "is natural in the present framework" (MP: 316). But no further, direct argument is given. All of this is basically just taken over from Hale and Keyser (1993).

It would presumably be a good thing to show that something about the actual patterns of argument alignment can be derived from minimalist assumptions, using minimalist reasoning. But this returns us to a familiar issue viz., whether such properties of the interface between the syntax and the lexicon are or need be within the domain of theory construction concerned with the syntax narrowly conceived.[22] There is no reason to rehash that discussion here. It is enough to make two points that push in opposing directions. One is that while it may ultimately be necessary to have some sort of minimalist accounting of argument alignment, it probably seems no big deal not to have it now, in MP. The second point is what I have called the fundamental idea of PS syntax:[23]

> The guiding idea here is that there must be some systematic relation between individual lexical requirements (i.e., argument structure) and syntactic structure – lexical items cannot appear in arbitrary places in a well-formed sentence – and that characterizing this relation is to some large degree what the theory of PS is about and for.

Now, in the context of MP, this second point serves to make the first a bigger deal than it originally seemed. This is because MP claims that "phrase structure theory is essentially 'given' on grounds of virtual conceptual necessity. . . ." (MP: 249) and that "we may be able to eliminate the theory of phrase structure entirely, deriving its properties on principled grounds" (MP: 378). While this *might* be true with respect to syntactic objects and their construction,[24] it is not true with respect to the theory of PS in the sense of the quote above. What is, perhaps, distinctive of MP is that it separates these two inquiries (syntactic objects and their construction and structuralization/argument alignment, respectively) and calls the first "phrase structure theory", whereas in earlier work – Speas (1990) being its zenith – the two together were "phrase structure theory". Whether this separation is a theoretical advance or not is unclear. That the terminological move may create confusion, and certainly changes the subject, is, once it is noticed, undoubtedly somewhat clearer.

3.2 Subjects

A version of the VP-internal structure is assumed in MP. Subjects are assumed to be in [Spec,*v*], the Specifier position of the light verb in the Larsonian shell structure (MP: 315). This position further "can be taken to express the causative or agentive role of the external argument" (MP: 315). While little more is directly said about Subjects, as such, in MP, this much in combination with what we have seen already about argument alignment does repay further examination.

A question we should ask is the following. Why should a "Larsonian shell" with a "light verb" be the favored structure for Subjects under minimalist assumptions and reasoning? Put slightly differently, we can ask why a verb could not have its (thematic) Subject internal to its projection (to use familiar terminology that may not be entirely appropriate to MP). More generally, the issue becomes why just a single complement and a single Specifier position are available. Notice that if a principled resolution to this last is forthcoming in MP, then we have gained some considerable insight into the lexical argument structure of verbs: there are no verbs with more than two (internal) arguments for minimalist syntactic reasons.

We can already see that given Noahistic Merge, the existence of single complement and Specifier positions can be accounted for. Merging a single item at the root of the existing PM means that there could not be more than one complement or Specifier, unless the structure being built were "flat" and not hierarchical, as we have argued MP must assume it is not. This takes us part of the way we want to go. But only part: it does not tell us what is *special* about these positions.

That is, it does not tell us why we could not simply continue doing Merge to add more and more arguments of a verb. Why, in other words, once the Specifier position has been "built" by Merge is (internal) argument alignment ended? To address this problem, we have to think a bit more directly about the structure itself.

Complement position is evidently special in that it is the sister of the verb. Notice that earlier P & P theories, in which all arguments must be sisters of the verb (see e.g., Carrier and Randall 1992), are ruled out in MP on account of Noahistic Merge. It is natural to interpret this structurally closest position to the verb as the position that the argument "semantically closest" to the verb occupies. It should be clear that the notion "semantically closest" is essentially metaphoric, and, therefore, while it is not without content, some care should be taken to make sure that it has independently testable content. Presuming this to be so, we can turn to Specifier position.

Specifier position is, of course, unique (as are all positions given Noahistic Merge). The question is whether there is anything about this particular unique position that suggests why it should be one occupied by an argument, even though it is not a sister of the verb. Our problem is not merely to explain why no further argument positions are available, though that is hardly trivial. It is also to explain why even this one further argument position is available, beyond that of the sister to the verb. It should go without saying that invoking the argument structure of verbs – pointing to the undeniable fact that verbs do have more than one (internal) argument – simply begs the question. We seek structural insight into why argument structure has precisely the range it does in terms of number of arguments.

Specifier position can be seen to have the following property. It is the structurally closest nonsister position to the verb. That is, any other position will have at least the Specifier position between itself and the verb. To which one can reply, "yes, but so what?" Such skepticism is not without force, and the answer to it must be conditionalized. If there were reason to have an element other than the sister in a relation with the verb, then the closest nonsister is arguably the most natural candidate for such a relatum. For any other candidate, one would have to explain why the structurally closer element(s), beginning with the closest one (that in Specifier position) was (were) passed over in favor of the structurally more remote choice. Within MP, this has obvious incarnations as the Minimal Distance and Minimal Link Conditions, as well as in the earlier Relativized Minimality of Rizzi (1990); and, indeed, something like these conditions might well be taken to rule out such "position skipping". A slightly different way to look at the situation is in terms of "asymmetric C-command", familiar from Chapter Three. The Specifier position is the first position to asymmetrically C-command the verb, so, if asymmetric C-command has some privileged status in syntax, then this may be a helpful analysis.

Where are we now? We have suggested that if any position were to structuralize an (internal) argument, it would be the sister (complement) position. We have now seen that if any further position were also to structuralize another argument, it would probably be the first nonsister (Specifier) position. While relatively heavy on the subjunctives, this is not too bad. But we are not home yet. We need to ask why the process should stop at the Specifier. Why should not yet another argument position be possible, once the Specifier position is given over for an argument? Notice that this might avoid a "no position skipping" solution, as no position seems to be skipped over. However, this depends precisely on how such "no position skipping" is formulated. Such ideas are often *modalized* (e.g., MP: 297 (84)), invoking elements or positions which *could* be a relatum in the relation in question. Much then depends on what the range of the modal is taken to be. That is, does *can* or *could* mean that the element or position in question is of the right type or category to, in principle, be in the relation in question (e.g., it is a noun and not a coordinate conjunction if the relation is "be an argument of"). Or does it mean that, in this particular structure and sentence, this particular element or position being in this particular relation would not in fact violate any principle or condition (e.g., a noun would receive two distinct theta roles or Cases). If the interpretation is of the first kind, then it follows that only the closest element or position of the right sort can ever be an actual relatum.

This may seem still unsatisfying. It appears to tell us that "closest" is special, which we might have believed, but when pressed as to why, the response seems to be "because it is closest". Again, this might be true, but is not inspiring. But we need now to recall just what sort of theory we are interested in here. It is PS theory. In such a theory, other than categorial information, the basic stuff is just structural information. In this sort of theory, a notion such as "closest" is exactly what one wants. If it is not a basic concept, it is nearly one, and easily, and precisely, constructible (e.g., using asymmetrical C-command). That it might seem unsatisfying perhaps tells more about how unpracticed analysts are in thinking with a basic, structural PS vocabulary than about the status of the concept. As PS objects are what mediate the relation between the lexicon and the conceptual system (viz., make up the "computational system"), the properties of PS objects ought to have some effect on that mediation.

We can pick out the complement and Specifier positions as follows, if we like. The complement position is that which uniquely stands in a mutual C-command relation with the verb. The Specifier position is that which stands in a unique asymmetrical C-command relation to the verb (viz., it asymmetrically C-commands the verb and nothing else which also asymmetrically C-commands the verb). These, then, are the positions which are closest to the verb in ways that are straightforwardly definable in terms of C-command relations. And as suggested, "closeness" is exactly the sort of structural relation that ought to play a role in constraining the space of available options for structuralizing lexical relations for interpretive purposes. Let us suppose, then, that we are (relatively) satisfied with why syntax provides (up to) two positions for positioning (internal) arguments, thus for why there are lexically (up to) two (internal) arguments.

We started out, however, not with internal arguments, but with Subjects. Specifically, we wanted to understand why a "Larsonian shell" with a "light verb" might be called for within MP's assumptions. This led us into our digression into why there are no more internal arguments than there are, which we now consider (more or less) resolved. So, we can now return to our original problem.

Having suggested (if not precisely established) that the minimal positions for a verb's arguments are the complement and Specifier positions, on account of their distinct "closest" structural positions to the verb, our original problem is now actually an even larger problem. Given that a thematic Subject is an argument of the verb, there is now literally no structural position for it to occupy if a verb has two other arguments. The justification for the "light verb" analysis must, presumably, go beyond this analytic inconvenience, however. And, indeed, it can. The "light verb" hypothesis can be seen as a structural means of capturing the "internal" versus "external" argument distinction. Subjects, though arguments of the verb, are not simply arguments of the verb in the way that other arguments are. In previous analyses, in fact, they are frequently taken as (syntactic) arguments of the verb phrase, rather than of the verb *simpliciter*. The "light verb" hypothesis reconstructs this idea, analyzing v's complement as the VP headed by the V in question and containing V's other (internal) arguments, and taking the Subject to occupy v's Specifier position (MP: 315). The Subject is a syntactic argument of the light verb v and semantic argument of the v-V complex. This seems to capture various intuitions about Subjects and reconstruct various ways of analyzing their peculiarities. There are, nonetheless, still a couple of issues to consider here.

We can begin by simply stating the issues. One is the status of the "light verb": is this at best an analytic convenience, at worst an analytic artifact? The second is why, if the status issue should be resolved in favor of the "light verb", there should be only one of them: if one is licit, why not an iterated structure of however many you like? Though they are interrelated, it is clearly natural to begin with the first issue.

As noted, the "light verb" hypothesis is not without analytic attraction. However, within minimalist theorizing, this simply is not enough justification. We might say that, in general, analytic usefulness and success is ultimately necessary, but it is not initially sufficient as theoretical justification. If an analyst thinks some idea or concept could or would be productive and useful, then the task is to discover independent theoretical grounds that, in the best minimalist case, require this idea or concept. The evident difficulty of this project is, of course, precisely the point.

Getting slightly more concrete, it is useful to consider whether there are alternatives to a presumptive analysis. In the case of Subjects, we might examine one of the alternatives rejected earlier, viz., another argument position "higher than" the Specifier position. It was suggested above that such a position would be illicit due to something like Minimal Distance/Link or Relativized Minimality. However, one of the major attractions of the "light verb" hypothesis is that it reconstructs the intuition that Subjects are importantly different from other arguments, viz., the "internal" versus "external" distinction. Now, we can ask whether it is not just as reasonable to reconstruct this intuition and distinction by having an argument that is distinguished exactly by *not* being structurally "closest" in either of the two significant ways discussed above.

Perhaps this seems peculiar, a purely "negative" characterization. But the logic is actually that of an "Elsewhere condition": internal argument if structurally "closest" (in the favored senses), external argument (Subject) Elsewhere. There is no violation of Minimal Link/Distance or Relativized Minimality, as the relations in question are distinct; the "closest" positions and the Elsewhere positions simply do not "compete", so the Minimality conditions do not come into play at all. It might be thought that this hypothesis would allow a Subject to be anywhere above the Specifier position, but this is not so. Despite the Minimality conditions being moot with respect to the internal versus external arguments, they are still in force when it comes to determining the position of the external argument. Thus, the interaction of Elsewhere with Minimality combines to place the external argument outside the Specifier position while constraining it to be as close to the verb as possible given this "outsider" status. As well, the Minimality conditions prevent iteration of such external argument positions, a consideration that will be significant presently, when we return to our second issue for the "light verb" hypothesis.

Theoretically, this alternative compares very favorably to the "light verb" hypothesis. No new entity or principle is summoned from offstage as a *deus ex machina*. The reconstruction of the distinction between the internal and external arguments in terms of "closestness" to the V is generally available (and used). Minimality conditions and Elsewhere are not special to this proposal, and are each entirely general, whatever the correct statement or status of either may ultimately be. Elsewhere pries open the hatch to let the external argument out, and Minimality shuts it down again before any more than one can escape, giving exactly the degree of freedom desired, in exactly the manner that is most valued.

The following objection might be raised. The hypothesis does not reconstruct the idea that the external argument is the syntactic argument of the verb phrase. This is because the Subject is now internal to the projection of the verb, rather than in the projection of the "light verb" (to which the full verb is ultimately adjoined). The answer to this is a familiar one: "true, but so what?" Distinct proposals will have different characteristics. The current proposal can reconstruct the desired distinction. It does so in terms of a structure that contains positions that are structurally "closest" to the verb (in the favored senses that both hypotheses need) and another structure which contains that verb-plus-closest-positions structure and another argument (the external argument). An objection that the hypothesis is wrong because the structure which contains the "closest" positions to the verb is not a maximal verb phrase just begs the question at hand.

We move now to the second issue for the "light verb" hypothesis. If one "light verb" can be pulled from the analyst's hat, why not more? Why should there not be iterated "light verb" shells? There would have to be verbs with many more arguments than are actually seen in order to move through these shells, but that is not a solution; it is rather the problem. If the syntax would allow them, then there ought to be such verbs. The suggested alternative, through the interaction of Minimality and Elsewhere conditions, had a solution, as the syntax would not allow such external argument iteration. The "light verb" hypothesis, by contrast, cannot rely on Minimality, because the separate "light verbs" prevent the application of Minimality: each "light verb"-plus-V complex would be a distinct entity and so a relation with one could not block a relation with any other under a Minimality condition.

The syntax would seem to allow iteration of "light verbs", and this means that there ought to be verbs to move through such shells. That there are no such verbs becomes a problem on this hypothesis. But the problem is an artifact of the analysis. The analysis is surely wrong. The issue will recur in our discussion of adjuncts below.

3.3   Adjunct(ion)s

As usual, there are two distinct, though related topics here: Adjuncts and adjunctions. Indeed, the two are not fully distinguishable in MP, with rather surprising results, as we shall see. We shall begin with Adjuncts, as that topic flows directly from the discussion in the previous section.

3.3.1   Adjuncts

We shall work our way through the MP approach to Adjuncts more or less backwards. We begin simply by presenting the proffered analysis. We then try to understand how and why this is what is on offer. Along the way, of course, we make our usual attempts to tidy up whatever seems messy. When we arrive at our end point, we will be in a position to move along naturally to the MP approach to adjunctions.

There is a sense in which there are no Adjunct structures in MP. All verbs except unaccusatives are analyzed by means of Larsonian shells and "light verbs".[25] The analysis of (VP) Adjuncts builds on this (MP: 331–2). VP Adjuncts (e.g., adverb(ials)) are hypothesized to be "between" the "light verb" and the main verb, as a sister to a projection of the main verb. The Adjunct and this main verb projection are themselves daughters of a further projection of the main verb, which will itself be sister (complement) of the "light verb" (MP: 331 (146)). In such a structure, then, there is only one maximal projection of the main verb (viz., the mother of the Adjunct and the projection of the main verb), so the characteristic "Adjunct structure" is apparently absent. There are a number of issues to clarify here, however.

First, we have been somewhat loose in our discussion in the following way. In MP, recall, the actual syntactic objects are sets constructed (ultimately) out of elements from the Numeration by Merge. And labels (if they exist) are themselves simply one of the two constituents of the new object – the one containing the Head. Actually, this is inaccurate, and our earlier discussion of labels was incomplete, in that the MP (246) position is that "it is natural, then, to take the label of K to be not alpha itself but rather H(K). . . ." That is, the label for a syntactic object K is the Head of K, not either of its immediate constituents (alpha or beta). Thus, in a NP the Head Noun would be the label for each nominal syntactic object in the Projection Chain (to use a term that does not appear in MP). In particular, there are no such things as e.g., XP, X', and X, though, to be sure, there are Minimal and Maximal Projections. These, however, are simply the beginning and ending of a given Projection Chain.[26] So, if this were all there were to the story, then there would be nothing distinctive about the labelling of the phrase structure of Adjuncts: all labelling looks effectively Adjunct-like, in that any mother has the same label as one of its daughters, the traditional *differentia* for Adjuncts. However, this is not the entire story.

MP (248) takes over from earlier work, specifically May (1985) and Chomsky (1986a), a distinction between *segments* and *categories*. The idea is that in adjunct(ion)s, there is formed "a two-segment category rather than a new category." Such an object is "constructed from K but with a label distinct from its head H(K). One minimal choice is the ordered pair <H(K), H(K)>." This suggestion would distinguish adjunct(ion)s from other structures, but it is not wholly unproblematic.

We should note "that <H(K), H(K)> . . . is not a term of the structure formed" (MP: 248). This is true of labels in general, as we have already pointed out. Because the labels are not Terms, it is not immediately clear how the difference in labelling between adjunct(ion)s and other objects can make a difference. But, in fact, it is also not clear that the claim that <H(K), H(K)> is not a Term is correct. Recall the definition for Terms (4), repeated here. The ordered pair <H(K), H(K)> would be a member of L, and ordered pairs have members, so each of H(K) and H(K) would be Terms. This then creates an odd asymmetry between adjunct(ion) labels and other labels.

(4)   For a syntactic object K
    a.   K is a Term of K
    b.   If L is a Term of K, then the members of the members of L are Terms of K
    c.   Nothing else is a Term

We should also notice that, while it is called *"one* minimal choice" (emphasis added) for a new label, the use of the ordered pair <H(K), H(K)> is simply stipulated. This is in keeping with its origin in May (1985), wherein the approach to adjunction is a mass of ad hoc stipulation masquerading as insight.[27] It is less than one asks of minimalist theorizing, which aims to provide THE minimal analysis, without stipulation. It is not clear, then, that a principled way of deriving traditional Adjunct structures is provided in MP.

A second point to note about the suggested analysis in terms of "light verbs" is that it seems entirely ungeneral. That is, not all Adjuncts are VP Adjuncts (e.g., relative clauses), and yet this hypothesis relies precisely on details of V projections.

Third, it seems as though the whole idea of "Adjuncts" has been lost. Adjuncts are exactly not arguments, and the traditional analysis provides a PS reconstruction of this difference, and does so in a way that explains central properties of Adjuncts, viz., that they "stack" (iterate) and can be interchanged. Here, however, there is an apparent obvious reply. Adjuncts are just those members of the Projection Chain which are not in either Specifier or complement position. Here the MP proponent could shadow the discussion above of Subjects without the "light verb" hypothesis using the notion of "closest" to the verb. That there is no special phrase structure for Adjuncts does not matter, on this view; it is enough that they do not have the phrase structure of arguments.

Finally, we have already cast aspersions on the "light verb" analysis, so any further hypothesis that builds on that analysis is, to that extent, suspect. And a pattern of argument with which we are familiar recurs: if the earlier attacks on the "light verb" analysis are on the right track, then anything built on that analysis should itself show cracks and weaknesses. Conversely, insofar as such "light verb" assuming analyses are sound, the earlier attacks are called into question.

Returning to the topic of Adjunct iteration, we note the following (MP: 333)

> Whatever may be involved in such cases, it is unlikely that proliferation of shells is relevant. Even if that analysis is assumed for multiple adjuncts, there is little reason to suppose that the verb raises repeatedly from deep in the structure; rather, if a shell structure is relevant at all, the additional phrases might be supported by empty heads below the main verb. . . .

It is not clear why "proliferation of shells" should be considered at all – except, of course, as was argued above with respect to Subjects, it is not clear how to stop them from proliferating in general. This could represent a relatively deep kind of problem for MP: having theoretical options that are analytically super-numerary. A potential response is the following. Suppose the earlier argument about "light verb" proliferation is correct. What the phenomenon of Adjunct iteration shows is that this theoretical option is, in fact, analytically necessary. That is, the earlier discussion shows that the qualms voiced in MP and quoted above with respect to "proliferation of shells" are misplaced. Shells cannot be stopped from proliferating, and this is a *good* thing, as they are needed to support Adjuncts. While endorsing the conclusion of an interlocutor's attempt at a *reductio* argument is certainly bracing, in this case it still leaves the earlier central objection to shell proliferation untouched: why is the external argument unique? That is, once there can be many "light verbs" why are there no verbs with many external arguments supported by these "light verbs"? And, in any event, it just is not clear what work the extra "light verbs" might be doing with respect to Adjuncts, as the original "light verb" is putatively present to support the external argument. So: with respect to the external argument, the "light verb" hypothesis and its concomitant shell proliferation gives too much, while with respect to Adjuncts, it gives nothing at all.

How then might Adjuncts be analyzed without "light verbs"? Adjuncts and the external argument would both be Merged into the V Projection Chain after all internal arguments. An apparently positive aspect of this is that Subjects and Adjuncts do, in fact, pattern together, and differently from internal arguments, with respect to Island (CED) phenomena. This is part of the argument for the approach to Islands taken in TPM, wherein Subjects have the PS by which Adjuncts are standardly analyzed. There are problems, however.

Recall that the analysis of Subjects without "light verbs" adumbrated above invoked Elsewhere and Minimality conditions in order to define a space that allowed just the single external argument. Now, the space will have to expand to allow (unlimited) iteration of Adjuncts, and there is nothing about either the phrase structure or the construction process that distinguishes external arguments from Adjuncts. It is not clear how to allow for iteration of the latter but not of the former in the same space.

There is, moreover, a question of positioning. The Adjuncts should presumably be between the external argument and the internal arguments, rather than outside the external argument. How this should be guaranteed is obscure.

These are serious, even devastating, problems, and they create a dilemma. The MP approach to Adjuncts, involving "light verbs", is, on account of this very property, basically a nonstarter. The alternative, without "light verbs", starts, maybe, but cannot get very far before running out of gas in a blind alley, it seems. The dilemma, then, is that neither a minimalist theory with "light verbs" or one without them works when Adjuncts are considered. And, as these types evidently exhaust the options, there appears to be no minimalist theory for/of Adjuncts.

Perhaps, then, we have to do the bracing thing, and endorse this conclusion. But we do not stop there; instead, we then ask *why* is there no minimalist theory for/of Adjuncts? The answer we are looking for is not the sort of argument just rehearsed, which shows *that* there is no such theory. To answer the "why question" we need to think again about what Adjuncts are, and what minimalist theorizing is.

Adjuncts are nonargument modifiers of a Head. They are optional. This is a crucial point, and bears repeating. They are optional. No sentence that contains an Adjunct would be ill-formed were the Adjunct absent. Minimalist theorizing is about trying to discover and use only that which is necessary. There might be, then, a principled tension between the phenomenon of Adjuncts and minimalist theorizing. Adjuncts might be simply the wrong sort of things for there to be a minimalist theory of. Minimalist theorizing aims to employ only operations that cannot be avoided, operating on objects that are mandatory. Adjuncts are not mandatory, and the operation Merge simply assimilated them to the form of mandatory objects (as in (6) above), and the special nature of Adjuncts entirely disappeared.

But what now? Two sorts of approaches suggest themselves. One is a theoretical architecture more like that of TPM. There, Adjuncts are added as part of creating the "Extended Base". D-structures are formed in a two-step/stage process. First, there is the "unextended base" without Adjuncts, and then Adjuncts are added by generalized transformation. In MP terms, Adjuncts would not be part of the (initial) Numeration. It would only be after the Numeration had been successfully mapped into a full (convergent) PM that Adjuncts would be added. Evidently, this could not be done by Merge, as this operation always applies "at the root". This is an advantage, however, as Merge necessarily elides the distinctiveness of Adjuncts, as we have already seen. Because Merge could not apply, there would have to be some other operation to add Adjuncts, and the nature of this operation (viz., its domain and range) would presumably help account for the distinctive properties of Adjuncts. While this does not seem to me entirely without merit, it is pretty much pure speculation at this point, and I currently have nothing more concrete to add.

It might, nonetheless, be objected that even this cursory sketch of the outline of an idea gives up too much to fit into any theoretical edifice that might reasonably be termed "minimal(ist)". Specifically, if postulation of a second stage and an "Extended Numeration" (or whatever it might be), along with a new, *sui generis*, operation can qualify as "minimal(ist)", then it is not clear what could not so qualify. These suggestions, the objection would say, go way beyond the bare requirements for a "computational component" imposed by the need to license fully interpretable PMs constructed out of lexical items. There is something to this; maybe quite a lot.

What is worth bearing in mind, however, is that what this approach is trying to do is to keep Adjuncts within the "computational component". The presupposition is that even if there is no direct minimalist theory of Adjuncts, nevertheless Adjuncts should, somehow, be a part of the syntax. This might well be incorrect, and is in direct contrast to the second sort of approach. If we recall from the Introduction that "Adjunct" is a term from dependency theory, then this second sort of approach becomes all the more intriguing. This second sort of approach leads to the conclusion that at least this dependency theory notion does not, and should not, get reconstructed within the core component of (minimalist) PS-based syntax. This is pretty interesting stuff, and does suggest that we ought to move beyond talk of "this second sort of approach", and get into the approach itself. As the second sort of approach comes out of, and leads us directly into, adjunctions in MP, we therefore turn immediately to that topic.

3.3.2 *Adjunctions*

Various forms and types of adjunction receive a fair amount of discussion space in MP. We shall begin with a conclusion about one apparent central case, "adjunction of YP to XP" (MP: 324). This operation "... may not really belong to the system we are discussing here ..." where "the system" refers to the "core computational properties" that are "highlighted by minimalist guidelines" (MP: 325). Instead, it, together with "extraposition, right-node raising [and] scrambling", falls into the class of "'stylistic' rules" (MP: 324). Internal to MP, the conclusion is couched as (7) (MP: 319 (119)) (H(K) is the Head of K), which effectively bars such an operation by placing the YP essentially outside of the syntax, hence unlicensable.[28]

(7) alpha adjoined to nonminimal K is not in the checking domain of H(K)

It should be stressed that the banishing of YP adjoining to XP from the computational component is not done either hastily or merely stipulatively in MP. Rather, various cases and instances are examined, and over and over again problems arise given minimalist assumptions if such an operation is legitimate.

This conclusion is a seductive one, given our discussion of Adjuncts in the previous section. The temptation is to move from this conclusion concerning adjunctions to a similar one for Adjuncts. However, such a move requires examination and analysis, both with respect to adjunctions and Adjuncts in general and with respect to the specifics of their respective treatments within MP.

The central conceptual difference between the two is that "adjunction" names a syntactic process, a particular form of PM construction or augmentation, while "Adjunct" names a phenomenon, a particular dependency relation. It is clear, then, that the former concept is a theory internal one, while the latter is not: so, for example, a pure dependency theory would, obviously, have no process of "adjunction" while it would, equally obviously, make use of the concept, and have some analysis, of "Adjuncts". The central similarity between the two is that the phrase structure configuration which the process gives rise to is also the phrase structure configuration with which the phenomenon is analyzed, though the phenomenon need not, in fact, be analyzed by means of the process. The question facing MP, and any minimalist theory, then, is whether the analysis of the phenomenon requires the use of the process. If so, then, apparently, the conclusion is established that "Adjuncts" are not a part of the core computational component. If not, then their syntactic status remains open.

I say "apparently" in the next to last sentence of the previous paragraph for the following reason. If "Adjuncts" must be analyzed by means of the "adjunction" process, this is an unprecedented analysis. In earlier P & P approaches, and in the transformational grammar from which P & P has grown, "adjunction" is a movement operation, and "Adjuncts" are not subject to this process. And, indeed, MP (329) agrees with this tradition: ". . . adverbs seem to have no morphological properties that require XP-adjunction. . . . The empirical evidence also suggests that adverbs do not form chains by XP-adjunction." The reason for this separation is quite clear. The phenomena typically analyzed by means of the "adjunction" operation have, as phenomena, pretty much nothing to do with the phenomenon of "Adjuncts". Thus, the theory internal analytic distinction mirrors a pre-theoretic descriptive distinction between types of phenomena. While this is attractive, it is not necessarily correct.

Assimilation of "Adjuncts" to "adjunctions", then, is neither immediate nor obviously correct. If it is done, a new syntactic kind is on view, one that crosscuts the pre-theoretic taxonomy in terms of functions and phenomena. This is, in itself, no argument against the assimilation, and may even be in its favor. That is because, in this specific case, the kind could arise directly from the bases of the theory: likeness of PS configuration and means of construction. As we have stressed throughout, a PS theory must be responsive to its particular primitive and derived concepts, and whether these reconstruct kinds from outside the theory is in part what the investigation is about. Failure to so reconstruct is perhaps as likely to be a theoretical advance, isolating the real kinds, as an analytic regression, missing some important datum.

Within MP, the crucial consideration is that Move "incorporates Merge" (MP: 378) within "the copy theory of movement" (MP: 251, 202), in which a "moved" element does not move, but instead a copy of that element is Merged into the PM at the "landing site". Given this, it is always Merge which constructs the relevant PS configurations, both in "adjunctions" and with respect to "Adjuncts", and so it is not at all implausible – indeed it may be unavoidable – that if Merge cannot construct such configurations for "adjunction" it also cannot do so for "Adjuncts".

Let us recap the argument. Move is actually Copy and Merge. The structures resulting from those movements previously called "adjunctions" are not licitly constructed by Move (viz., Merge). The structures for "Adjuncts" are identical to these unconstructible structures. Therefore, Merge cannot construct them, either. Thus, because there is only one operation for PM construction (Merge), neither "adjunctions" nor "Adjuncts" can be part of the core computational component.

The only apparent alternative, sketched at the end of the previous section, is an architecture more like that in TPM, which accepts that some further operation (and component) is necessary for the licensing of Adjuncts. In either case, there is no straightforward minimalist account of Adjunct(ion)s. The issue between the approaches comes down, ultimately, to how and to what degree Adjuncts need to be incorporated into the computational component (the syntax). MP offers some theoretical grounds for grouping "adjunctions" and "Adjuncts" together. However, there seems to be less reason, theoretical or empirical, to group Adjuncts with "such operations as extraposition, right-node raising . . . and scrambling" (MP: 324) with which they would now fall outside of the core computational component. Regardless of how this is finally resolved, we have arrived at some challenging and unexpected, if still tentative, conclusions.

4.0   Heads

With respect to Heads, the goal of a PS-based approach to syntax is, of course, to provide a PS-based notion of "Head". Beyond that, the goal is that this notion should itself reconstruct, or at least be articulable with a reconstruction of, the dependency concept of "Head". Thus, recall that while the approach to Heads in AS is syntactically impeccable but does not reconstruct the dependency concept, it does converge and cohere with such a reconstruction, that from Speas (1990).

There is, however, more still that we can ask of a PS theory of Heads, and minimalist theorizing well brings out this further something. In the best possible PS world, the concept of "Head" would not merely be reconstructed, but would also be, at least to some degree, explained. More specifically, we want the reconstruction of the concept to offer some insight into *why* the concept plays a significant role in syntax. This could be done by, so to say, *naturalizing* the concept. By this is meant that the closer the reconstruction comes to "virtual conceptual necessity" in the PS system, the more we can claim to have explained the fact that the concept plays however central a role it does in syntax. Conversely, "mere" reconstruction leaves the concept dangling.

MP (244) defines Heads by means of labels: the label for a syntactic object is, in the first instance, one of the two constituents of that syntactic object, and that constituent *"projects* and is the *head"*. MP (245) further restricts "the term *head* to terminal elements drawn from the lexicon . . ." and, as we have already noted, ultimately requires labels to be Heads: "H(K) is the head of alpha and its label as well" (MP: 246). This is a bit tricky seeming: a Head projects, which means it determines the label, and labels are restricted to being Heads. We appear to have to know what the Head is to determine the label, while the label must be a Head. However, the restriction of Heads to terminals can straighten out the seeming circularity, if a terminal can be termed a "Head". We could then say that all terminals are Heads, and any (but not every) Head can project. A Head which does project is the constituent which determines (is) the label of a larger syntactic object. The label of such a syntactic object is also its Head. So, given two "terminal elements drawn from the lexicon" that are Merged as the constituents of a new syntactic object, while both will be Heads, only one will project, becoming the label of its projection, the new syntactic object. This label is also the Head of the new object, which means the projecting Head is the Head of its projection. This new object is then available for further Merging, and its Head can further project, becoming the label (and Head) for a new object/projection, etc., etc.

Despite its convolutedness, then, we will assume that there is nothing incoherent or viciously circular going on here, and we can ask whether these notions do the work required of a PS-based investigation of Heads. It seems that they do. If "terminal elements drawn from the lexicon" are not licit starting points for this syntactic theory, then probably nothing will be. The dependency relations between a mother and its Head daughter are reconstructed by means of the identity between their labels, the projection of the constituent as the label. This does suggest, however, that the analysis may be vulnerable given our findings that labels are not Terms, and thus (presumably) are inert in the computational component, and that the definition of "Term" itself was untenable (section 2.2.4).

This is potentially very important, as it leads us to the issue of *naturalizing*. Within a PS-based approach to syntax, as we have said, if the dependency notion of "Head" is a useful or necessary one, then it must be reconstructed in PS terms. However, this brings us immediately to the problem of naturalizing: what is the theory internal status of whatever the reconstruction turns out to be? As has been stressed, if one *can* reconstruct the dependency notion, the issue becomes, why *should* one do so, internal to the workings of the PS-based theory. Minimalist theorizing highlights this issue, as purely empirical considerations cut far less ice in such an environment than in others, even earlier P & P approaches. In minimalist theorizing, the *should* ought not to be something like "because it gets such-and-such-a-result". Rather, we want a *should* that is due, as much as possible, to "virtual conceptual necessity".

In order to understand how close, if at all, MP takes us to this goal, it seems we have to return to the MP account of derived syntactic objects and their labels. The closer these approach "virtual conceptual necessity", the more we will find that the concept of "Head" has been naturalized into the MP theory, hence explained. This, then, appears to lead us back to our earlier qualms about both the status of labels and the definition of Terms. These objections then may derail the MP explanatory express. Or perhaps not; perhaps these somewhat technical considerations are not the proper locus of attention and analysis.

In fact, the crucial concept in this area is *inclusiveness*. It is the fact (if it is a fact) that derived syntactic objects satisfy this condition that provides the possibility of an explanatory PS account of headedness. Inclusiveness requires, in an older idiom, that a mother be related to its daughter(s), and this is just what the reconstruction of "Head" must also guarantee. The problem now becomes the status of inclusiveness. In MP (228) it is an assumption: "Let us assume that this condition holds (virtually) of the computation from N[umeration] to LF. . . ." This effectively forecloses the possibility of an explanatory account of Heads. If inclusiveness were not assumed, but rather were a property that held in virtue of the (minimalist) architecture and processes of the computational component, then an explanatory account could be claimed. Thus, even if our technical objections to labels and Terms were rejected, the MP approach would still not be an explanatory one, given the assumed (i.e., stipulated) rather than derived (i.e., emergent) status of inclusiveness. It is only because they must meet the inclusiveness condition that the construction processes for derived syntactic objects even seem to provide an explanatory approach to "Heads".

Endocentricity, that all syntactic objects are headed, has always had to be assumed (or stipulated) in PS-based theories.[29] Inclusiveness appears to be the form this takes in MP.

5.0 Functional Categories

Functional Categories play a central role in the theory of movement in MP, and discussion of justification of Functional Categories occupies some considerable space; yet, at the same time, there seems to be little to connect the analysis of Functional Categories in MP with the tradition that we have discussed in earlier chapters. We take up these items in turn.

5.1 Functional Categories and movement

In MP, "all applications of Move are forced by the requirement that a functional head that has been introduced into a structure by Merge has a feature that must be checked" (Johnson and Lappin 1997: 279). Overt movement is the further result of a Functional Category being "strong" where this means there is "a non-intrinsic categorial feature in the head, where this feature is non-intrinsic if it is distinct from the categorial feature of the head" (Johnson and Lappin 1997: 281). The idea here is that such a feature must be "checked" by another category that also has such a feature, and that therefore, when a Functional Head with such a feature is introduced by Merge, such a second category must appear in the Functional Head's "checking domain". "Feature checking consists in matching the feature of a head H with the feature of a lexically headed phrase in the minimal syntactic domain of H (roughly, in SPEC of H or adjoined to H) and the elimination of this feature at least from H's feature set" (Johnson and Lappin 1997: 279). This is based on the premise that movement is one of the (few) areas of variation between grammars, and that variation should be localized to parameters "restricted to formal features of functional categories" (MP: 6). The underlying reasoning is that "[v]ariation in language is essentially morphological in character" (MP: 7) and that therefore "the operation Move is driven by morphological considerations: the requirement that some feature F must be checked" (MP: 262).

There are a number of points to make about this set of ideas. First, it is relatively unclear what is particularly *minimalist* about it. I suppose it might be claimed that restricting the locus of cross linguistic variation to "morphology" is, in general, minimalist, and that in MP specifically this is realized as the restriction to formal features of Functional Heads. However, no actual argument is made for either part of this hypothetical position, and one might wonder why, exactly, "formal features of functional heads" reconstructs the domain of "morphology".[30]

Second, as Johnson and Lappin (1997) (281) point out, and as is basically conceded in MP (233), the account of overt movement in terms of "strong features" "remains a stipulation of the system. These features do not explain the distinction between overt and covert movement, but simply provide a device for encoding it." A familiar argument form recurs here: if the general ideas which shape the overall theoretical space are untenable, then we should expect specific attempts to work out their implications to reveal problems, rather than yield insights. In this case we have our objection that there is nothing particularly minimalist about the unargued for identification of "formal features of functional heads" with "morphology" and the subsequent discovery that the crucial mechanism providing for the central distinction between overt and covert movement is nothing but a stipulative encoding scheme.

Finally, we have already argued that Move is itself conceptually ill-founded. If this is correct, then there is something fundamentally flawed with this entire line of inquiry "having to do with the formal features that advance the computation (primarily strength, which drives overt operations . . .) and the functional categories that consist primarily (sometimes entirely) of such features . . ." (MP: 349). If there is no Move, then there is no need to try to identify "formal features of functional heads" with "morphology" so that movement is localized for parametric variation, nor any reason to stipulate a distribution of "strong" features in order to encode the distinction between overt and covert movement. As usual, filtering out flotsam and jetsam upstream allows for smoother and safer downstream activities.

5.2   Functional Categories: fact or fiction?

There are four[31] Functional Categories discussed in MP: T, C, D and AGR (MP: 240, 349, 378). A primary conclusion is "that Agr does not exist" (MP: 377). More generally, "the only functional categories are those with features that survive through the derivation and appear at the interfaces, where they are interpreted" (MP: 378). Such "Interpretable features[ ] provid[e] 'instructions' at either or both interface levels." AGR lacks such features: "it consists of -Interpretable formal features only . . . [and] is present only for theory-internal reasons" (MP: 349). This suggests that AGR could and should be eliminated because "[p]ostulation of a functional category has to be justified, either by output conditions (phonetic and semantic interpretation) or by theory-internal operations. It bears a burden of proof, which is often not so easy to meet" (MP: 240). Moreover, if a postulated Functional Category has only theory internal justification, then it is in principle possible that it can be eliminated, unlike those which are interpreted at an interface. And, given that the category is in principle eliminable, minimalist theorizing both dictates investigation of whether it is eliminable in fact and prefers the more abstemious inventory.

From the point of view of the Functional Category tradition reviewed in section 3 of Chapter One, the outlined MP position may seem somewhat surprising. Let us recall two representative statements from that tradition, the first from Speas (1990: 116), the other from Abney (1987: 65), repeated here.

A functional head is in an informal sense semantically parasitic on a predication, and so although it has Kase features to assign, it has no relevant variable in its LCS to which these might be linked.

(v) Functional elements lack . . . "descriptive content". Their semantic contribution is second-order, regulating or contributing to the interpretation of their complement. They mark grammatical or relational features, rather than picking out a class of objects.

What is surprising is the following. In the tradition as represented by Speas and Abney, the semantic interpretability of Functional Categories is always understood to be dependent on some Lexical Category or other: it is "parasitic" or "second-order". In MP, as we have seen, it is interpretability at an interface (concretely taken to mean semantic interpretability) that serves as the ultimate justification for postulation of a Functional Category. While there may be no strict contradiction between these positions – MP does not say that the interpretations are *not* "parasitic" or "second-order", and the tradition does not say that Functional Categories without interpretation are to be *preferred* – the difference in emphasis is nonetheless striking. Insofar as semantic interpretability of Functional Categories is stressed in the tradition, it is for its derivative and system regulating character. That is, Functional Categories are "relational" acting as the "glue" or "frames" which bind together the Lexical Categories in a sentence. In MP, by contrast, (semantic) interpretability becomes the *sine qua non* for Functional Categories, and their (only?) system regulating property is their role in forcing movement. If there is no Move, as we have argued, then it is no longer entirely clear, in MP, what Functional Categories are *for*.

Nonetheless, it is good to bear several points in mind. One is that there may be nothing contradictory between the tradition and MP, as noted. The second is that we argued in Chapter One that the tradition is not in such wonderful theoretical shape and that some sort of rethinking is in order. Minimalist theorizing generally requires rethinking, and MP specifically appears to offer some with respect to Functional Categories, as suggested in the immediately preceding paragraph. Finally, as the elimination of AGR indicates, the requirement that Functional Categories have interpretable features provides a relatively principled way to limit their proliferation, something we argued was desirable in Chapter One.

6.0   X-Bar Theory

The two subareas for discussion are, as usual, the status of the results of X-Bar Theory and branching. We take up each in turn.

6.1   *"Additional elements"*

The goal with respect to X-Bar Theory is, we might say, to have no cake and to eat it, too. In other words: eliminate X-Bar Theory as such, but retain its desirable effects as a by-product of minimalist requirements. We have already seen, for the most part, how this is meant to work.[32] One aspect of the MP approach that has not been stressed so far is that syntactic structures do not involve "additional elements such as nodes, bars, primes, XP, subscripts and other indices, and so on" (MP: 244). Instead, there are only the basic syntactic objects translated from the lexicon and the derived syntactic objects constructed under inclusiveness, including labels; "empirical evidence would be required to postulate the additional elements" (MP: 245). A somewhat puzzling detail of the discussion is the following.

> Thus, with sufficiently rich formal devices (say, set theory), counterparts to any objects (nodes, bars, indices, etc.) can readily be constructed from features. There is no essential difference, then, between admitting new kinds of objects and allowing richer use of formal devices; we assume that these (basically equivalent) options are permitted only when forced by empirical properties of language. (MP: 381, fn. 7)

Now, set theory *is* the formal device in which the MP approach to syntactic structure is couched: lexical items are sets of features, derived syntactic categories are sets containing their two constituents, and the options entertained for labels include the union and the intersection of the constituents. What is puzzling is that, on the one hand, "nodes, bars, indices, etc." are castigated as "additional elements" which need special justification, while, on the other, the formal resources of the theory as developed apparently allow "counterparts" of these elements to be "readily" constructed, and the two approaches are "basically equivalent". This situation seems to cry out for further examination and analysis.

The uncharitable interpretation is that this is a conceptual shell game. The text makes heavy weather about "additional elements" and trumpets its minimalism with respect to syntactic objects, while in a footnote it is declared that as much nonminimal complexity as you like is obtainable with the resources at hand. On this view, the best that can be said is that at least the "essential equivalence" was not entirely ignored or denied. But arguably nothing of substance has been achieved.

But there is a more generous interpretation possible. It would go as follows. It has been shown that within MP's particular assumptions, minimalist theorizing leads to a set theoretic interpretation of (the construction of) syntactic objects. One cannot do without this. Suppose one also wants (some subset of) "nodes, bars, indices, etc." for some (analytic) reason or other. On minimalist grounds, this would be a serious disappointment: what is necessary should be sufficient, but here apparently is not. However, footnote to the rescue: using the resources minimalist theorizing allows and requires is enough, because if, for some (analytic) reason, one wants "nodes, bars, indices, etc." then "counterparts" of these elements are able to be "readily" constructed. And, for analytic purpose, that is all that is needed.

The problem with the generous interpretation is the following. Suppose the situation is as suggested in the previous paragraph. Then we should be unsatisfied in that there are analytically useful or necessary concepts which are not ones the theory immediately, or even, perhaps, straightforwardly, delivers. Indeed, without the existence of a different (by hypothesis, nonminimalist) theory that included the "additional elements" there would be nothing to suggest that the MP approach was missing anything at all. This is another instance of the need for theoretical naturalization: that it is possible to reconstruct an alien concept does not by itself provide any obvious insight into why such a concept is useful, a serious failing in minimalist theorizing. As is well known, in general theories which are "essentially equivalent" may very well have quite different foci and emphases, leading to analyses which, while stateable in either theory, are likely to arise endogenously only in one.

But now suppose the situation is not as suggested two paragraphs ago. That is, suppose it is not the case that there is any (analytic) reason to want "nodes, bars, indices, etc." It is nevertheless still true that "counterparts" of these elements can be "readily" constructed and that the two theories are "essentially equivalent". What we have now are unnecessary degrees of freedom. In this situation, set theory allows more than we want or need; it is more powerful than is required. If it is also what is minimally necessary to do what is needed, then, apparently, to this extent language fails to be "'perfect'" where for this latter notion "[t]he essential question is whether, and to what extent . . . the computational system . . . is . . . in some interesting sense optimal" (MP: 9).

We thus see that regardless of the interpretation, "mingy" or kind, there is a problem given the footnote. The unkind reading sees a conceptual confidence game. The forgiving interpretation ends up in a dilemma. The MP theory may do too little, merely reconstructing analyses involving "nodes, bars, indices, etc." that it would not itself generate, or it could do too much, allowing construction of "counterparts" of unnecessary "additional elements". In either case, it would fail to explain why what was necessary was necessary, the fundamental goal in minimalist theorizing.

6.2   *Branching*

Given Noahistic Merge, there is (an equivalent of) exactly binary branching. And, as we have argued, Noahistic Merge is well-motivated in MP (section 2.2.5 above). This, then, is a notably successful instance of naturalization. A desideratum that arose antecedent to the advent of minimalist theorizing has been shown to follow directly from what is required by the minimalist theorizing in MP. There is not much more to be asked for, nor any more to be said.

7.0   **PM ordering**

"[T]here is no linear order in the N[umeration] → LF computation" (MP: 335). Instead, linear order is part of "the phonological component" (MP: 340). This is an entirely reasonable position, but still leaves open the question on which AS is founded, viz., what, if anything, is the relation of hierarchical structure to linear order (see Chapter Three). This issue is taken up in MP by an attempt to reconstruct (and naturalize) the Linear Correspondence Axiom (LCA) of AS.

The conclusion reached is that the LCA "can be accommodated in a straightforward way" (MP: 340). However, MP points out that there are two sorts of support for the LCA in AS, only one of which carries over into MP. These are conceptual and empirical, respectively, with only the latter valid in MP (MP: 335–6, 340). This is significant because it means that naturalization of the LCA in fact fails, and the empirical results, while "accounted for" are entirely unexplained.

The conceptual arguments which do not carry over into MP "show how certain stipulated properties of X-bar theory can be derived from the LCA" (MP: 335) yet "crucially rely on . . . standard X-bar-theoretic assumptions [(8)]" that are given up in MP (Chomsky 1995a: 414). In MP, there is "no head-terminal distinction" (MP: 336), there are no bar levels, and it is not the case that "certain features project".

(8)   Certain features (categorial features) project from a terminal element to form a head, then on to form higher categories with different bar levels.

It is correct, then, that the conceptual arguments do not hold in MP.

But, of course, in minimalist theorizing it is precisely conceptual arguments that carry the most weight. With only empirical support, the LCA provides at best a research problem, at worst an embarrassment for MP. If, indeed, the relation between hierarchical structure and linear order is constrained in ways predicted by the LCA, then minimalist theorizing is obliged to offer some conceptual reasons for why this should be so. There are no coincidences.

This concludes our discussion of MP, and of the three approaches to PS in the P & P tradition. I think we can hardly do better, in summing up MP, than this:

> [T]he Minimalist Program, right or wrong, has a certain therapeutic value. It is all too easy to succumb to the temptation to offer a purported explanation for some phenomenon on the basis of assumptions that are of roughly the same order of complexity as what is to be explained. If the assumptions have broader scope, that may be a step forward in understanding. But sometimes they do not. Minimalist demands at least have the merit of highlighting such moves, thus sharpening the question of whether we have a genuine explanation or a restatement of a problem in other terms. (MP: 233–4)

This chapter, I hope, has contributed to the therapeutic project.

Notes

1   Here and throughout, I ignore phonology and the derivation to PF.
2   Johnson and Lappin (1997: 278) take such pairs to be *ordered* pairs, MP (225) does not explicitly do so.

3 There is also "Spell Out", but this begins the phonological derivation, which we are ignoring.

4 This is because "Merge always applies in the simplest possible form: at the root" (MP: 248, 254).

5 Uniformity says that "a chain is uniform with regard to its phrase structure status." Last Resort "expresses the idea that Move is driven by feature checking, a morphological property" (MP: 253).

6 Following MP, we are assuming that there is a substantive issue of some sort with respect to presence or absence of Move, though it is noted in MP (223) that "[t]hese questions are not only imprecise but also rather subtle; typically, it is possible to recode one approach in terms of others."

7 Quoted from section 1.1 above.

8 In MP's sense – see 1.1 above and 2.1 below.

9 We should note that Johnson and Lappin (1997: 285–7) argue that using the numeration as the reference set for economy-of-derivation purposes leads to unacceptable computational explosions, apparent moves to the contrary in MP (227–8) notwithstanding.

10 TPM (153–65) presents relatively detailed criticism of the earlier work exactly for its stipulative nature with respect to the theory of phrase structure.

11 See section 3.0 of the Introduction.

12 In fact, this is not so clear. Inclusiveness rules out adding anything new in the course of the derivation, but deletion is one of the allowed violations of inclusiveness (see section 1.1 above). So, the strict identity between the label and one of the parts of the derived object is evidently not guaranteed.

13 This ensures a version of exactly binary branching.

14 This is obscure, as there is no notion of "contradiction" with respect to union. There is an operation with precisely the property gestured at: *unification* (Shieber 1986). This is, in fact, one reason that some syntacticians prefer unification based approaches to grammar.

15 Actually it is not entirely clear that Merge is so limited by what is said in MP (243): "Applied to two objects [a] and [b], Merge forms the new object K, eliminating [a] and [b]. . . ." This does not strictly require that Merge *can* only apply to pairs; it merely assumes that Merge *will* only apply to pairs – due, presumably, to the operation of Select (and Merge itself). See below.

16 This sort of reasoning should be familiar, as it is essentially that employed to reduce various specific transformations to Move Alpha in the course of the development of generative syntax.

17 Noted on p. 113.

18 See section 1.3 above.

19 This need not embarrass MP, however, as, with respect to a somewhat different issue the following point is made. "This is not, of course a logical necessity; Martian could be different. Rather, it is an assumption about how *human* language works . . ." (MP: 243, emphasis in original).

20 But see note 6 above.

21 We discuss external arguments in section 3.2 below.

22 See section 2 of Chapter Three.

23 Quoted from Chapter One, section 1.0 and repeated in section 2 of Chapter Three.

24 Recall that in section 2.2.5 we argued that MP must make the background representational assumption that sentences are hierarchically structured objects in order to achieve these goals.

25 See section 3.1.1 above.

26   This account of labels is basically identical to that found in Speas (1990).

27   This is shown in Chametzky (1994), TPM: chapter 4, and Chapter Two, section 2.3.

28   MP allows for adjunction of Heads to Heads, i.e., X^0 to X^0. We shall not discuss this.

29   Postal (1964: 27) argues that Zellig Harris (1946, 1951) introduced "raised super-scripts" in his substitutibility equations "to reconstruct this notion [Head]." Postal further, and most interestingly for our purposes, argues that if this reconstruction works "we would be forced to reject a PSG interpretation for Harris equations involving superscripts and say that these involved some other type of . . . system." That is, if you have Heads, then you are not using a Phrase Structure Grammar (PSG). While we are not now concerned with PSGs, i.e., phrase structure rule systems, we are investigating PS-based syntax, and "Head" remains something of a conceptual interloper.

30   We might guess that this has something to do with the connection between Functional Categories and "Closed Class" items. However, as we have seen in our discussion in section 3 of Chapter One, this is not an area of settled theory, so guesswork with respect to the intended position (if any) in MP is unsatisfying.

31   Or five: Johnson and Lappin 1997 (279) list three, but include the "light causative verb v".

32   See sections 2 and 4 above.

Conclusion

Beginning of the End

We really need to wrap this up. We will therefore look at just a couple of issues that give us a way to bring together the separate discussions of the previous chapters. One is a comparison of the "derivationalist" MP with a (hypothetical?) "representational" alternative. This is something that has been touched on already, but the conclusion reached there was entirely internal to MP.[1] Here, we shall bring in considerations from AS. The second issue is the status of "phrase structure" itself. Again, this has been touched on before;[2] we will here generalize the discussion.

1.0 "Derive," he said

Prima facie, it seems that "derivational" theories are less desirable than "representational" ones. This is because *everyone* assumes there is some sort of representation – a "final" object of some sort. Given this, that there is **also** a *derivation of* this object is, presumably, an extra that must be justified – at least if one is committed to, say, minimalist theorizing. Within minimalist theorizing, this justificatory burden could, in principle, be met if otherwise arbitrary properties of the representation would be explained by the fact of its derivation. That is, if the nature of the derivation were such that it necessarily gave rise to the otherwise arbitrary properties of the representation, then the primacy and necessity of the derivation would be established.

Here is the argument for derivationalism developed earlier.[3] (1) if MP is to have a derivation for hierarchically structured objects (and not one that just, say, concatenates), then it must assume such objects *ex ante* and (2) MP does provide a derivational explanation for the binarity of branching in the objects. From (1) it is argued that derivationalism is no better off than representationalism.[4] From (2), however, the argument is made that derivationalism does what it needs to: it explains an otherwise arbitrary property of the object in a principled manner that is unavailable to representationalism. It is this second argument that we now examine.

The argument is vulnerable on two fronts: factual and theoretical. For the first, the issue is whether it is *correct* to limit branching to being (no more than) binary. It is widely assumed that this is correct, but there is some empirical evidence against the claim.[5] Unsurprisingly, I will not pursue this line, other than to say that those who have already leapt might at least hazard a brief, belated peek, even if they feel it too late for a full look. The theoretical issue is whether a representationalist can derive (no more than) binary branching in a way that seems as principled as the MP derivation. Recall that all the representationalist needs is a local tie to claim the overall advantage. We turn, then, to the theoretical issue.

1.1 The Derivationalist's case

The argument is basically the following. Given that sentences have, by hypothesis, hierarchical structure, it then follows that Merge **must** be what we termed *Noahistic*:

> if it were not, then, for some sized numeration, it would (or could) fail to construct a hierarchically structured object, which, by assumption, it cannot do. Put somewhat differently, Noahistic Merge is the only version of Merge-as-set-formation that guarantees a hierarchically structured object regardless of the size of the numeration, and such a guarantee is precisely what is required.[6]

We thus have an explanation for (no more than) binary branching in the fact that *Noahistic* Merge is what is necessary to ensure derivation of a hierarchically structured object given an arbitrary numeration. This is quite an accomplishment, resting, as it does, on only the relatively weak background assumption of hierarchical structure for sentences. The challenge for a representationalist is to do as well.

1.2 A Representationalist alternative

The problem, then, is whether representationalism can come up with as principled a way to derive (no more than) binary branching as derivationalism has. Note that it need not be the *same* way, or even a particularly similar way, or even a way that is about the same thing. We previously concluded that:

> a representational theory should have to countenance either (1) arbitrary restrictions on the form of syntactic objects or (2) arbitrary forms for syntactic objects. Given that syntactic objects do not, in fact, have arbitrary (though hierarchical) forms, the theory of grammar must provide some principled (minimal) way of accounting for this. The Noahistic derivational theory does this; a purely representational theory does not.[7]

This conclusion was premature, however. It was not based on a wide enough exploration of alternative ways in which representationalism might, in fact, arrive at a principled accounting of (no more than) binary branching. Indeed, we need not look all that far to find such an alternative: only as far as Chapter Three, as it happens.

AS provides a principled, non-stipulative explanation for (no more than) binary branching. The argument comes down to the following.[8]

(1)   The central intuition of AS (131): "that a parsimonious UG would not have linear order and hierarchical structure be as independent of one another as syntactic theory normally assumes . . ." hence the LCA.

(2)   The need for there to be some relation that mediates between structure and string.

(3)   The conclusion that whatever the mediating relation (2) is, it must be *locally linear*, in order that it be formally "close to" precedence.

(4)   The conclusion that the relation in (2) is (some form of) C-command.[9]

(5)   Given (4) and (3), the relation must be *asymmetric* C-command.

(6)   The fact that asymmetric C-command is locally linear in binary branching PMs.

(7)   The fact that given (1) (the LCA), (5) (asymmetric C-command) *guarantees* that PMs are (no more than) binary branching (deriving (6)).

The important parts of the argument are these. Its goal is not to ensure (no more than) binary branching (7), but rather to derive a locally linear version of C-command (6). It is based squarely in the "central intuition" of AS, itself independent of branching. Arriving at (5), the conclusion that asymmetric C-command is the mediating relation, is also entirely independent of any consideration of branching. The situation was summed up in the following way. "No more than binary branching, then, is not stipulated in AS. Rather, it follows from its guiding intuition and an independently motivated way of realizing that intuition."[10]

In the present dialectic, this is a powerful position for two reasons. The first is quite obvious: there is evidently nothing "derivational" about it. It is entirely available to the representationalist, which means that the only advantage for the derivationalist has apparently disappeared. Both views now can claim that PMs are no more than binary branching for principled reasons.

The second reason is rather more subtle. Recall from section 7 of Chapter Four that the LCA does not receive "conceptual support" in MP. In the terms of Chapter Four, the LCA fails to be *naturalized* into MP. If the central intuition of AS is granted, and if the LCA seems empirically supported, then, as noted, "minimalist theorizing is obliged to offer some conceptual reasons for why this should be so." If the derivationalist can claim binary branching follows from the nature of the derivation itself, then the representationalist can claim that it follows from independently justified conditions on the representation(s) which are not available to the derivationalist.

The dialectic need not end here, however. The derivationalist can respond as follows. Suppose one could naturalize the LCA into MP. Then there would be two distinct guarantees of (no more than) binary branching: Noahistic Merge and the asymmetric C-command argument. But within minimalist theorizing this would itself be a large problem. There simply should not be two such entirely distinct means to arrive at this single conclusion. We therefore conclude that within derivationalism, the LCA should not be naturalized, and that the conclusion reached in MP is the correct one, as far as it goes. What is still left is either to explain in some other way whatever empirical support the LCA has or to deny the central intuition and show that the LCA's support is only apparent, not real.

But now we see that, by a final twist, this second strand leads us back again to precisely where the first left us, viz., in a standoff. And, as we have stressed, such a seemingly equipollent situation in fact tilts in favor of the representationalist.

2.0 *Now* you tell us?

Maybe there isn't any phrase structure. No doubt a disconcerting suggestion to make at this point in our voyage, but make it any earlier and who would not have jumped ship? Anyway, we will examine this idea from two angles. First, from inside minimalist theorizing. Then we will move back a bit to P & P more generally.

2.1 *REALLY minimalist phrase structure*

The initial moves in the discussion have already been made.[11] First it was argued that "concatenate" was at least as "minimal" as Merge, probably more so. But "concatenate" was then claimed to be TOO minimal: sticking strings next to one another to make a new, bigger string does not provide the means for analyzing sentences as hierarchically structured objects. And since, *by hypothesis*, sentences are hierarchically structured objects, "concatenate" cannot be the operative process. This argument, however, is presumably only as strong as the hypothesis that sentences are hierarchically structured objects. While that seems like a pretty strong, though corrigible, assumption, in fact the situation is worse still.

Let us assume that sentences are hierarchically structured objects. Let us also assume that MP is the right *kind* of theory for syntax (though not THE right theory). Suppose now that we had been lucky or smart enough to begin our inquiries with the right kind of theory (rather than with, e.g., *The logical structure of linguistic theory*). We would then be in the embarrassing position of our theory not allowing us to discover one of the basic facts about its domain, viz., that sentences are hierarchically structured objects. Instead, our theory would lead us to "concatenate" as the basic process, with the result that either we would go about asserting falsehoods as truths about sentences or we would recognize (somehow) these falsehoods as false, and wrongly give up the theory which led us to them in favor of some other (kind of) theory that allowed us to assert truths. In either case, we are in serious trouble.

Now, perhaps it will be rejoined that this is just how sciences work in point of historical fact. We *always* start with the wrong sort of theory, and yet we discover truths with them, which truths get carried over into the right kind of theory once, or if, we figure out what that might be. Well, maybe so. But the point here is stronger, I think, than this response allows. The present point is not that we *do* start with the wrong sort of theory, it is that we *have* to, or else we would get things irreparably wrong. The right kind of theory here in fact makes the wrong sort of claim about the domain. This strikes me, at least, as a singularly terrible thing for the right kind of theory to do.

Moreover, why accept this (or any) particular result from the wrong kind of theory as something to carry over into the right kind? Answer: because it is empirically extremely well motivated. Rebuttal: but that's all *within* the wrong sort of theory; shouldn't we accept only those refugees from the bad theory that are both empirically well motivated *and* derivable within the good theory, and doesn't the second condition count for at least as much as the first? Isn't that, after all, largely what makes the new (kind of) theory *new*?

In other words, within MP the right conclusion might be that the assumption that sentences are hierarchically structured objects is not merely corrigible, but "corriged".

2.2   ... *made to be broken*

Phrase structure rules are one of the villains of the piece. They are redundant and stipulative. Redundant: combinatoric information they encode is already available in the lexical entries of lexical items. Stipulative: they simply *say* that this or that is the mother of these or those; they do not provide insight into or explanation of the mother/daughter relations they encode. Redundancy and stipulation being among the prime demons in the P & P anti-pantheon, phrase structure rules have been marked for elimination ever since Timothy Stowell's 1981 unpublished dissertation.

But if phrase structure rules go, is there really nothing lost with them? No one evidently thinks that anything (important) has disappeared. Is this true? One thing that phrase structure rules provided was a specific place/module/component of the grammar where generalizations about phrase structure could be *explicitly stated*. So, for example, generalizations about the distribution of syntactic categories were explicitly stated in phrase structure rules – that, say, NPs (or DPs) are sisters (complements) of Ps. If there are no phrase structure rules, then this is something that the grammar just cannot explicitly represent. If there are real generalizations of this sort, do we prefer a grammar that in principle cannot express them?

Two responses suggest themselves. The first is that the rules are gone because we have, in whatever version we accept, found a way to derive and explain the fact that the grammar conforms to the requirements of X-Bar Theory. The second response is that the sorts of generalizations pointed to are spurious or, at best, epiphenomena.

The first response just changes the subject. The sorts of generalizations that would be missed are not ones that X-Bar Theory would address, so deriving X-Bar advances the dialectic not at all.[12] The second response forces us deeper into our subject. It leads us to ask the following: if there really are no such generalizations, what, exactly, is the point of phrase structure?

Consider: if there are no significant statements to be made in terms of phrasal categories and their constructional occurrences, why should we want our syntax to be built up and out of *precisely* these? Phrase structure theories are about the part/whole relation of constituency. Phrase structure rules allow for explicit statements about these relations, and the extraction and encoding of generalizations pertaining thereto. Getting rid of the phrase structure rules (for independent reasons) leads to the conclusion that there are no (worthwhile) such generalizations. And, as suggested, once you arrive here, the (not so?) obvious next step is to ask why think in terms of phrase structure at all, since the grammar does not let you talk about it.[13]

Notice now that this line of thought pulls us back to where the last section left off. We were wondering there how and why the right kind of theory, concessively agreed to be MP, could incorporate something (viz., phrase structure) from the wrong kind of theory that it could not naturalize. We were skeptical that it either should or could. But if the suggestions just sketched are at all compelling, then it seems that the wrong kind of theory, properly understood, also demotivates phrase structure. Moreover, it is precisely those aspects of earlier P & P work that most create the lineage with MP (viz., abhorrence of redundancy and stipulation) that provide the grounds for eliminating phrase structure rules, and thus the questioning of phrase structure itself. This is certainly a suggestive convergence. One thing it suggests, for example, is that the title of this work has a mostly ironic appropriateness.

Notes

1 See the close of section 2.2.5 of Chapter Four.
2 See section 2.2.5 of Chapter Four.
3 See (again) section 2.2.5 of Chapter Four.
4 What was not noted previously is that, given the *prima facie* advantage of the latter over the former, ties go to the representationalist.
5 See e.g., Carrier and Randall (1992), Pesetsky (1995: chapter 7), noted in section 4.2 of Chapter One.
6 Quoted from section 2.2.5 of Chapter Four.
7 Quoted from section 2.2.5 of Chapter Four.
8 The argument is made in section 5.2 of Chapter Three.
9 See also section 1.1 of Chapter Three.
10 Quoted from section 5.2 of Chapter Three.
11 See sections 2.2.3 and 2.2.5 of Chapter Four.
12 Supposing, for example, that we want the specific statement that NP can be the sister of P, X-Bar tells us only the general statement that YP can be the sister of X.
13 Worueber man nicht sprechen kann, darauf kann man schreiben? (*gratia* Anthony Bruck).

References

Abney, Steven. 1987. *The English Noun Phrase in its Sentential Aspect*. Ph.D. dissertation, MIT.

Bach, Emmon. 1974. *Syntactic Theory*. New York: Holt, Rinehart, and Winston.

Bach, Emmon. 1988. "Categorial grammars as theories of language." In Oehrle et al., eds., 17–34.

Baker, Mark. 1988. *Incorporation*. Chicago: University of Chicago Press.

Bar-Hillel, Yehoshua, C. Gaifman, and E. Shamir. 1960. "On categorial and phrase structure grammars." Reprinted in Y. Bar-Hillel, ed., *Language and Information*, 99–114. Reading, MA: Addison-Wesley, 1964.

Barker, Chris, and Geoffrey Pullum. 1990. "A theory of command relations." *Linguistics & Philosophy* 13, 1–34.

Bloch, Bernard. 1946. "Studies in colloquial Japanese II: syntax." Reprinted in Martin Joos, ed., *Readings in Linguistics*, 154–84. New York: ACLS, 1957.

Bloomfield, Leonard. 1933. *Language*. New York: Henry Holt.

Borer, Hagit. 1986. "I-subjects." *Linguistic Inquiry* 17, 375–416.

Borer, Hagit. 1994. "The projection of arguments." In E. Benedicto and J. Runner, eds., *University of Massachusetts Occasional Papers* 17, 19–48. Amherst: GLSA.

Bouchard, Denis. 1991. "From conceptual structure to syntactic structure." In K. Leffel and D. Bouchard, eds., *Views on Phrase Structure*, 21–36. Dordrecht: Kluwer Academic Publishers.

Bouchard, Denis. 1995. *The Semantics of Syntax*. Chicago: University of Chicago Press.

Bresnan, Joan, ed., 1982. *The Mental Representation of Grammatical Relations*. Cambridge, MA: MIT Press.

Brody, Michael. 1994. "Phrase structure and dependence." *University College London Working Papers in Linguistics*, #6.

Carrier, Jill, and Janet Randall. 1992. "The argument structure and syntactic structure of resultatives." *Linguistic Inquiry* 23, 173–234.

Chametzky, Robert. 1985. "Coordination & predication." *ESCOL '84*, 165–80.

Chametzky, Robert. 1987. *Coordination and the Organization of a Grammar*. Ph.D. dissertation, University of Chicago.

Chametzky, Robert. 1987a. "Syntax without the *S*." *ESCOL '86*, 71–85.

Chametzky, Robert. 1994. "Chomsky-adjunction." *Lingua* 93, #4, 245–64.

Chametzky, Robert. 1995. "Dominance, precedence, and parameterization." *Lingua* 96, #2–3, 163–78.

Chametzky, Robert. 1996. *A Theory of Phrase Markers and the Extended Base*. Albany: SUNY Press.

Chomsky, Noam. 1963. "Formal properties of grammars." In R. Duncan Luce, R. Bush, and E. Galanter, eds., *Handbook of Mathematical Psychology*, volume 2, 323–418. New York: John Wiley.

Chomsky, Noam. 1965. *Aspects of the Theory of Syntax*. Cambridge, MA: MIT Press.

Chomsky, Noam. 1970. "Remarks on nominalization." In R. Jacobs and P. Rosenbaum, eds., *Readings in English Transformational Grammar*, 184–221. Waltham, MA: Ginn & Co.

Chomsky, Noam. 1981. *Lectures on Government and Binding*. Dordrecht: Foris.

Chomsky, Noam. 1986a. *Barriers*. Cambridge, MA: MIT Press.

Chomsky, Noam. 1986b. *Knowledge of Language*. New York: Praeger.

Chomsky, Noam. 1993. "A minimalist program for linguistic theory." In K. Hale and S. Keyser, eds., *The View from Building 20*, 1–52. Cambridge, MA: MIT Press.

Chomsky, Noam. 1995. *The Minimalist Program*. Cambridge, MA: MIT Press.

Chomsky, Noam. 1995a. "Bare phrase structure." In G. Webelhuth, ed., *Government and Binding Theory and the Minimalist Program*, 385–439. Oxford and Cambridge, MA: Blackwell Publishers.

Corbett, Greville, Norman Fraser, and Scott McGlashan, eds., 1993. *Heads in Grammatical Theory*. Cambridge: Cambridge University Press.

Croft, William. 1996. "What's a head?" In J. Rooryck and L. Zaring, eds., *Phrase Structure and the Lexicon*. Dordrecht: Kluwer Academic Publishers.

Dworkin, Ronald. 1977. *Taking Rights Seriously*. Cambridge, MA: Harvard University Press.

Emonds, Joseph. 1976. *A Transformational Approach to English Syntax*. New York: Academic Press.

Emonds, Joseph. 1985. *A Unified Theory of Syntactic Categories*. Dordrecht: Foris.

Emonds, Joseph. 1987. "The invisible category principle." *Linguistic Inquiry* 18, 613–32.

Ernst, Thomas. 1992. "The phrase structure of English negation." *The Linguistic Review* 9.

Farmer, Ann. 1984. *Modularity in Syntax*. Cambridge, MA: MIT Press.

Fillmore, Charles. 1968. "The case for case." In E. Bach and R. Harms, eds., *Universals in Linguistic Theory*, 1–88. New York: Holt, Rinehart, & Winston.

Fodor, Janet. 1989. "Learning the Periphery." In R. Matthews and W. Demopoulos, eds., *Learnability and Linguistic Theory*, 129–54. Dordrecht: Kluwer Academic Publishers.

Frost, Robert. 1934. "Neither out far nor in deep." Reprinted in R. Frost, *A Further Range*. New York: Henry Holt, 1936.

Fukui, Naoki, and Margaret Speas. 1986. "Specifiers and projections." In N. Fukui, T. Rappaport, and E. Sagey, eds., *MIT Working Papers in Linguistics* 8.

Fukui, Naoki. 1995. *Theory of Projection in Syntax*. Stanford: Center for the Study of Language and Information.

Gazdar, Gerald, Ewan Klein, Geoffrey Pullum, and Ivan Sag. 1985. *Generalized Phrase Structure Grammar*. Cambridge, MA: Harvard University Press.

Gazdar, Gerald, and Geoffrey Pullum. 1981. "Subcategorization, constituent order, and the notion 'Head'." In M. Moortgat, H. v. D. Hulst, and T. Hoekstra, eds., *The Scope of Lexical Rules*, 107–23. Dordrecht: Foris.

Goodall, Grant. 1987. *Parallel Structures in Syntax*. Cambridge: Cambridge University Press.

Grimshaw, Jane. 1979. "Complement selection and the lexicon." *Linguistic Inquiry* 10, 279–326.

Grimshaw, Jane. 1981. "Form, function, and the language acquisition device." In C. L. Baker and J. McCarthy, eds., *The Logical Problem of Language Acquisition*, 165–82. Cambridge, MA: MIT Press.

Grimshaw, Jane. 1990. *Argument Structure*. Cambridge, MA: MIT Press.

Grimshaw, Jane. 1991. "Extended projection." Unpublished manuscript, Rutgers University.

Hale, Kenneth, and Samuel Keyser. 1993. "On argument structure and the lexical expression of syntactic relations." In K. Hale and S. Keyser, eds., *The View from Building 20*, 53–109. Cambridge, MA: MIT Press.

Harris, Zellig. 1946. "From morpheme to utterance." Reprinted in Martin Joos, ed., *Readings in Linguistics*, 142–53. New York: ACLS, 1957.

Harris, Zellig. 1951. *Methods in Structural Linguistics*. Chicago: University of Chicago Press.

Hawkins, John. 1982. "Notes on cross category harmony, X-bar and the predictions of markedness." *Journal of Linguistics* 18, 1–35.

Hays, David. 1964. "Dependency theory." *Language* 40, 511–25.

Higginbotham, James. 1982. "A note on phrase-markers." *Revue Quebecoise de Linguistique* 13, 147–65.

Higginbotham, James. 1985. "On semantics." *Linguistic Inquiry* 16, 547–93.

Higginbotham, James. 1989. "Elucidations of meaning." *Linguistics & Philosophy* 12, 465–87.

Hornstein, Norbert. 1996. *LF: from GB to Minimalism*. Oxford and Cambridge, MA: Blackwell Publishers.

Huck, Geoffrey. 1985. "Exclusivity and discontinuity in phrase structure grammar." *WCCFL* 4, 92–8.

Hudson, Richard. 1987. "Zwicky on heads." *Journal of Linguistics* 23, 109–32.

Hudson, Richard. 1990. *English Word Grammar*. Oxford: Blackwell Publishers.

Iatridou, Sabine. 1990. "About Agr(P)." *Linguistic Inquiry* 21, 551–77.

Jackendoff, Ray. 1972. *Semantic Interpretation in Generative Grammar*. Cambridge, MA: MIT Press.

Jackendoff, Ray. 1977. *X'-Syntax*. Cambridge, MA: MIT Press.

Jackendoff, Ray. 1983. *Semantics and Cognition*. Cambridge, MA: MIT Press.

Janda, Richard. 1993. "Checking-theory, syntactic feature-geometry, and the structure of IP." *WCCFL* 12.

Janda, Richard, and David Kathman. 1992. "Shielding morphology from exploded INFL." *CLS* 28–2, 141–55.

Johnson, David. 1977. "On Keenan's definition of 'Subject of'." *Linguistic Inquiry* 8, 673–92.

Johnson, David, and Shalom Lappin. 1997. "A critique of the Minimalist Program." *Linguistics & Philosophy* 20, 273–333.

Joseph, Brian, and Jane Smirniotopoulos. 1993. "The morphosyntax of the Modern Greek verb as morphology and not syntax." *Linguistic Inquiry* 24.

Kayne, Richard. 1981. "Unambiguous paths." Reprinted in R. Kayne, *Connectedness and Binary Branching*, 129–63. Dordrecht: Foris, 1984.

Kayne, Richard. 1994. *The Antisymmetry of Syntax*. Cambridge, MA: MIT Press.

Keenan, Edward. 1976. "Towards a universal definition of subject." In C. Li, ed., *Subject and Topic*, 303–33. New York: Academic Press.

Kitcher, Philip. 1983. *The Nature of Mathematical Knowledge*. New York and Oxford: Oxford University Press.

Kornai, Andras, and Geoffrey Pullum. 1990. "The X-bar theory of phrase structure." *Language* 66, 24–50.

Lakoff, George, and Stanley Peters. 1969. "Phrasal conjunction and symmetric predicates." In D. Reibel and S. Schane, eds., *Modern Studies in English*, 113–42. Englewood Cliffs: Prentice-Hall.

Lapointe, Steven. 1993a. "Constraints on the morphological forms of gerundive nominalizations." Paper presented at the annual meeting of the Linguistic Society of America, January 1993.

Lapointe, Steven. 1993b. "Dual lexical categories and the syntax of mixed category phrases." *ESCOL '93*, 199–210.

Larson, Richard. 1988. "On the double object construction." *Linguistic Inquiry* 19, 335–91.

Lasnik, Howard, and Joseph Kupin. 1977. "A restrictive theory of transformational grammar." *Theoretical Linguistics* 4, 173–96.

Lebeaux, David. 1988. *Language Acquisition and the Form of the Grammar*. Ph.D. dissertation, University of Massachusetts, Amherst. Amherst: GLSA.

Lebeaux, David. 1990. "The grammatical nature of the acquisition sequence: adjoin-alpha and the formation of relative clauses." In L. Frazier and J. de Villiers, eds., *Language Processing and Language Acquisition*, 13–82. Dordrecht: Kluwer Academic Publishers.

Lebeaux, David. 1991. "Relative clauses, licensing, and the nature of the derivation." In S. Rothstein, ed., *Syntax & Semantics 25: Perspectives on Phrase Structure*, 209–40. San Diego: Academic Press.

Levin, Beth, and Malka Rappaport Hovav. 1995. *Unaccusativity*. Cambridge, MA: MIT Press.

Lyons, John. 1968. *Introduction to Theoretical Linguistics*. Cambridge: Cambridge University Press. 391–416.

Manaster-Ramer, Alexis, and Michael Kac. 1990. "The concept of phrase structure". *Linguistics & Philosophy* 13, #2.

Matthews, P. H. 1993. *Grammatical Theory in the United States from Bloomfield to Chomsky*. Cambridge: Cambridge University Press.

May, Robert. 1985. *Logical Form*. Cambridge, MA: MIT Press.

May, Robert. 1989. "Bound variable anaphora." In R. Kempson, ed., *Mental Representations*, 85–104. Cambridge: Cambridge University Press.

McCawley, James. 1968. "Concerning the base component of a transformational grammar." *Foundations of Language* 4, 243–69.

McCawley, James. 1982. "Parentheticals and discontinuous constituent structure." *Linguistic Inquiry* 13, 91–106.

McCawley, James. 1988. *The Syntactic Phenomena of English*. Chicago: University of Chicago Press.

Mel'cuk, Igor. 1988. *Dependency Grammar*. Albany: SUNY Press.

Munn, Alan. 1993. *Topics in the Syntax and Semantics of Coordinate Structures*. Ph.D. dissertation, University of Maryland, College Park.

Oehrle, Richard, Emmon Bach, and Deirdre Wheeler, eds., 1988. *Categorial Grammars and Natural Language Structures*. Dordrecht: Kluwer Academic Publishers.

Partee, Barbara, Alice ter Meulen, and Robert Wall. 1990. *Mathematical Methods in Linguistics*. Dordrecht: Kluwer Academic Publishers.

Perlmutter, David, and Paul Postal. 1984. "The 1-advancement exclusiveness law." In D. Perlmutter and C. Rosen, eds., *Studies in Relational Grammar, 2*, 81–125. Chicago: University of Chicago Press.

Pesetsky, David. 1982. *Paths and Categories*. Ph.D. dissertation, MIT.

Pesetsky, David. 1995. *Zero Syntax*. Cambridge, MA: MIT Press.

Pollard, Carl. 1988. "Categorial grammar and phrase structure grammar." In Oehrle et al., eds.

Pollard, Carl, and Ivan Sag. 1987. *Information-based Syntax and Semantics*. Stanford: Center for the Study of Language and Information.

Pollock, Jean-Yves. 1989. "Verb movement, Universal Grammar, and the structure of IP." *Linguistic Inquiry* 20, 365–424.

Postal, Paul. 1964. *Constituent Structure*. Bloomington: Indiana University Research Center in Anthropology, Folklore, and Linguistics.

Pullum, Geoffrey. 1985. "Assuming some version of the X-bar theory." *CLS* 21–1, 323–53.

Pullum, Geoffrey. 1989. "Formal linguistics meets the boojum." *Natural Language & Linguistic Theory* 7, 137–43.

Pullum, Geoffrey. 1991. "English nominal gerund phrases as Noun Phrases with Verb Phrase heads." *Linguistics* 29, 763–99.

Rawls, John. 1971. *A Theory of Justice*. Cambridge, MA: Harvard University Press.

Richardson, John. 1982. "Constituency and sublexical syntax." *CLS* 18, 466–76.

Richardson, John. 1984. "Let X'=X'." *CLS* 20, 321–33.

Richardson, John, and Robert Chametzky. 1985. "A string based reformulation of C-command." *NELS* 15, 332–61.

van Riemsdijk, Henk, and Edwin Williams. 1981. "NP structure." *The Linguistic Review* 1, 171–217.

Rizzi, Luigi. 1990. *Relativized Minimality*. Cambridge, MA: MIT Press.

Robinson, Jane. 1970. "Dependency structure and transformational rules." *Language* 46, 259–85.

Rosen, Carol. 1984. "The interface between semantic roles and initial grammatical relations." In D. Perlmutter and C. Rosen, eds., *Studies in Relational Grammar*, 2, 38–77. Chicago: University of Chicago Press.

Rothstein, Susan. 1985. *The Syntactic Forms of Predication*. Bloomington: Indiana University Linguistics Club.

Rothstein, Susan. 1991a. "Heads, projections, and category determination." In K. Leffel and D. Bouchard, eds., *Views on Phrase Structure*, 97–112. Dordrecht: Kluwer Academic Publishers.

Rothstein, Susan. 1991b. "Syntactic licensing and subcategorization." In S. Rothstein, ed., *Syntax & Semantics 25: Perspectives on Phrase Structure*, 139–58. San Diego: Academic Press.

Sadock, Jerrold. 1991. *Autolexical Syntax*. Chicago: University of Chicago Press.

Shieber, Stuart. 1986. *An Introduction to Unification-based Approaches to Grammar*. Stanford: Center for the Study of Language and Information.

Speas, Margaret. 1990. *Phrase Structure in Natural Language*. Dordrecht: Kluwer Academic Publishers.

Speas, Margaret. 1991. "Generalized transformations and the D-structure position of adjuncts." In S. Rothstein, ed., *Syntax & Semantics 25: Perspectives on Phrase Structure*, 241–57. San Diego: Academic Press.

Speas, Margaret. 1994. "Null arguments in a theory of economy of projections." In E. Benedicto and J. Runner, eds., *University of Massachusetts Occasional Papers* 17, 179–208. Amherst: GLSA.

Spencer, Andrew. 1992. "Nominal inflection and the nature of functional categories." *Journal of Linguistics* 28, 313–41.

Stabler, Edward. 1992. "Implementing Government Binding theories." In R. Levine, ed., *Formal Grammar*, 243–75. Oxford and New York: Oxford University Press.

Steedman, Mark. 1985. "Dependency and coordination in the grammar of Dutch and English." *Language* 61, 523–68.

Steedman, Mark. 1987. "Combinatory grammars and parasitic gaps." *Natural Language & Linguistic Theory* 5, 403–39.

Steedman, Mark. 1988. "Combinators and grammars." In Oehrle et al., eds., 417–42.

Steedman, Mark. 1990. "Gapping as constituent coordination." *Linguistics & Philosophy* 13, 207–63.

Stowell, Timothy. 1981. *Origins of phrase structure*. Ph.D. dissertation, MIT.

Stowell, Timothy. 1992. "The role of the lexicon in syntactic theory." In T. Stowell and E. Wehrli, eds., *Syntax & Semantics 26: Syntax and the Lexicon*, 9–20. San Diego: Academic Press.

Stuurman, Frits. 1985. *Phrase Structure Theory in Generative Grammar*. Dordrecht: Foris.

Tesniere, Lucien. 1959. *Elements de Syntaxe Structurale*. Paris: C. Klincksieck.

Venneman, Theo. 1977. "Konstituenz und Dependenz in einigen neueren Grammatik-theorien." *Sprachwissenschaft* 2, 259–301.

Wall, Robert. 1972. *Introduction to Mathematical Linguistics*. Englewood Cliffs: Prentice-Hall.

Wells, Rulon. 1947. "Immediate constituents." Reprinted in Martin Joos, ed., *Readings in Linguistics*, 186–207. New York: ACLS, 1957.

Wexler, Kenneth, and Peter Culicover. 1980. *Formal Principles of Language Acquisition*. Cambridge, MA: MIT Press.

Williams, Edwin. 1980. "Predication." *Linguistic Inquiry* 11, 203–38.

Williams, Edwin. 1981. "Argument structure and morphology." *The Linguistic Review* 1, 81–114.

Williams, Edwin. 1994. *Thematic Structure in Syntax*. Cambridge, MA: MIT Press.

Wood, Mary. 1993. *Categorial Grammars*. London and New York: Routledge.

Zwicky, Arnold. 1985. "Heads." *Journal of Linguistics* 21, 1–29.

Index

Page numbers in **bold** type indicate major references. The various approaches to phrase structure outlined in this book have no index entries. See relevant chapters for details.